EU Health Systems and Distributive Justice

EU Health Systems and Distributive Justice uses theories of distributive justice to examine tensions created by the application of the Internal Market rules to the provision of health care services within the European Union (EU).

Using the concepts and principles embedded in the theories of egalitarianism and libertarianism, this book analyses the impact of the Internal Market rules on common values and principles shared by EU health systems, such as universality, accessibility, equity and solidarity. This analysis is conducted using the specific issue of cross-border health care.

This book makes innovative contributions to the study of the relationship between EU health systems and the Internal Market – it encompasses the analysis of all principles recognised by EU institutions as guiding principles of European health systems; it integrates human rights law and practice into the discussion of the EU Court of Justice's approach to patient mobility cases; and it assesses the potential impact of the Internal Market over EU health systems through the lens of distributive justice, looking at the underlying principles of these systems that are mostly concerned with social justice.

Ultimately, this is not a book on EU law and health care, but it is a book on distributive justice, health care and the principles and policies guiding European health systems.

Danielle da Costa Leite Borges is an Associate Professor at Fundação Getulio Vargas Law School, Rio de Janeiro, Brazil.

Routledge Research in EU Law

Available titles in this series include:

EU Health Systems and Distributive Justice

Towards New Paradigms for the Provision of Health Care Services?

Danielle da Costa Leite Borges

Routledge
Taylor & Francis Group

LONDON AND NEW YORK

First published 2017 by Routledge

2 Park Square, Milton Park, Abingdon, Oxfordshire OX14 4RN
711 Third Avenue, New York, NY 10017

Routledge is an imprint of the Taylor & Francis Group, an informa business

First issued in paperback 2018

British Library Cataloguing in Publication Data
A catalogue record for this book is available from the British Library

Library of Congress Cataloging-in-Publication Data
Names: Borges, Danielle da Costa Leite, author.
Title: EU health systems and distributive justice: towards new paradigms
for the provision of health care services? / Danielle da Costa Leite Borges.
Other titles: European Union health systems and distributive justice
Description: New York: Routledge, 2016. | Series: Routledge research in
EU law | Includes bibliographical references and index.
Identifiers: LCCN 2016003341 | ISBN 9781138645172 (hbk) |
ISBN 9781315628301 (ebk)
Subjects: LCSH: Medical care – Law and legislation – European Union
countries. | Medical policy – European Union countries. | Medical laws
and legislation – European Union countries. | Public health – European
Union countries.
Classification: LCC KJE6206 .B67 2016 | DDC 344.2403/21–dc23
LC record available at http://lccn.loc.gov/2016003341

ISBN: 978-1-138-64517-2 (hbk)
ISBN: 978-1-138-61409-3 (pbk)

Typeset in Baskerville by
Florence Production Ltd, Stoodleigh, Devon

MIX
Paper from
responsible sources
FSC
www.fsc.org   FSC™ C013985

Printed in the United Kingdom
by Henry Ling Limited

To Mario, Lorenzo and Antonio,
the best part of my life

Contents

Acknowledgements

In writing this book I received the help of many people and I owe a significant intellectual debt to all of them. I am particularly indebted to Professor Marise Cremona, who gave me support and guidance. I am also indebted to Professor Christopher Newdick, who helped me a lot in understanding the dynamics of health care services provision.

Writing a book, however, is not just a matter of working, and some of the most valuable experiences I have had during my stay in Florence are the friendships that I have developed. These friends are: from the EUI (apologies if I have forgotten someone), Norberto Andrade, Ida Federica Pugliese, Adriana Bessa, Alessandro Chechi, Samantha Ribeiro, Timo Hiller, Lucas Lixinski, Lúcio Feteira, Marco Botta, Rozeta Karova, Vassilis Tzevelekos, Edurne Iraizoz, Claire Staath, Jonathan Murray Bright, Evaldo Xavier Gomes, Marcílio Toscano Franca Filho, Alessandra Franca, Alessandra Becucci, William Baugniet, Devina Saha, Ana Espírito Santo, Hélder Ferreira do Vale, Fabiano Corrêa and Alessandra Vannini; from Florence (outside the EUI community), Gabriele Mazzota, Isabella Mariani, Mike Wiesmeier, Donatella Costantini (*in memorium*), Laura Mencherini, Jacopo Ceccarelli, Rosa Iuliano and Sonia Brogi.

I am also thankful to four friends from Brazil, who have always supported this life project: Mercedes Schumacher, Isabela Soares Santos, Marcelo Cidade and Tulio Faraco.

I would also like to say a special thank you to all the teachers from the European University Institute's Language Centre, who were always available, both to review papers and clarify any doubts regarding a specific language. Those that I had the pleasure to have as teachers are: Edurne Iraizoz, Nicky Owtran, Nicki Hargreaves and Sylvain Capelli.

A special thanks goes also to the administrative staff of the EUI, especially to Alessandro Coccioli, Natasha Tsigler, Saverio Bertaccini, Antonio Corretto, Siobhán Gallagher, Eleonora Masella and Françoise Thauvin, who have always tried to make things easier for me. The same gratitude goes to the *mensa* team: Antonella, Fiamma, Loredana, Cinzia, Paola, Guia and Lorena, who have made my life in the EUI more 'tasteful' and pleasant.

I am also thankful to Ana Beatriz D'Anna, who helped me with the final revision of the manuscript.

Now more than ever I recognise the importance of family in my life, and in the period that I was in Florence, apart from my husband, I am very thankful to my cousins Márcia and João and to their daughters Gabriella and Giovanna for providing me with family support.

Finally, my deepest gratitude goes to my mother, Arlene, and to my grandmother, Arlette, who made the conclusion of this work possible after the birth of my children, Lorenzo and Antonio.

Cases

European Court of Justice

Case C-175/78, *R. v Saunders* [1979] ECR 1129

Case C-263/86, *Belgian State v Humbel* [1988] ECR 5365

Case C-215/87, *Schumacher v Hauptzollamt Frankfurt am Main-Ost* [1989] ECR 617

Case C-62/90, *Commission v Germany* [1992] ECR I-2575

Joined cases C-159/91 and C-160/91 *Poucet and Pistre v AGF and Cancava* [1993] ECR I-00637

Joined Cases C-363/93, C-407/93, C-409/93 and C-411/93, *Lancry* [1994] ECR I–3957

Joined Cases C-485/93 and C-486/93, *Simitzi* [1995] ECR I-2655

Case C-70/95, *Sodemare* [1997] ECR I-3395

Joined cases C-64/96 and C-65/96, *Ueker and Jacquet* [1997] ECR I-3171

Case C-120/95, *Decker* [1998] ECR I-1831

Case C-158/96, *Kohll* [1998] ECR I-1931

Case C-266/96, *Corsica Ferries* [1998] ECR I-03949

Case C-376/98, *Germany v Parliament and Council (Tobacco Advertising)* [2000] ECR I-8419

Case C-368/98, *Vanbraekel and others* [2001] ECR I-5363

Case C-157/99, *Smits and Peerbooms* [2001] ECR I-5473

Case C-184/99, *Grzelczyk* [2001] ECR, I-6193

Case C-475/99, *Ambulanz Glöckner* [2001] ECR I-8089

Case C-491/01, *British American Tobacco* [2002] ECR I-11453

Case C-60/00, *Carpenter* [2002] ECR I-6279

Case C-56/01, *Inizan* [2003] ECR I-12403

Case C-148/02, *Garcia Avello* [2003] ECR I-11613

Case C-385/99, *Müller-Fauré and van Riet* [2003] ECR I-4509

Case C-156/01, *Van der Duin* [2003] ECR I-7045

Case C-72/03, *Carbonati Apuani Srl v. Comune di Carrara* [2004] ECR I-8027

Joined Cases C-264/01, C-306/01, C-354/01 and C-355/01, *AOK Bundesverband and Others* [2004] ECR I-2493

Case C-8/02, *Leichtle* [2004] ECR I-02641

Case C-145/03, *Keller* [2005] ECR I-2529

European Court of Human Rights

Constitutional Court of South Africa

Supreme Court of Canada

U.S. Supreme Court

Epigraph

Oui à l'économie de marché, dit un jour Lionel Jospin, non à la société de marché!»
La formule me convient. L'économie de marché, je n'ai rien contre, et même je
suis pour: on n'a pas trouvé mieux pour créer la richesse – et comment, sans
richesse, faire reculer la pauvreté? Mais le marché a aussi sa limite, qui est stricte:
il ne vaut que pour les marchandises, autrement dit que pour ce qui est à vendre
(les marchandises et les services, donc, mais dès qu'un service est à vendre, ce n'est
qu'une marchandise comme une autre)

La reconnaissance de cette limite, c'est ce qui distingue, à mon sens, les libéraux
des ultralibéraux. Si vous croyez que tout se vend, que tout s'achète, alors soyez
ultralibéral: le marché suffit à tout. Si, au contraire, vous pensez qu'il y a des choses
qui ne sont pas à vendre (la vie, la santé, la justice, la liberté, dignité, l'éducation,
l'amour, le monde . . .), alors, on ne peut pas tout soumettre au marché: il faut
résister à la marchandisation de toute notre vie, aussi bien individuellement (c'est
le rôle de la morale et de l'éthique) que collectivement (c'est le rôle de la politique).
Les trois sont nécessaires. Mais à l'échelle de la société, c'est la politique qui est la
plus efficace: nous avons besoin d'un État pour organiser la part non marchande
de la solidarité – pour veiller, exactement, à ce qui n'est pas à vendre.

André Comte-Sponville (*Le capitalisme est-il moral?*
2009, pp. 131–2)

Introduction

This book deals with the tensions created by the application of the Internal Market rules to the provision of health care services within the European Union (EU). In distinction to other works on this subject, this book uses theories of distributive justice and their relationship with the underlying – and common – principles of EU health systems in order to develop its main arguments and explain any tensions. The choice of the subject is, in a wider perspective, justified by the importance that health care has gained in individuals' lives and societies' policy agendas in the last decades for its role in improving and maintaining human health. The concern modern society devotes to health is explained by the fact that individuals want to be and remain healthy because this is viewed as one of the most valuable assets a person possesses.[1] According to Gostin, '[h]ealth is necessary for much of the joy, creativity and productivity that a person derives from life'.[2] Moreover, in terms of societies, healthy populations are not only economically more productive, but also socially more cohesive, because health enables individuals to lead a socially and economically productive life.[3] Considering that health care services contribute to improvements in health, both through its prevention and promotion, and can indeed be considered as a determinant of health,[4] the provision of health care has become an important issue for individuals as well as an important item on today's policy agendas.

From a narrower perspective, the subject choice is important because it can point to a trend regarding the underlying values and ideologies that are being used to develop health care policies in the very special space of the EU. Despite its particularities as an economic bloc, the EU is a reference for the exportation of models to other parts of the world. In the case of health care, this is very real because the solidarity-based model of EU health systems was in fact exported to overseas countries, which reformed their health systems using EU Member States'

1 BARAK-EREZ, D. & GROSS, A.M. 2007. *Exploring social rights: between theory and practice*, Oxford; Portland, OR: Hart, p. 289.
2 GOSTIN, L.O. 2000. *Public health law: power, duty, restraint*, Berkeley; New York: University of California Press; Milbank Memorial Fund, p. 8.
3 International Conference on Primary Health Care, Alma-Ata, USSR, 6–12 September 1978.
4 RUGER, J.P. 2004. Health and social justice. *The Lancet*, 364: 1075–80.

health systems as paradigms. Moreover, some of these overseas countries are also now part of economic blocs and are therefore likely to face some of the problems already encountered by the EU.[5]

The concerns of individuals and societies regarding health issues are reflected in the health policies[6] developed by specific governments. In terms of ideology, it can be argued that health systems are shaped according to different theories of distributive justice. For example, egalitarian and libertarian viewpoints lead to quite different health care systems: in the egalitarian system, equal opportunity of access for those in equal need is the determining rule, independently of who is paying for the care, and this is best accomplished in a publicly provided system. By contrast, in the libertarian system, willingness and ability to pay is the determinant of access and it is most successfully accomplished in a market-oriented private system. Even though the egalitarian and libertarian ideologies are not to be considered as 'ideal types', and, in practice, in most countries it is possible to find traces of both ideologies in the policies regarding the organisation and delivery of health care, the principles behind these policies are likely to be systematically related to the nature of equity concerns that have been dominant in the past, and are also likely to reflect the ideology which generated those concerns.[7] In modern democracies and especially in European welfare states,[8] people expect their governments to protect them against illness and disease, to guarantee safe and healthy food and environmental conditions, to reflect these expectations in national policies, and to be politically responsible for their achievement.[9]

---

5   This is the case of Brazil, for example, which is part of Mercosur and has had a public health system since 1988. 'The current Brazilian public-sector health system was introduced under the new Federal Constitution (1988) which, inspired by the idea of a national health system, created the Sistema Único de Saúde (SUS, or Unified Health System), whose principles are free and universal access to health care, comprehensiveness, and public financing'. UGÁ, M.A. D. & SANTOS, I.S. 2007. An Analysis of Equity in Brazilian Health System Financing. *Health Affairs*, 26: 1017–28.

6   'Health policy as a concept is also broad enough to capture the expansive terrain of health because it encompasses all aspects of government policy that affect the protection and promotion of health. Thus, health policy includes traditional public health activities designed to protect community health, the provision and regulation of health care services to individuals, the financing of health services, and efforts to improve social determinants of health. To manage health adequately given the enormous range of issues involved, governments require sufficient policy space and flexibility'. FIDLER, D.P., CORREA, C. & AGINAM, O. 2005. *Draft* Legal Review of the General Agreement on Trade in Services (GATS) from a Health Policy Perspective. *Globalization, Trade and Health Working Papers Series.* World Health Organization. Available at www.who.int/trade/resource/GATS_Legal_Review_15_12_05.pdf?ua=1 [Accessed 28 November 2015].

7   WILLIAMS, A. 1993. Equity in health care: the role of ideology. *In:* WAGSTAFF, A., RUTTEN, F. & DOORSLAER, E.K.A.V. (eds) *Equity in the finance and delivery of health care: an international perspective.* Oxford: Oxford University Press, p. 292.

8   A basic definition of welfare state comprises the idea of state responsibility in providing basic modicum welfare for its citizens. This idea stems from the concept of social citizenship developed by T.H. Marshall, which implies the granting of social rights by the state. ESPING-ANDERSEN, G. 1990. *The three worlds of welfare capitalism.* Cambridge: Polity, p. 21.

9   LAMPING, W. 2005. European integration and health policy. *In:* STEFFEN, M. (ed.) *Health governance in Europe: issues, challenges and theories.* London: Routledge.

The differences between the implementation of egalitarian and libertarian viewpoints in the organisation of health systems becomes clear when, for example, EU health systems are compared to the American one. Despite cultural and economic differences among EU nation states, they have typically become welfare states, where the social rights of citizenship play a crucial role and are no less important than civil and political rights.[10] Therefore, EU health systems are much more inclined towards the egalitarian viewpoint. By contrast, in the United States the idea of liberty plays a more important role than social rights and the involvement of the state in providing welfare is restricted to minimum standards of care for the elderly and poor.

Although the egalitarian ideology in the organisation of health care systems still prevails in Europe and, in fact, is most widely supported by and widespread amongst health professionals and policy makers,[11] the formation of an EU citizenship together with the Internal Market project has had an impact on the way in which Member States organise their health systems. The application of the Internal Market freedoms to issues related to health care can have a direct or indirect effect on national laws and policies.[12] In the case of cross-border health care, for example, the option of granting subjective rights to treatment to patients, as can be seen from the jurisprudence of the European Court of Justice (ECJ)[13] and from Directive 2011/24/EU on the application of patients' rights in cross-border health care,[14] reflects a specific approach to health care which promotes individual rights as a dominant value, being associated with the idea that health care is not different from other market goods and that patients are consumers in a health care market. Therefore, it is possible to say that the Internal Market rules have introduced new values into the field of health care, which can be argued to be more concerned with a libertarian view of health care.

The impact of the Internal Market rules on the way in which Member States organise and deliver social welfare, including health care, has already been explored by scholars.[15] These works are mostly concerned with the principle of

---

10 DE BÚRCA, G. 2005. *EU law and the welfare state: in search of solidarity*. Oxford: Oxford University Press, p. 11.
11 Most studies of equity in the delivery of health care start from the premise that health care ought to be distributed according to need rather than ability to pay. WAGSTAFF, A. & DOORSLAER, E.K.A.V. 1993. Equity in the Finance and Delivery of Health Care: concepts and definitions. *In:* WAGSTAFF, A., RUTTEN, F. & DOORSLAER, E.K.A.V. (eds) *Equity in the finance and delivery of health care: an international perspective.* Oxford: Oxford University Press, p. 9.
12 DE BÚRCA, G. 2005. *Op. cit.*
13 See, for example, *Decker*, Case C-120/95 [1998] ECR I-1831; *Kohll*, Case C-158/96 [1998] ECR I-1931; *Vanbraekel and others*, Case C-368/98 [2001] ECR I-5363;*Smits and Peerbooms*, Case C-157/99[2001]ECR I-5473; *Müller-Fauré and van Riet*, Case C-385/99 [2003] ECR I-4509; and *Watts*, Case C-372/04[2006] ECR I-4325.
14 EUROPEAN PARLIAMENT AND THE COUNCIL OF THE EUROPEAN UNION 2011. Directive 2011/24/EU on the application of patients' rights in cross-border healthcare.
15 See, for example, DOUGAN, M. & SPAVENTA, E. 2005. *Social welfare and EU law*, Oxford: Hart and DE BÚRCA, G. 2005. *Op. cit.*

solidarity and the way that Internal Market rules might affect the application of this principle in relation to welfare services at the national level. However, in the case of health care, solidarity is not the only principle guiding EU health systems. There are other principles that are widely accepted as common values of these systems, such as universality, accessibility and equity, which might also be affected by the Internal Market rules. These principles are recognised by EU institutions as a way of contributing to social cohesion and social justice, as the 'Council Conclusions on Common values and principles in European Union Health Systems' demonstrates.[16] Considering the importance of these other principles for national health systems, this work will examine not only the way in which the Internal Market rules might affect the application of the principle of solidarity, but also how it affects the application of universality, accessibility and equity as well.

Therefore, this book makes innovative contributions to the study of the relationship between EU health systems and the Internal Market. First, because it encompasses the analysis of all principles recognised by EU institutions as guiding principles of EU health systems; second, because it integrates human rights law and practice into the discussion of the ECJ's approach to patient mobility cases; and third, because this book assesses the potential impact of the Internal Market over EU health systems through the lens of distributive justice, looking at the underlying principles of these systems that are mostly concerned with social justice. Furthermore, this book can be distinguished from other works dealing with the actual or potential impact of the application of EU law to health care services because these focused on specific national health systems.[17] In addition, it provides a historical overview of the development of national health systems in western EU countries.

---

16 COUNCIL OF THE EUROPEAN UNION 2006. Council Conclusions on Common values and principles in European Union Health Systems. 2006/C 146/01.
17 Kostera's research on the implications of cross-border patient mobility for the German and Danish health care systems (KOSTERA, T. 2008. Europeanizing Health Care: Cross-Border Patient Mobility and Its Consequences for the German and Danish Health Care Systems. Bruges Political Research Papers, 7, Bruges: College of Europe); Sieveking's analysis on the implementation of the ECJ rulings in Germany (SIEVEKING, K. 2007. ECJ Rulings on Health Care Services and Their Effects on the Freedom of Cross-Border Patient Mobility in the EU. *European Journal of Migration and Law*, 9: 25–51); Földes' analysis regarding the impact on Slovenia and Hungary (FÖLDES, M.É. 2009. A Legal Analysis of the Influence of Internal Market Implementation on Access to Health Care in Hungary and Slovenia. Dissertation submitted to Central European University, Department of Legal Studies and Department of Political Science, in partial fulfilment of the requirements for the degree of Doctor of Philosophy, Central European University); a research commissioned by the European Parliament explored the impact of the ECJ judgements on seven national systems (EUROPEAN PARLIAMENT 2007b. The Impact of the European Court of Justice Case Law on National Systems For Cross-Border Health Service Provision. DG Internal Policies of the Union – Policy Department Economic and Scientific Policy); and OBERMAIER, A.J. 2009. *The End of Territoriality? The Impact of ECJ Rulings on British, German and French Social Policy*. Aldershot, UK: Ashgate.

Considering the above, the general scope of this work will be to analyse, in light of the theories of distributive justice applied to the field of health care, the impact of the Internal Market rules on common values and principles shared by EU health systems, such as universality, accessibility, equity and solidarity. This analysis will be conducted using the specific issue of cross-border health care. This phenomenon encompasses the mobility of patients, professionals and services,[18] but this book focuses on patient mobility under EU law and its implications. The choice of using this issue is due to the fact that; 'access to health care has become an EU law topic through the phenomenon of cross-border care'.[19] Moreover, although cross-border health care represents a low percentage of national public budgets, indications are clear that it is moving at a fast pace with yet still immense potential to grow in the years ahead.[20] Hence, it is by using this specific phenomenon as an example that this work aims to demonstrate how solid values guiding EU health systems can be affected by EU law and libertarian ideas. In order to develop this analysis, the work will be presented as follows. The first chapter will be devoted to a literature review regarding the questions of the special moral importance of health care and of theories of distributive justice used to justify the distribution of this special good among individuals. It is important to highlight that this work deals specifically with health care. Even when it refers to health and not to health care, it is implied that health and health care are directly related, since the idea supported here is that health care is a social determinant of health and that the former, thus, plays a role in influencing the latter. The discussion about theories of distributive justice and health care will also include the argument concerning the role of the market in health care provision. The second chapter will focus on the development of social rights of citizenship and its relationship with the welfare state. This will also include an analysis of the meaning of solidarity. Then, the concepts of European citizenship and supranational solidarity will be analysed and compared to the meanings that these concepts have at the national level. The third chapter will concentrate on the provision of health care services at the national level. It will begin with a historic overview of the development of welfare services in the field of health care in Europe. Then, the models for financing and delivering health care, and their guiding principles, will be explained. The meaning of each principle will be explored through the illustration of its role in the organisation and delivering health care. Following this, it is intended to demonstrate that these systems use the egalitarian theory of justice to distribute health care. In the fourth chapter the framework of health services provision at the EU level will be analysed. It will include an analysis of EU legislation, such as

18 FOOTMAN, K. *et al*. 2014. *Cross-border healthcare in Europe*. Policy Summary 14, WHO Regional Office for Europe and European Observatory on Health Systems and Policies.

19 FÖLDES, M.É. 2009. *Op. cit*, p. 31.

20 ZUCCA, G. *et al*. 2015. *Evaluative study on the cross-border healthcare Directive (2011/24/EU)*. Luxembourg: Publications Office of the European Union. Available at http://ec.europa.eu/health/cross_border_care/docs/2015_evaluative_study_frep_en.pdf [Accessed 14 December 2015].

Treaty provisions and secondary legislation, as well as the jurisprudence of the ECJ on health services, as for example, cross-border health care and competition law cases. The fifth chapter will look at human rights law and documents in the field of health, outlining their relationship with theories of distributive justice and the provision of health care. Finally, in the last chapter, I will identify the new paradigms introduced by the Internal Market rules in the field of health care and outline their relationship with a libertarian view of health care. In this part it will also be examined how these new paradigms affect the principles of universality, accessibility, equity and solidarity at the national level, and conclusions will be drawn about the role of the EU in the realm of health care. Ultimately, this book aims to contribute to a more comprehensive and balanced interpretation of the role of the provision of health services in the context of the Internal Market and EU law.

It must be noted, however, that the theories of distributive justice considered in this work, namely egalitarianism and libertarianism, will be used here as analytical tools. Therefore, these two theories will not be directly applied as ideal models to the analysis of EU health systems; instead, the concepts and principles embedded in these theories will be used in the identification and comprehension of the new arrangements established by the application of the Internal Market rules into the health care services field.

In terms of methodology, this work can be considered exploratory documental research, whose main methods consist of bibliographic review and analysis of legal documents. Regarding the analysis of legal documents, the sources are the jurisprudence of the ECJ on health care services and other social issues, the jurisprudence of other Courts when relevant for the research aims, and legislation and other legal documents from the European Commission and the Council of the EU, such as regulations, proposals, and Green and White Papers.

Finally, it is important to point out that this research does not aim at comparing Member States' health systems; instead, the focus is on the common characteristics embedded in these systems. Although in many parts of this work specific features of some health systems are described, this has only an illustrative purpose. Furthermore, the fact that health systems from Western European countries are used more often as examples is due to the fact that the literature on these systems is more extensive than that relating to Eastern European countries.

1 Ideology in the field of health care

A general overview

This chapter starts by explaining why health and health care have special moral importance. Then, by distinguishing egalitarianism from libertarianism, theories that can be used to justify the distribution of benefits – as is the case of health care – within society, it shows that public health systems which provide universal access to health care, such as EU health systems, tend to use the egalitarian theory as the basis for their policies. It concludes by analysing the role of the market in the delivery of health care.

The special importance of health and health care

One of the reasons leading to the discussion of ideology and ethics of distribution in the field of health policies is the moral importance attached to health and health care as special benefits or goods. Since the ancient world, health has been recognised as a special good: Ancient Greek poetry and the Hippocratic texts already mention and attribute a special importance to health. In the 17th century Descartes, in his *Discours de la Méthode*, ascertained that 'the preservation of health is . . . without doubt the first good and the foundations of all other goods'.[1]

Although it resembles other forms of human capital, such as education, professional knowledge or athletic skills, it is fundamentally different from them in several crucial respects: first, it is subject to strong and unpredictable risks, which are mostly independent of one another. Also, health cannot be accumulated in the same way as knowledge and skills.[2]

This idea has evolved through time and by the end of the 19th century, when the treatment of infectious diseases became possible through the discoveries of bacteriologists, health became a question of medicine and also science.[3] Accordingly, this special importance was expanded to include health services, since

1 Apud ANAND, S., PETER, F. & SEN, A.K. 2004. Public health, ethics, and equity. Oxford; New York: Oxford University Press, p. 17.
2 WORLD HEALTH ORGANIZATION 2000. *The world health report 2000 – Health systems: improving performance.* Geneva: World Health Organization, p. 4.
3 GOSTIN, L.O. 2000. *Op. cit.*, p. 10.

one of the fundamental objectives of these services is to improve the health of the population they serve.

Even if health care is not the only determinant of health and is sometimes not the most effective and efficient way to protect and promote health,[4] it is still extremely important for people because health care services can supply some critical needs in case of illness and can reduce people's anxiety about payment for the coverage of catastrophic illness.[5] In fact, in modern society chronic diseases tend to affect and disable people frequently and thus the use of health care services tends to be necessary for a wide range of problems. As Tom Beauchamp points out, 'medical needs deserve special attention because they are unpredictable, randomly distributed, underserved, and overridingly important when they appear'.[6] Moreover, considering the different kinds of interventions that health systems are able to develop and apply against a large number of diseases, evidence indicates clearly that health systems make a large difference to health.[7]

In recent years, several authors have developed research concerning the special moral importance of health and health care. Norman Daniels, for example, who expanded Rawls' appeal to the principle assuring fair equality of opportunity,[8] attributes a moral importance to health care by arguing that the maintenance of the normal functioning of the body contributes to protecting the range of opportunities that individuals can reasonably exercise. Even if health is not the only factor affecting the range of opportunities open to people, 'the loss of functioning or premature death that may come with ill health clearly diminish the range of plans of life people can reasonably choose among in a given society. Accordingly, protecting health protects opportunity, even if it is not the only thing that does so'.[9]

A similar approach is proposed by the capability view of health, developed from Amartya Sen's capability theory,[10] which also supports the view that health and health care – due to its role in influencing health – are special goods. Resting on the Aristotelian ethical principle of 'human flourishing', this view considers that health is an end of political and societal activity,[11] emphasising that it is important because it is directly constitutive of a person's well-being and enables that person to pursue the various goals and projects in life that he or she values.[12] Instead of

---

4 In effect, other social determinants of health, such as sanitation, income and education are more effective in improving health indicators. BEAUCHAMP, T.L. & CHILDRESS, J.F. 1983. *Principles of biomedical ethics*. New York: Oxford University Press, p. 204.

5 *Ibid.*, p. 204.

6 *Ibid.*, p. 203.

7 WORLD HEALTH ORGANIZATION. 2000. *Op. cit.*, p. 9.

8 RAWLS, J. 1999. *A theory of justice*. Cambridge, MA.: Belknap Press of Harvard University Press.

9 DANIELS, N. 2008a. Justice and Access to Health Care. *Stanford Encyclopedia of Philosophy*. Available at http://plato.stanford.edu/entries/justice-healthcareaccess/ [Accessed 14 December 2015].

10 SEN, A. 1985. Well-Being, Agency and Freedom: The Dewey Lectures 1984. *The Journal of Philosophy*, 82: 169–221.

11 RUGER, J.P. 2004. *Op. cit.*

12 ANAND, S., PETER, F. & SEN, A.K. 2004. *Op. cit.*, p.17.

focusing on means (income, for example), the capability approach focuses on the opportunity to fulfil ends. As Sen illustrates:

> if a person has a high income but is also very prone to persistent illness, or is handicapped by some serious physical disability, then the person need not necessarily be seen as being very advantaged, on the mere ground that her income is high. She certainly has more of one of the means of living well (that is, a lot of income), but she faces difficulty in translating that into good living (that is, living in a way that she has reason to celebrate) because of the adversities of illness and physical handicap. We have to look instead at the extent to which she can actually achieve, if she so chooses, a state of good health and wellness, and being fit enough to do what she has reason to value. To understand that the means of satisfactory human living are not themselves the ends of good living helps to bring about a significant extension of the reach of the evaluative exercise. And the use of the capability perspective begins right here.[13]

Besides considering that the benefits of health are indispensable to individuals, the capability approach also supports the view that health is important for political communities, because 'without minimum levels of health populations cannot fully engage in the political process, generate wealth and assure economic prosperity, and provide for common defense and security'.[14] In effect, when used as a supportive theory for the development of social policies and for the solution of actual policy problems, the capability approach shows some advantages over other theories. First, because it recognises that human flourishing does not only depend on resources and, thus, that social policy should not only be concerned with material resources; and second, because this approach focuses on outcomes that are valuable in themselves. In this connection, for example, an index based on this approach would not consider only GDP per capita as a variable representative of development; it would also include other variables, such as literacy, education and life expectancy.[15]

In a similar vein, other authors recognise the importance of health as a universal need. According to this view, together with autonomy, physical health works as a 'universal precondition' to meaningful social participation. Hence, the provision of this basic need is essential to enable people 'to engage in the social activities that are central to the human condition'.[16]

Accordingly, once it is recognised that health and health care have a special status, the criteria for the distribution of these goods within the society will be

13   SEN, A.K. 2009. *The idea of justice.* London: Allen Lane, p. 234.
14   GOSTIN, L.O. 2000. *Op. cit.*
15   BURCHARDT, T. 2007. Welfare: what for? *In:* HILLS, J., LE GRAND, J. & PIACHAUD, D. (eds) *Making social policy work.* Bristol: The Policy Press.
16   DWYER, P. 2004. *Understanding social citizenship: themes and perspectives for policy and practice.* Bristol: Policy Press, p. 14.

different from the criteria applied to the distribution of non-special goods. Considering that theories of distributive justice tell us what goods justice is concerned with and how justice requires them to be distributed,[17] theories of distributive justice must be approached when talking about the distribution of health and health care. Therefore, the work turns now to the question concerning the theories of distributive justice used to justify the distribution of health and health care within society. The focus will be specifically on health care services and, as already pointed out, the intrinsic relationship existing between these services and health.

Health care and theories of distributive justice

Theories of social or distributive justice are the philosophical foundations used to justify the distribution of benefits and burdens within society. As opposed to the idea of retributive justice,[18] which is concerned with private relations and is the business of courts and the legal profession, distributive justice is the 'justice owed by community to its members, including the fair allocation of common advantages and the sharing of common burdens'.[19] Hence, it is seldom the business of courts, but primarily the business of government and public policies. Different theories of distributive justice will reflect different moral principles as the basis (or the meaning) for what is just (or fair) and what distinguishes these various theories are the principles used to give material content to the idea of justice. Although there are other principles and theories to justify the distribution of health care,[20] here I will deal only with the principles related directly with egalitarian and libertarian theories of justice. This choice is due to the fact that this book is concerned *inter alia* with the contrast between egalitarian and libertarian values within health care systems. The material principles of justice considered here are:[21]

- to each person an equal share;
- to each person according to individual need;
- to each person according to individual effort;
- to each person according to societal contribution;
- to each person according to ability to pay;
- to each person according to merit.

---

17 HURLEY, S. 2007. The 'What' and the 'How' of Distributive Justice and Health. *In:* HOLTUG, N. & LIPPERT-RASMUSSEN, K. (eds) *Egalitarianism: new essays on the nature and value of equality.* Oxford: Oxford University Press, p. 308.

18 'Justice concerned with the relation between persons and especially with the fairness in the exchange of goods and the fulfilment of contractual obligations'. BLACK, H.C. & GARNER, B.A. 2009. *Black's Law Dictionary.* St. Paul, MN: Thomson Reuters, p. 942.

19 *Ibid.,* p. 942.

20 See, for example, STANTON-IFE, J. 1999. *Health care allocation in ethics and law: a defence of the need principle.* Thesis submitted for assessment with a view to obtaining the degree of Doctor of Laws of the European University Institute, p. 17.

21 BEAUCHAMP, T.L. & CHILDRESS, J.F. 1983. *Op. cit.,* p. 187.

Considering that the distribution of health care is primarily a political issue, each government invokes one or more of these material principles for public policy purposes, applying different principles to different contexts.

Egalitarianism

Egalitarian theories of justice emphasise equal access or equal distribution of social goods as a material principle of justice. A traditional and common criterion used by egalitarians is the Aristotelian principle of equality that equals ought to be treated equally and unequals may be treated unequally.[22] However, this basic idea of equality is merely formal since no reference is made to what is to be considered equal. Thus, formulated in this way, the principle lacks substance, and in order to specify the relevant grounds on which people are to be treated equally, it is necessary to give some specification of the kind of equality that is under consideration.

The classic material principle of equality in terms of the distribution of goods corresponds to the idea of to each an equal share. However, an extreme equality in the distribution of resources, though desirable, can be said to be unfeasible. First, because the way modern societies are organised in terms of legal, political and economic structures cannot allow for a completely equal distribution of resources without also implying a breach of individual property rights. Second, even if equality were achieved, inequality would probably emerge again because people's capacities, qualities and wants differ.

In the field of health care, this type of extreme egalitarianism or 'strong egalitarianism'[23] is avoided since it could lead to absurd situations in which a healthy individual receives the same amount of care as one in real need of care. Therefore, if the objective is to obtain an egalitarian result in the distribution of resources without violating individual rights or leading to absurd situations, other rules and principles must be applied in order to obtain the equalisation of differences between individuals. In this regard, another rule used by egalitarians is the principle of equality of opportunities. According to this rule, equalisation is achieved by giving people equal access to positions in society, i.e. any individuals in society with the same native talent and ambition should have the same prospects of success in competition for positions that confer special benefits and advantages.[24]

The principle of equality of opportunity was disseminated in the late 20th century by the most influential theory of justice of this time – that of John Rawls.[25] Although a philosopher in the liberal tradition, the distribution of social goods proposed by

---

22 *Ibid.*, p. 186.
23 OLSEN, J.A. 1997. Theories of justice and their implications for priority setting in health care. *Journal of Health Economics*, 16(6): 625–39.
24 ARNESON, R. 2002. Egalitarianism. *Stanford Encyclopedia of Philosophy*. Available at http://plato.stanford.edu/entries/egalitarianism/ [Accessed 14 December 2015].
25 RAWLS, J. 1999. *Op. cit.*

Rawls' theory is associated with egalitarianism. According to Rawls, there are two basic principles of justice:

> First: each person is to have an equal right to the most extensive scheme of equal basic liberties compatible with a similar scheme of liberties for others.
>
> Second: social and economic inequalities are to be arranged so that they are both (a) reasonably expected to be to everyone's advantage, and (b) attached to positions and offices open to all.[26]

Since then, some authors have continued to elaborate and expand Rawls' principle to some variants of equality of opportunity to welfare or advantage.[27] In the field of health care, for example, Norman Daniels broadened Rawls' notion of opportunity to include health care institutions among the basic institutions involved in providing for fair equality of opportunity.[28] Therefore, the provision of health care resources by the state is important because of the role it can play in furnishing an adequate range of opportunities to pursue valuable options for everyone. The idea behind it is to restore the fair opportunity range for individuals to what they would have if social arrangements were more just and less unequal. A similar idea applies in protecting opportunity against ill health. The impairment of normal functioning by significant pathology or disability restricts individuals' opportunity relative to the portion of the normal range that their skills and talents would have made available to them were they healthy. If individuals' fair shares of the normal range are the life plans they may reasonably choose, given their talents and skills, the disease and disability reduce their shares from what is fair.[29]

In the same light, John Stanton-Ife used Rawls' equality of opportunity to argue that at the heart of individual well-being is the idea of adequate opportunity to pursue successful lives, and health care provision in turn has an important role to play in this idea.[30] Therefore, even if Rawls does not include health or health care amongst what he calls primary social goods, i.e. things that any rational man would want whatever else he wants, and that can assure greater success in one's life intentions and ends,[31] his theory and the principles arising from it are very often used in the field of health care.

A second influence in the field of health care of Rawls' principles lies in the idea of need. Rawls advocates that special attention must be devoted to the

26   *Ibid.*, p. 53.
27   See, for example, ARNESON, R. 1989. Equality and Equal Opportunity for Welfare. *Philosophical Studies*, 56(1): 77; COHEN, G.A. 1989. On the Currency of Egalitarian Justice. *Ethics*, 99(4): 906–44.
28   DANIELS, N. 2008b. *Just health: meeting health needs fairly.* Cambridge; New York: Cambridge University Press, p. 57.
29   *Ibid.*, p. 44.
30   STANTON-IFE, J. 1999. *Op. cit.*, p. 9.
31   According to Rawls, primary social goods, given in broad categories, are rights, liberties, and opportunities, and income and wealth. RAWLS, J. 1999. *Op. cit.*, p. 79.

worst-off because 'in order to treat all persons equally, to provide genuine equality of opportunity, society must give more attention to those with fewer native assets and to those born into less favorable positions. The idea is to redress the bias of contingencies in the direction of equalities'.[32] This is what Rawls calls the difference principle, which, expanded into the field of health care, can be understood through the idea of need. The need for health is a crucial concept for the discussion of the distribution of health care insofar as it is one way of measuring equitable access to health services, as it builds on the idea that the utilisation of services should reflect actual need for care.[33] Therefore, translating Rawls' difference principle into the principle of need leads to the idea that the greater the health need, the greater the reason to meet it.[34]

One difficulty found in the application of the need principle lies in how to define need. Indeed, there is much discussion and disagreement between health economists and scholars regarding the concept of need, and an accepted working definition of need has not yet been reached. Despite these disagreements, there are two components of need that stand out as important, even if they too will sometimes conflict with each another: the first is the definition embraced by most clinicians, according to which what counts as need is the pre-treatment state of the individual's health, with greater ill health equating to greater need; and the second is the definition embraced by most health economists, which holds that the individual's capacity to benefit from health care determines the size of his or her need.[35]

Defining a technical concept of need is, however, beyond the scope of this work. Moreover, it should be considered that each country will refine the notion of health need in order to give more consistency and put in practice action based on this principle by, for example, developing formulas for the purpose of informing regional health care allocations.[36] Therefore, for the purposes of this work it is sufficient to merely acknowledge that need comprises the idea of necessity and indispensability; it is different from preferences and wants[37] and it is not to be

---

32   *Ibid.*, p. 86.
33   GULLIFORD, M., FIGUEROA-MUNOZ, J., MORGAN, M., HUGHES, D., GIBSON, B., BEECH, R. & HUDSON, M. 2002. What does 'access to health care' mean? *Journal of Health Services Research & Policy*, 7(3): 186–8.
34   STANTON-IFE, J. 1999. *Op. cit.*, p. 9.
35   OLIVER, A. & MOSSIALOS, E. 2004. Equity of access to health care: outlining the foundations for action. *Journal of Epidemiology and Community Health*, 58: 655–8.
36   *Ibid.*
37   Norman Daniels refers to health needs as those things required to maintain, restore or provide the normal species functioning. His set of health needs includes: adequate nutrition, sanitary, safe, unpolluted living and working conditions, exercise, rest; important lifestyle features such as avoiding substance abuse and practising safe sex; preventive, curative, rehabilitative and compensatory personal medical services and devices; non-medical personal and social support services; and an appropriate distribution of other social determinants of health. DANIELS, N. 2008a. *Op. cit.*, pp. 42–3.

elucidated in terms of individually perceived and felt needs.[38] Callahan and Wasunna illustrate this idea of medical necessity very well by stating that '[t]here is no debate about the necessity of surgery for a ruptured appendix, but plenty of squabbling about Viagra as a necessity for ageing males, with or without some clear medical pathology'.[39] In Chapter 3 I will come back to the idea of need when discussing equity in access to health care.

As can be seen, the achievement of fairness in the distribution of health care according to the egalitarian theory of justice requires the application of the need principle together with the fair opportunity rule. Making use of the material principles of justice stated above, it is possible to say that an egalitarian theory of distributive justice in the field of health care recognises the special importance of this social good and, in order to distribute it, combines the formal principle of justice with the fair opportunity rule and the principle of need, leading, thereby, to the idea that people with equal health needs should be treated equally by having equal access to health care, i.e. by having access to the same kind of health care services in regard to the satisfaction of their needs.

For matters of ideology and ethics, public health systems that provide universal access to health care tend to use the egalitarian theory as the basis for their policies. However, even countries that do not use the egalitarian theory as a general policy supporting the whole health system have egalitarian concerns behind the development of some specific policies. This is the case, for example, of the Medicaid and Medicare Programmes in the United States.[40]

In the EU, this egalitarian ideology is shared across Member States and is used as a basis for the development of social policies, including those concerning health. This ideology is actually a corollary of the principle of solidarity, which is a core value of the EU health systems. However, it is not only solidarity that reflects the egalitarian ideology of EU health systems; there are other values and principles recognised by EU institutions that also reflect this ideology. In this regard, the Council of the European Union recognises that universality, access to good quality care, equity and solidarity are overarching values widely accepted in the work of the different EU institutions and shared across Europe. Universality means that no one is denied access to health care; solidarity is closely linked to the financial arrangement of national health systems and the need to ensure accessibility to all; equity relates to equal access according to need, regardless of ethnicity, gender, age, social status or ability to pay. By using this set of values, EU health systems aim to reduce the gap in health inequalities, which is a concern of EU Member States.[41]

38 STANTON-IFE, J. 1999. *Op. cit.*, p. 73.
39 CALLAHAN, D. & WASUNNA, A.A. 2006. *Medicine and the market: equity v. Choice.* Baltimore, MD: John Hopkins University Press, p. 8.
40 Health care programmes specially designed for the poor and the elderly, respectively.
41 COUNCIL OF THE EUROPEAN UNION 2006. Council Conclusions on Common values and principles in European Union Health Systems. 2006/C 146/01, p. 3.

It is worth noting that not only material principles coming from the egalitarian ideology are used in the development of EU health systems and policies. In fact, none of the EU countries have systems that would fit exclusively with the egalitarian or libertarian ideologies. To give an example, the countries which use the social insurance model (or conservative welfare states, as we will see in the next chapter) also make use of the material principle, 'to each person according to societal contribution'. In these countries the law determines the categories of persons who are compulsorily insured, the premiums to be paid (which are usually income-related), the benefit package and the rules governing the administration of the systems. Even using non-egalitarian principles, there is still the government commitment to provide universal access for all the population, and above all the appeal to solidarity. For this reason, also people who for some reason do not contribute to the social security scheme, such as the unemployed, have access to benefits on the basis of solidarity, equal treatment and progressive cover according to need.

Therefore, although Member States have different approaches to turning the application of the principles of universality, access to good quality care, equity and solidarity into a practical reality – and, in effect, some have relied on market mechanisms and competitive pressures to strategically manage their health systems – the commitment to provide everyone with full access to an adequate range of health care services, based on the material principle of equal access according to need, still prevails as a strong value in EU health systems. None of the EU Member States has chosen fully to entrust the supply of medical care to market principles. The adoption of market mechanisms has not reduced the long-term role of the state but rather has shifted the requirements for the satisfactory fulfilment of that role.[42] Therefore, governments regulate and subsidise the health care sector, and in many Member States insurance for medical care is mandatory and health care facilities are provided by state institutions.[43] The reason for this is the fact that the concept of solidarity remains at the heart of the European model, which works not only as a founding principle but also as a moral premise that encompasses the idea of citizens' mutual responsibility for each other's health care and that of equitable access to care. In Chapter 3 the principles of universality, access to good quality care, equity and solidarity will be explored thoroughly.

Equity and equality

A last point related to the egalitarian theory that must be clarified before we move ahead is the difference between the terms equity and equality.[44] These are two

42   SALTMAN, R.B. 1997. Balancing state and market in health system reform. *European Journal of Public Health*, 7(2): 119–20.

43   VAN DER MEI, A.P. 2003. *Free movement of persons within the European Community: cross-border access to public benefits*. Oxford; Portland, OR: Hart, p. 223.

44   BRAVEMAN, P. & GRUSKIN, S. 2003. Defining equity in health. *Journal of Epidemiology and Community Health*, 57: 254–8.

terms that represent quite different concepts, but in the field of health care they are often used interchangeably. Equality means '[t]he quality or state of being equal';[45] meanwhile, equity means fairness, impartiality or the body of principles constituting what is fair.[46] Accordingly, when the concept of equality is used for the distribution of a given resource, as health care for example, this implies that everyone will be provided with an identical amount of it. As mentioned before, in the field of health care the pure use of the principle of equality, what some authors call 'strong' egalitarianism, is avoided, since it could lead to absurd situations in which people who do not have the same need of health care would benefit in the same way as those who are in greater need.

In turn, if the objective is to achieve equity in the distribution of goods, health care included, first we will have to agree upon what we believe to be the most fair. Then, a distribution will only be equitable once there is a previous agreement on the relevant criteria for a fair distribution, such as the material principles of justice listed at the beginning of this chapter. Therefore, equity may involve distributing a resource equally or unequally, depending upon the relevant criteria for fairness requirements in a given situation.

In the field of health care, equity is usually identified as having two forms: vertical equity, which means preferential treatment for those with greater needs, and horizontal equity, which means equal treatment for equivalent needs.[47] Considering these two forms of equity and the discussion developed concerning egalitarian theories and health care, we can conclude that need is the relevant criterion for achieving an equitable distribution in the field of health care.

Although equity and equality are different concepts, they can have similar meanings if equal shares or equal treatment are chosen as the relevant criteria of fairness. This is, in effect, what happens between equality and the horizontal form of equity, insofar as this provides for the equal treatment of persons. The difference, however, between strict equality and the idea of horizontal equity is that the latter is complemented by the concept of need, which is used together with equal treatment as a criterion of equalisation.

In addition to the use of equity as a principle of distribution of health care, it can also be applied to all of the health policies of a given health system. Equity is a concept that also regards access to the health care system as well as its funding. In terms of funding, health systems are equitable insofar as they provide a

---

45 BLACK, H.C. & GARNER, B.A. 2009. *Op. cit.*, p. 616.

46 As defined by Black's Law Dictionary, equity, indeed, has five different definitions. Equity also means 'The recourse to principles of justice to correct or supplement the law as applied to particular circumstances', 'The system of law or body of principles originating in the English Court of Chancery and superseding the common and statute law', or even 'A right, interest, or remedy recognizable by a court of equity'. However, these are definitions of equity applied to the legal field and here we are interested in the more general concept of equity, which is related to fairness. *Ibid.*, p. 619.

47 MACINKO, J. & STARFIELD, B. 2002. Annotated Bibliography on Equity in Health, 1980–2001. *International Journal for Equity in Health*, 1: 1.

redistribution of resources, providing health care services to the whole population, and are funded from a large percentage of the resources of those with increased income. In effect, those with higher incomes pay for the care of those who have lower incomes, but equal or greater need.[48]

Equity in terms of access to health care is another important aspect of an equitable health system. This is, in fact, the focus of this work, since equity of access is recognised as a common value of EU health systems. This topic will be better explored in Chapter 3, in which the common values of EU health systems will be examined. On this point there is much literature, though little agreement has been reached on a commonly accepted definition of equitable access.[49] In order to conclude this part, it is enough to say that it is not possible to settle questions about equity in access until there is more clarity on what we mean by access to health care.

Libertarianism

Originally grounded in the ideas of the invisible hand proposed by Adam Smith and on *laissez-faire* theories, libertarian ideas of justice have a different view of the distribution of health care. These theories emphasise social and economic liberty as strong and dominant values, and concentrate on the individual rights of persons to enter and withdraw freely from arrangements in accordance with the perception of their interests.[50] The social reality is framed by the primacy of the individual, who is a rational being able to be the best judge of his or her interests. Accordingly, a just society for libertarians is not one that seeks to promote the general good or an equal distribution; on the contrary, it is one that promotes individual rights and freedoms and that protects its individuals from any kind of state intervention which might interfere with citizens' rights of freedom and the entitlement to choose.

In the economic sphere, libertarian theories sustain that the state should only ensure the operation of a competitive market system. It is for the market to meet the requirements of efficiency and equity. The distribution of goods is left to the market and is assumed to be just insofar it will reflect individual abilities and efforts.[51] As Callahan and Wasunna summarise, '[i]n essence, their argument is that the market is the key to the spread and success of democracy, prosperity, and human freedom; it is more than an instrumental tool'.[52]

During the 20th century, the American philosopher Robert Nozick was one of the most important authors supporting the libertarian view in terms of distributive justice. According to his ideas, a distribution is just provided it has the appropriate history; provided it did in fact come about in accordance with the rules of

---

48 KLUTHE, J. 2002. Equity and equality: core values in Canadian health care. *In touch: Journal of the Provincial Health Ethics Network*, 5(7).
49 OLIVER, A. & MOSSIALOS, E. 2004. *Op. cit.*
50 BEAUCHAMP, T.L. & CHILDRESS, J.F. 1983. *Op. cit.*, p. 190.
51 DWYER, P. 2004. *Op. cit.*, pp. 24–5.
52 CALLAHAN, D. & WASUNNA, A.A. 2006. *Op. cit.*, p. 11.

acquisition, transfer and rectification of holdings.[53] What might seem unequal according to egalitarianism is not unequal according to Nozick's ideas, because his entitlement theory does not merely look at the prevailing pattern of distribution, but also looks at the history of how the distribution came about. If it came about in accordance with the rules of acquisition, transfer and rectification, i.e. if people do not cheat, steal or violate someone's right in acquiring goods, then whatever distribution results will be a just distribution, however unequal it might be.

Libertarianism does not attach any special moral importance to health care. On the contrary, this kind of service is viewed as a service or commodity, to be purchased in a market like any other service or commodity. Having this in mind, the American philosopher Ronald Dworkin developed a model for the distribution of health care in which he identifies how much society should spend on health and how it should be distributed.[54] According to his ideas, health care cannot be considered the chief among all goods (the 'insulation' model of health care) because in this case it would require society to spend all its resources on health care. He also rejects the idea of need, arguing that it is a philosophically controversial idea. By imagining a society where there is fair equality in the distribution of resources, where people in general know about the costs and value of medical procedures, and health care is not provided by the government, he proposes, then, that whatever this society spends as its total health care budget and however it distributes health care would be a just distribution for that society.[55]

When designing his model for a just distribution of health care, Dworkin probably had in mind American society and a market-oriented health system since one of the premises of his hypothetical society is that health care is not provided by the government. In practice, market-oriented health systems have libertarianism as their basis and the material principle implicit in the distribution of health care is the ability to pay. In these systems the state does not play a role in the distribution of health services and goods, and the term choice, as the essence of economic and social freedom, is a leading value. In market systems, choice means not only the choice of a doctor by the patient but also a personal choice about how much to pay for health care. Thus, on the one hand, there is the choice of the individual to shop around and buy the health insurance plan and health package that best suits her or him. On the other hand, however, there is the fact that not all citizens will be able to afford any kind of coverage, thus remaining without access to health care.

This is, for instance, one of the problems in the use of the libertarian ideology in the field of health care, because these systems usually end up creating a two-tier health system in which wealth grants some patients access to medical services that others with the same need cannot obtain. A paradigm of this kind of system

53   NOZICK, R. 1974. Distributive Justice. *In:* AVINERI, S. & DE-SHALIT, A. (eds) *Communitarianism and individualism.* Oxford; New York: Oxford University Press, pp. 138–9.
54   DWORKIN, R. 1993. Justice in the Distribution of Health Care. *McGill Law Journal,* 38(4): 883–98.
55   *Ibid.,* p. 889.

is the American health system and, as a consequence, in the United States public health coverage is limited and most Americans rely upon insurance they receive from their employers or can afford to purchase on their own. Many American insurance products are specifically designed with different tiers of service. For more money, people can access more services, have limited prior approvals and gate-keeping, and have greater choice of physicians and hospitals.[56] Although many changes have been recently introduced by the Patient Protection and Affordable Care Act (PPACA), commonly called the Affordable Care Act (ACA) or colloquially Obamacare, which is briefly analysed in the following pages, the basis of the American health system is private health insurance.

The market and health care

Nowadays the discussion between egalitarian and libertarian theories of justice can no longer be viewed in a 'black and white' perspective, since the influence and role of the market even in the most egalitarian health systems and policies cannot be avoided. Therefore, discussions about theories of distributive justice no longer reflect the two contrasting prospects represented by the market versus the state; instead, these discussions should depart from the premise that the market does in fact play an important role in present-day health systems and policies. The focus is then on the role and the value of the market in different types of health systems, i.e. of how market mechanisms are incorporated by health systems which use different ideologies to develop their health policies. In this regard, it is possible to say that some countries seem far more prone than others to incorporate and develop market ideas within their health systems, whereas others try to cope with the introduction of market values while maintaining the government's role. The idea is not to make a judgement of the different uses of the market within health systems, instead the intention is to analyse whether this use of the market is compatible with the principles and values on which EU health systems are grounded. Furthermore, it must be noted that this work is not criticising the market as an institution. In effect, the idea supported here is that there is nothing wrong with introducing market ideology into the health care field, provided that everyone can afford to participate in that market.[57]

It must be noted that the health care 'market' is quite different from a normal market. While in a normal market the primary objective of producers and consumers is naturally selfish, since the former aim to maximise profit and the latter utility, in the health care 'market' things do not work with this same logic due to the distinctive features that characterise this sector. Many of these distinctive features are related to the asymmetries of information that exist between a provider

56 KROHMAL, B.J. & EMANUEL, E.J. 2007. Tiers without tears: the ethics of a two-tier health care system. *In:* STEINBOCK, B. (ed.) *The Oxford handbook of bioethics.* Oxford; New York: Oxford University Press, p. 176.
57 GOOIJER, W.D. 2007. *Trends in EU health care system.* New York: Springer, p. 2.

and the patient. The patient does not know what kind of treatment he or she may need and is completely reliant upon the advice of his or her doctor. The result is that health care is a market where suppliers determine demand rather than well-informed consumers. The reliance upon health professionals transforms 'consumers' into 'patients'.[58] This is the reason why going to the doctor is very different from buying any other service. Therefore the application of market mechanisms to the health care field should take into account the particularities of this rather special sector and cannot be based solely on the experience of usual markets.

Although the United States has always been far more prone to using market mechanisms within its health system, it is not only in this country that the market plays a role in the health care sector. In Europe, some background conditions which started in the 1970s led to a more prominent role for the market in EU health systems from the 1980s. Economic background conditions, such as the economic crisis of the 1970s, which culminated in the oil crisis, affected the countries' economies leading to unemployment. Social changes, such as the new role of women in the market place, associated with medical progress creating a long life expectancy led to demographical changes in the structure of society. Furthermore, within the health care sector, an increasing role for medical technology in the provision of health care opened the door for the most sophisticated and expensive medical devices, including expensive pharmaceuticals, creating a link between the health care sector and the industrial economy, subjecting health care to the industrial imperatives of expanding the demand for goods and services.[59]

These economic, social and sector changes associated with a political environment, known as the Thatcher and Reagan era, fostered the advocacy of the so called *neoliberal* agenda, which promoted amongst its main ideas a prominent role for the market and a reduction in the role of the state as a way to increase employment rates, adjust economies and reduce public expenditures.[60] These ideas circulated with growing force particularly in the United States and the United Kingdom, but in the rest of Europe a parallel market stream also took place, influenced by globalisation and aiming at providing financial sustainability of the economy and public services.[61] Therefore, throughout the 1980s, radical, neoliberal economic policies were undertaken in many OECD countries. Policy innovations included the liberalisation of labour and capital markets, the removal of import

58 NICKLESS, J. 2002. The Internal Market and the Social Nature of Health Care. *In:* MOSSIALOS, E., MCKEE, M. & BAETEN, R. (eds.) *The impact of EU law on health care systems.* Bruxelles: P.I.E.-Peter Lang.

59 FREEMAN, R. & MORAN, M. 2000. Reforming health care in Europe. *West European Politics,* 23: 35–58, p. 36.

60 SANTOS, I. S. 2009. *O Mix Público-Privado no Sistema de Saúde Brasileiro: elementos para a regulação da cobertura duplicada.* Thesis submitted for assessment with a view to obtaining the degree of Doctor of Public Health of the Escola Nacional de Saúde Pública Sergio Arouca-ENSP/FIOCRUZ, p. 21.

61 CALLAHAN, D. & WASUNNA, A.A. 2006. *Op. cit,* p. 9.

restrictions, the deregulation of industry and the privatisation of state enterprises. In the public sector, departments were restructured and down-sized, many functions were contracted out to private suppliers and a vast array of new public management tools were introduced. These years were thus characterised by a worldwide move away from command-and-control systems towards entrepreneurial, market-based arrangements.[62]

The health care sector was also affected by these neoliberal ideas. In fact, over the last 30 years almost all EU health systems have undertaken some health reforms, seeking efficiency and cost containment, and introduced market mechanisms in the funding and provision of health services. These market mechanisms comprise, for example, the use of competition, co-payments or user fees, private health insurance, for-profit versus not-for-profit institutions, medical savings accounts and physician incentives.[63] The introduction of market mechanisms in EU health systems was a gradual process and can be viewed indeed as 'waves' of reforms,[64] each aiming at different objectives and resulting in different outputs. The first wave of reforms took place between the 1970s and the 1980s and was aimed basically at containing costs. Some authors view it as a kind of fiscal imperative, since the volume of costs consumed by the health sector doubled between the 1960s and the 1970s.[65] This was pursued via different strategies applied by national governments in varying combinations of policies, among which it is possible to identify control over the number of health professionals, changes in the way of remunerating these professionals, the decentralisation of services and control over the use of health services by the introduction of user charges.[66]

The wave of reforms which took place between the 1980s and 1990s was also aimed at containing costs, but by introducing greater competition and fostering efficiency within the system. The idea of managed competition introduced by the American health economist, Alain Enthoven, became incorporated into a general discourse of health policy and planning.[67] In this second wave of reforms it is possible to identify the privatisation of some health services and consequently the contracting of private providers in order to promote competition within the health systems. Some countries created specific agencies, which were distinct from state

---

62   TOTH, F. 2010. Healthcare policies over the last 20 years: Reforms and counter-reforms. *Health Policy*, 95: 82–9.

63   CALLAHAN, D. & WASUNNA, A.A. 2006. *Op. cit.*, p. 112.

64   TOTH, F. 2010. *Op. cit.*

65   As Freeman and Moran explain: 'By 1975, in France, Germany and Sweden, public spending on health absorbed more than twice the proportion of GDP it had in 1960: in Italy, health spending had grown by more than two-thirds and in the UK by more than half'. FREEMAN, R. & MORAN, M. 2000. *Op. cit.*, p. 37.

66   'Co-payments were increased in conjunction with other legislation in Germany in 1981–82, 1983–84, 1989 and 1993, while a small additional health insurance contribution was levied for hospital maintenance between 1997 and 1999. In France, charges were raised in 1986 and 1993, and in the UK most notably in 1989, when they were introduced for eye tests and dental checks (though NHS prescription charges have been raised at other times, too)'. *Ibid.*, p. 39.

67   *Ibid.*, p. 43.

bodies, in order to act as intermediaries and purchase health services.[68] Other types of mechanism introduced during this period were the creation of lists of services and the introduction of more patient choice.

The third wave of reforms that took place from the mid-1990s onwards can be viewed as a step back in relation to competition and market mechanisms. This phase is characterised by more regulation and integration of the various components of the health system as a response to the retreat of market-oriented experiments. According to Federico Toth, '[i]n part, this was motivated by disillusion with market as a tool for increasing efficiency and responsiveness in health care, and in part it was a response to the election of governments with an ideological preference for regulation over competition'.[69]

In effect, authors who analysed the outcomes resulting from the market reforms undertaken by European welfare states have concluded that the changes introduced by market-oriented mechanisms had not changed the nature of the welfare state and thus had not implied the loss of social rights or diminution of the universal social protection guaranteed by these systems.[70] They suggest that the reforms were of a more managerial and administrative nature, which far from diminishing the role of government, engaged it in a different set of activities. Thus, health policy continues to be made at the national level, accompanied by tight aggregate expenditure and quality controls, and strong government control still prevails in all instances of the health system – financing, organisation and delivery. The central strategy behind these reforms relies upon two key concepts. First, they have sought to add micro-economic (institutional-level) efficiency to previously achieved macro-economic (health system level) efficiency by introducing better managerial mechanisms within provider institutions in order to contain health care costs; and second, they have sought solutions that can combine entrepreneurial behaviour with solidarity. National policymakers across Western Europe have pursued mechanisms that can harness the innovation and efficiency benefits of entrepreneurialism within what they insist must remain an overall health system structure based on social equity.[71]

Therefore, it is possible to argue that EU health systems remain under government domination and have focused on the goal of solidarity and universal access, even if entrepreneurial activities are accepted or encouraged. As the metaphor proposed by Callahan and Wasunna well illustrates:

---

68   This is what the OECD calls the public contract model, according to which public payers – state agencies or social security funds – contract with private health-care providers. DOCTEUR, E. & OXLEY, H. 2003. Health-Care Systems: Lessons from the Reform Experience. *OECD Health Working Papers*.

69   TOTH, F. 2010. *Op. cit.*, p. 84.

70   See, for example, FREEMAN, R. & MORAN, M.P. 2000. *Op. cit.* and ESPING-ANDERSEN, G. 1999. *Social Foundations of Postindustrial Economies*. Oxford: Oxford University Press.

71   SALTMAN, R.B. 2002. The Western European Experience with Health Care Reform. *European Observatory on Health Systems and Policies*. Available at www.teamgrant.ca/M-THAC%20Greatest% 20Hits/M-THAC%20Projects/All%20info/mthac%20lectures/Saltman%20Paper.pdf [Accessed 21 December 2015].

It is as if the European solidarity systems, whether of Bismark or Beveridge type, are saying to market ideas, in effect, 'we will sometimes accept you into our house and occasionally even welcome you – just keep in mind that it is *our* house not yours. Do not rearrange the furniture in any drastic way, and be sure to take off your shoes before entering'.[72]

In this sense, the reforms undertaken by EU health systems did not imply the expansion of the market into what has traditionally been the role of the state. That is the reason why some countries in the EU identify themselves as 'social market states',[73] in which 'public philosophy favours a creative blend of government and market forces in organizing society and tackling its problems'.[74] This implies a special relationship between market forces and the government, and a good way of looking at it and identifying its specificities is by comparing the relationship between market forces and the state's role in EU health systems to that of the American system. The United States leans much more towards the libertarian model and, even if the government runs programmes for the provision of health care to the poor and the elderly, its role is still reduced *vis-à-vis* the role of the market. The government not only plays a reduced role in the provision of health care, but also encourages the market. Therefore, the use of the private insurance/private provider model[75] is the general rule for the majority of the population, which may remain without coverage in many situations. This not only leaves space for an excessive market influence, but also conditions the right to access to health services to the socio-economic condition of the individual.

However, the American market approach to health is not synonymous with efficiency. For instance, data on many common health indicators suggests that 'the US health system is highly inefficient, yielding poor outcomes despite high levels of expenditures'.[76] Comparing the American and EU health systems, it is possible

---

72 CALLAHAN, D. & WASUNNA, A.A. 2006. *Op. cit.*, p. 116.
73 For example, Article 20 paragraph 1 of the German Basic Law characterises Germany as a 'social federal state'. In economic terms, this idea is associated with a 'social market economy', an expression invented by the German Professor of Economics Alfred Müller Armak, who presented in an article of 1948 the 'social market economy' as a third way between 'laissez-faire liberalism' and 'planned economy' with the threat of socialisation. JOERGES, C. & RÖDL, F. 2004. 'Social Market Economy' as Europe's Social Model? *In:* MAGNUSSON, L. & STRÅTH, B. (eds) *A European social citizenship?: preconditions for future policies from a historical perspective.* Brussels; New York: P.I.E. – Peter Lang, p. 139.
74 BROWN, L.D. & AMELUNG, V.E. 1999. 'Manacled competition': market reforms in German health care. *Health Affairs*, 18: 76–91, p. 78.
75 The use of private insurance combined with private (often for-profit) providers. According to this model, insurance can be mandatory, as in Switzerland, or voluntary, as in the United States, and in the case of the latter, affordable insurance may not be available to some individuals. DOCTEUR, E. & OXLEY, H. 2003. *Op.cit.*, p. 10.
76 SCHMITT, J. & ZIPPERER, B. 2007. Is the United States a good model for reducing social exclusion in Europe? *In:* NAVARRO, V. (ed.) *Neoliberalism, globalization, and inequalities: consequences for health and quality of life.* Amityville, NY: Baywood, p. 248.

to say that in the former there is excessive 'commodification'[77]. This is due to the fact that solidarity is not universally embraced as a foundational principle of the health system as it is in the EU, which has remained focused on the goal of solidarity, seeing market mechanisms as a possible means to achieving this goal rather than an end in itself.[78] Therefore, the American system stands as a poor model for countries seeking equality and the combatting of social exclusion.

In fact, problems of access to health services faced by the American system, such as the fact that 86.7 million people under the age of 65 went without health insurance for some or all of the period from 2007 to 2008,[79] led the government to propose a health reform in 2009. Following that, in March 2010, the American Congress passed a health care bill, the Patient Protection and Affordable Care Act, informally referred to as Obamacare. This health reform is the most significant one in the United States since Medicare. Generally speaking, this law sought to improve coverage, extending it to about 30 million uninsured Americans, and to provide greater protection for those considered underinsured.[80] The primary means for doing that would be by expanding Medicaid and providing federal subsidies to help lower- and middle-income classes buy private insurance.[81] This bill was subject to the scrutiny of the United States Supreme Court.[82] On 28 June 2012, the Court upheld President Obama's law. However, the decision of the Court restricted the part regarding Medicaid by giving individual states the flexibility not to expand their Medicaid programs. This health reform, although intended to increase the number of people with health insurance coverage by creating a new insurance marketplace that allows people without insurance and small businesses to compare plans and buy insurance at competitive prices, and to offer a public health insurance option to provide the uninsured who cannot find affordable coverage with a real choice, is not intended to change the market-oriented logic of the American system. It will certainly reduce the number of Americans without insurance, but it is far from providing a solidarity-based model.

Therefore, we can conclude that in all health systems there is a role for the market and from system to system what changes is the space that the market occupies, that is, whether it is an end itself or just an instrument. This represents

77   Esping-Andersen refers to this term as the 'process by which both human needs and labour power became commodities and, hence, our well-being came to depend on our relation to the cash nexus'. ESPING-ANDERSEN, G. 1990. *Op. cit.*, p. 35.

78   JOST, T.S., DAWSON, D. & EXTER, A.D. 2006. The role of competition in health care: a western European perspective. *Journal of Health Politics, Policy and Law*, 31(3): 687–703.

79   FAMILIES USA 2009. *Americans at risk: one in three uninsured.* Washington, DC: Families USA. Available at www.ckfindiana.org/files/news/Americans%20At%20Risk%20report%20-%20 March%202009.pdf [Accessed 23 November 2015].

80   RICE, T., ROSENAU, P., UNRUH, L.Y., BARNES, A.J., SALTMAN, R.B. & GINNEKEN, E.V. 2013. United States of America: Health system review. *Health Systems in Transition*, 15(3): 1–431.

81   For details on President Obama's health care law reform, see http://housedocs.house.gov/ energycommerce/ppacacon.pdf [Accessed 7 January 2016].

82   For the full decision of the US Supreme Court, see www.supremecourt.gov/opinions/11pdf/ 11–393c3a2.pdf [Accessed 7 January 2016].

two different views of the market: one that emphasises its commercial use, focused on economic growth and preferences satisfaction, and another that focuses on the use of the market as a more or less neutral behavioural and managerial tool to manage social institutions efficiently, including health care.[83]

Quasi-markets and the delivery of health care

The delivery of public services in general, including health care, can be done through different models. These models are designed to achieve the aims or objectives of public service, which can include for example equity, quality and efficiency. The model works as a means for the achievement of the ends of the system. Popular models used within the health care field are the trust model, the targets and performance management model (also termed command-and-control) and the voice model. The first, as its name suggests, is based on trust, and professionals in the public sector are trusted to deliver a good service with no interference from the government. The targets model is the opposite of the trust model; professionals are part of a management hierarchy and the organisations for which they work are expected to achieve targets set by the government, which can be then rewarded or penalised. The voice model is based on forms of communication with users, which are encouraged to express their opinion about a specific service.[84]

All of these models present advantages and disadvantages and that is why, in practice, most health systems use some combination of them.[85] For example, the voice model, which is relevant in the context of this book as will be seen in the following chapters, presents advantages because users can express their own opinions about the system – satisfaction or dissatisfaction – communicating directly or indirectly with providers. Therefore, it takes direct account of users' needs and wants.[86] However, this model has the disadvantage of favouring the educated and articulate. Considering that the better-off have more voice, better contacts and sharper elbows, the middle classes are more used to using their voice to demand access to more extensive services, such as specialist outpatient consultations, diagnostic tests and inpatient treatments. Consequently, middle-class patients are more articulate, more confident and more persistent than their poorer equivalents. Even in situations in which the middle classes cannot rely upon their voice to get their way – as for example in systems where there is no public system of choice – they are able nonetheless to exercise forms of choice. First, in most countries there is always the possibility of opting out of the public system, that is, to use one's own funds to buy private health care (Canada, where private health is outlawed in some

---

83 CALLAHAN, D. & WASUNNA, A.A. 2006. *Op. cit.*, p. 3.
84 LE GRAND, J. 2007. *The other invisible hand: delivering public services through choice and competition*, Princeton, NJ: Princeton University Press.
85 *Ibid.*, p. 15.
86 *Ibid.*, p. 31.

provinces, is a partial exception, although even there there is the possibility of crossing the border). Second, there is always the possibility of moving so as to benefit from good schools or hospitals.[87]

Another model for the delivery of health care is the so-called quasi-market model.[88] This model has been applied in many countries in Europe with public health systems in the last years, such as Norway, Denmark, France, Germany and the United Kingdom.[89] It is based on the use of two main market mechanisms: choice and competition. It resembles a market in many ways, since there are independent providers competing for customers. However, different from a normal market, the services are paid for by the state and the money follows the users' choice through the form of a voucher, an earmarked budget or a funding formula.[90]

In the view of Le Grand, the use of the choice and competition model can better deliver good public services in terms of quality, efficiency, responsiveness and equity.[91] Moreover, it offers also the advantage of increasing the motivation of professionals working in the public sector, being either knights or knaves.[92] Nevertheless, this model is also subject to criticism. The main complaints regard the issue of the middle classes getting a greater share of public services, increasing inequalities within the system, and the dismantling of the public sector.[93] In order to avoid these problems, Le Grand asserts that public health systems using the choice-and-competition model must adopt a specific policy design. This includes, first, the provision of services free at the point of use, which avoids the inequalities that can arise in a normal market due to the differences in people's purchasing power. Furthermore, patients must be informed in order to make appropriate judgements and the system must provide arrangements to advise patients on various aspects and not only about the choice of provider – as for example, special needs regarding travel and disability, communication problems in terms of language and

---

87   *Ibid.*, pp. 32–3.
88   The term, as Le Grand and Bartlett explain, 'derives from an intervention by Glen Bramley in one of the early discussions that led to the setting up of the SAUS Quasi-Market Programme. However, we have subsequently discovered that it was originally used in this kind of context by Oliver Williamson'. LE GRAND, J. & BARTLETT, W. 1993. *Quasi-markets and social policy*, Basingstoke, UK: Macmillan, p. 2.
89   LE GRAND, J. 2007. *Op. cit.*, p. 100.
90   *Ibid.*, p. 41.
91   *Ibid.*
92   This terminology was used by Le Grand to explain the motivation of people working in the public service. So, knaves would be those motivated primarily by their own self-interest and knights refer to those altruistic public servants. The author also uses the terms pawns and queens to differentiate between recipients of services who receive benefits as passive agents (the former) and those who receive them as active recipients. LE GRAND, J. 2003. *Motivation, agency, and public policy: of knights and knaves, pawns and queens.* Oxford: Oxford University Press.
93   For more about these arguments, see MARQUAND, D. 2004. *Decline of the public: the hollowing-out of citizenship,* Cambridge, Polity; TITMUSS, R.M., OAKLEY, A. & ASHTON, J. 1997. *The gift relationship: from human blood to social policy,* London: London School of Economics & Political Science.

transport and navigation in the health system.[94] The system must also provide help with transport and travel costs; this both promotes equity and helps to make competition real.[95]

It is, therefore, possible to conclude that the quasi-market model, although structured in market mechanisms and thereby attached to liberal values, can offer solutions for the delivery of health care services in publicly provided systems based on solidarity. Accordingly, the discussion about this model is important for this book not only because of the health reforms adopted by many EU health systems in the last few decades, which comprised the use of some of the elements present in the quasi-market model, but also because some of these elements are also present in the context of the process of EU integration in relation to health services.

As will be discussed in the following chapters, the process of EU integration has spilled over the principles governing the Internal Market into the field of health care. As the waves of reforms described above, it can be viewed as another challenge to EU health systems, insofar as market integration also involves discussion about a more prominent role of the market in the provision of health care. However, it is different from these 'waves' in many ways: first, because it is a process centred in the EU, second because it is an ongoing process and third because the process of EU integration, although strongly focused on economic integration, was not initiated exclusively for this reason. Furthermore, this process of integration is accompanied by a new legal framework which establishes another set of legal rules, different from national ones, but also binding on national states. Considering that the influence of the Internal Market on EU health systems will be explored in Chapter 4, for the moment it suffices to say that the analysis of the Internal Market's influence is different from that of the 'waves' of reforms and cannot be guided only by the discourse concerning the role of the market; instead, it must also consider other aspects related to the process of EU integration, such as the role of citizenship.

Conclusion

The aim of this chapter was to develop part of the theoretical framework of the book, by defining some of the paradigms and values – as well as basic concepts – which will be built upon in the discussions of the following chapters. The discussion about the special moral importance of health and health care works as a justification for the study of the subject. Moreover, the theories of distributive justice analysed in this chapter, namely egalitarianism and the libertarianism ideologies, and the

---

94   LE GRAND, J. 2007. *Op. Cit.*, p. 119.
95   It is important to note that competition is different from the privatisation of services. In fact, as Le Grand points out, 'it is perfectly possible to have competition between publicly owned or non-profit entities without any participation of the private sector'. *Ibid.*, pp. 42 and 108.

discourse on the role of the market in the provision of health care, will be used as paradigms for the analysis which will be developed in Chapter 6 concerning the impact of EU Internal Market policies on national health systems. Before developing this analysis, however, it is important to understand other concepts linked to the provision of social rights, especially health care rights, which offer an explanation of the development of welfare services in Europe.

2 National and European approaches to social citizenship and solidarity

This chapter is devoted to the study of two important concepts in the field of health care: social citizenship and solidarity. The main idea of the chapter is to analyse these two concepts from a national perspective and then to approach them from a supranational (EU) point of view. By confronting these two dimensions, I attempt to show that the concept of European citizenship was developed without including a social dimension. Recent improvements in the interpretation of this concept have aimed at extending the scope of rights that have a social nature. Yet, the concept of European citizenship may not be sufficient to include health care-related rights.

The role of (social) citizenship

Citizenship is a concept used in different contexts, which entails different ideas. A legal definition of citizenship, for example, is confused with the idea of nationality. In philosophical terms, it is concerned with questions of the best way to achieve a just society. Although recognising other definitions and contexts for the concept of citizenship, this work is concerned with citizenship as a status, denoting membership to a society, and the rights deriving from this membership.[1] For this discussion, the notions of the individual and the community embedded in the analysis of theories of distributive justice elaborated in Chapter 1 will be useful.

The first idea related to citizenship dates back to the Ancient Greek city-states and lies in the concept that citizens are not isolated from the community. During this period, the status of citizen was identified with the notions of loyalty and engagement, and the 'wider public interest takes precedence over any personal considerations; such public-spirited virtue becomes the guarantee of good government'.[2] This is called the civic republican tradition of citizenship and,

---

1 Here citizenship is regarded as a status denoting a membership to a certain community. However, citizenship can be also regarded as a legal or philosophical concept. For a more detailed analysis of these different meanings of citizenship, see FAULKS, K. 1998. *Citizenship in modern Britain*. Edinburgh: Edinburgh University Press.
2 DWYER, P. 2004. *Op. cit.*, p. 21.

although it is argued by some authors that the traces of this view of citizenship lasted only until the modern period,[3] others consider that communitarianism is the lasting legacy of civic republicanism.[4]

In the modern period, citizenship gained different functions and forms. With the development of capitalism and the nation state, the communal duty entailed in the civic republic tradition became less demanding, giving rise to the libertarian liberal tradition of citizenship. Within this new approach the citizen has individual rights and preferences, and his or her link to the community is represented by membership to the nation state, which is 'a much larger and looser community than that required by civic republicans'.[5] The libertarian liberal tradition is thus recognised as a citizenship of civil and political rights.

Nevertheless, this tradition then took a step further to acknowledge the issues of equality and distributive justice. The differences between these liberal traditions recall those discussed in Chapter 1 between egalitarian and libertarian theories of distributive justice. While the libertarian liberal approach maintains that the responsibilities of the state to its citizens are limited to the promotion of individual civil and political rights, the egalitarian liberal tradition takes account of distributive justice as part of state responsibilities, acknowledging the provision of social rights as a central aspect of citizenship.

Within the egalitarian liberal tradition, T.H. Marshall is the most influential author and his work is essential for the understanding of welfare rights as they currently stand. In his famous work *Citizenship and Social Class*[6], developed in the period following the end of World War II, Marshall proposes that citizenship can be divided into three parts or elements: civil, political and social. The civil element comprises the rights related to individual freedom and liberty, including not only freedom of speech, thought and faith, but also the right of property, the right to conclude contracts and the right to justice. The political element refers to the right to exercise political power, as a member of a body or as an elector. The social element, which this work is concerned with, comprises 'the whole range from the right to a modicum of economic welfare and security to the right to share to the full in the social heritage and to live the life of a civilised being according to the standards prevailing in the society'.[7]

Marshall maintains that, historically, these three elements of citizenship were blended because the institutions concerned with their provision were amalgamated. However, their meaning and conceptualisation are different when compared to the concept of modern citizenship. It was thus the evolution of these three

---

3 As Faulks explains, the development of citizenship can be divided into distinct stages. The first stage begins with the Greeks and ends 'with the onset of modernity, marked above all by the French Revolution of 1789'. FAULKS, K. 2000. *Citizenship*. London: Routledge, p. 14.

4 DWYER, P. 2004. *Op. cit.*, p. 26.

5 *Ibid.*, p. 23.

6 First published in 1950 and reprinted in 1992. MARSHALL, T.H. 1950. *Citizenship and social class and other essays*. Cambridge: Cambridge University Press.

7 MARSHALL, T.H. 1992. *Citizenship and social class*. London: Pluto, p. 8.

elements – civil, political and social – that led to the modern concept of citizenship. Hence, he departs from the idea of the historical evolution of citizenship[8] by arguing that each of these elements became independent and gained substantive content at a given moment as a result of the evolutionary process of political, social and economic contexts. In this regard, civil rights were the first to arise in the 18th century, followed by political rights in the 19th century and social rights in the 20th century.

Social rights are, therefore, a fundamental aspect of Marshall's theory and it is essentially what distinguishes it from the libertarian liberal tradition. In his view, by developing the notion of citizenship 'to include rights to welfare (the social element), it may be possible to remove some of the inequalities generated by the continuing operation of an essentially capitalist market system'.[9]

The rise of social rights of citizenship presented in Marshall's theory is directly related to the rise of the welfare state. In effect, the issue of membership to a community – nowadays the nation state – is central both to Marshall and to contemporary ideas of citizenship. However, for a number of reasons Marshall's theory is subject to criticism by specialists in contemporary welfare regimes. For example, it is often argued that his theory is time and place limited, insofar this was based on the British experience and developed considering the reality of the post-war period.[10] Moreover, others, such as Powell, argue that the content and scope of social rights is rather vague in Marshall's theory.[11]

This is not to deny, however, the importance of Marshall's theory in relation to contemporary approaches to citizenship. Even nowadays it is still possible to distinguish between libertarian and egalitarian models of citizenship, and Marshall's theory is quite important for this latter model. For example, within the social democratic political tradition, welfare rights are an essential element of the status of citizenship. By guaranteeing the universal provision of these rights, the state ensures effective membership to society even for the most marginalised groups.[12]

Accordingly, the provision of social rights is also a central question in contemporary welfare states. Even if a contemporary concept of citizenship goes beyond Marshall's trilogy of rights,[13] the provision of social rights by the state

---

8   Another author who works with the idea of the evolution of rights regarding citizenship is Norberto Bobbio. See BOBBIO, N. 1996. *The age of rights*, Cambridge, UK; Oxford, UK; Cambridge, USA, Polity; Blackwell.

9   DWYER, P. 2004. *Op. cit.*, p. 39.

10   See, for example, HEATER, D.B. 1999. *What is citizenship?* Cambridge, UK; Malden, MA: Polity; Blackwell Publishers; and DWYER, P. 2000. *Welfare rights and responsibilities: contesting social citizenship.* Bristol: Policy Press.

11   POWELL, M. 2002. The Hidden History of Social Citizenship. *Citizenship Studies*, 6 (3): 229–44.

12   *Ibid.*, p. 53.

13   Mullard suggests, for example, that the notion of citizenship should be built upon four central components: universal human rights, the right to be different, a public dimension and a social dimension. MULLARD, M. 1999. Discourses on citizenship: the challenge to contemporary citizenship. *In:* BUSSEMAKER, J. (ed.) *Citizenship and welfare state reform in Europe.* London; New York: Routledge, p. 21.

became a common strand in welfare states, especially in Europe. In fact, European countries have typically become welfare states in which social rights of citizenship are as important as civil and political rights. This social element of citizenship can be said to confer rights to a minimum standard of living, and includes, for example, education, housing and health care. Different from civil and political rights, the purpose of social rights is not simply to promote liberty, but also to promote redistribution, reciprocity, mutuality and the notion of community. Therefore, the provision of social rights aims at promoting equality and justice, and reducing inequality.[14] Furthermore, social rights are also considered important because they create the conditions for individuals to enjoy and exercise their civil and political rights freely.[15]

Due to their redistributive nature, social rights conferred by citizenship in the context of modern welfare states are determined 'not solely by reference to fundamental principles, but also to economic and government policy, affected as it often is with politics and the squalls of electoral anxiety'.[16] Nevertheless, social rights play an important role in strengthening the notions of citizenship because they capture 'the duty to have regard for others and the responsibility to devise systems capable of doing so'.[17]

In the context of this book, the concern is with one specific type of social right: the provision of health care. Moreover, the work is centred on the provision of these services within the EU. Therefore, in order to examine health care rights in a broader EU context it is necessary to look at the meaning of the right to access health care services within its historical interpretations, as well as within contemporary conceptions of differentiated citizenship.[18] This incorporates not only the two dimensions of citizenship, territorial and personal, but also the concept of European citizenship, since one of the elements of analysis in this work is the provision of health services in a EU cross-border context.

---

14 NEWDICK, C. 2006. Citizenship, free movement and health care: cementing individual rights by corroding social solidarity. *Common Market Law Review*, 43: 1645–68.
15 'Another way to support the importance of social rights is to show their importance to the full implementation of civil and political rights. If a government succeeds in eliminating hunger and providing education to everyone this promotes people's abilities to know, use, and enjoy their liberties, due process rights, and rights of political participation. This is easiest to see in regard to education. Ignorance is a barrier to the realization of civil and political rights because uneducated people often do not know what rights they have and what they can do to use and defend them. It is also easy to see in the area of democratic participation. Education and a minimum income make it easier for people at the bottom economically to follow politics, participate in political campaigns, and to spend the time and money needed to go to the polls and vote'. NICKEL, J. 2006. Human Rights. *The Stanford Encyclopedia of Philosophy*. Available at http://plato.stanford.edu/entries/rights-human/ [Accessed 21 December 2015].
16 NEWDICK, C. 2008. The European Court of Justice, Trans-National Health Care, and Social Citizenship – Accidental Death of a Concept? *Wisconsin International Law Journal*, 26 (3): 844–67.
17 *Ibid.*
18 REDDEN, C.J. 2002. Health Care as Citizenship Development: Examining Social Rights and Entitlement. *Canadian Journal of Political Science / Revue canadienne de science politique*, 35(1): 103–25.

The welfare state and social rights of citizenship: territorial v. personal dimensions

As discussed above, the status conferred by citizenship entails the provision of rights by the state to all its members. In this regard, the concept of citizenship comprises three elements: the first is a set of rights that guarantees and protects the holder of the status, i.e. freedoms, powers and means to exercise basic capabilities within the society; the second is a set of obligations and duties required by the holder of the status, such as the payment of taxes and engagement in military service; and the third is the membership in a certain political community, which distinguishes citizens from non-citizens.[19]

This third element of citizenship is the one which defines the territorial and personal limits of the status of citizen: the membership and the consequent grant of rights are restricted to citizens who possess the status and live within a certain territorial boundary (the political community). Therefore, the territorial dimension means the status acquired through some form of territorial attachment defined by a geographical boundary. In relation to the personal (or membership) dimension, citizenship specifies the criteria for the 'insiderhood' and the sense of belonging to a certain community.

These dimensions of citizenship become especially important with regard to social rights of citizenship. In Europe, social rights including health-related rights are usually enshrined in states' constitutions and are conferred to citizens belonging to the specific nation state. In practice, most constitutions enshrine social rights, although varying considerably in the degree of the social provision they mention and protect as well as on the level of justiciability regarding these rights. For example, the right to health is present in several national constitutions, such as Belgium, Finland, Italy, Luxembourg, the Netherlands, Portugal and Spain,[20] but its content and implementation vary from country to country.[21]

In the EU context, social rights of citizenship have played a crucial role in the process of state-building, insofar as the conferring of such rights helped the process of closure which marked the boundaries of the welfare state. As Ferrera argues, 'The fusion between territorial control and identity, mass democracy, and the welfare state produced very solid and highly integrated political systems, functioning according to distinct internal logics'.[22]

---

19 LUKES, S. 1999. Solidarity and Citizenship. *In:* BAYERTZ, K. (ed.) *Solidarity.* Dordrecht; London: Kluwer Academic Publishers. In a slightly different vein, Bellamy maintains that citizenship comprises also the element 'participation', which corresponds to 'the right to have rights' and 'indicates how access to numerous rights depends on membership of a political community'. BELLAMY, R. 2008b. *Citizenship: a very short introduction.* New York: Oxford University Press, p. 15.

20 HERVEY, T.K. & MCHALE, J.V. 2004. *Health law and the European Union,* Cambridge: Cambridge University Press, p. 9.

21 EXTER, A.D. & HERMANS, H. 1999. *The right to health care in several European countries.* The Hague; London; Boston, MA: Kluwer Law International.

22 FERRERA, M. 2005. *The boundaries of welfare: European integration and the new spatial politics of social protection,* Oxford: Oxford University Press, p. 25.

Based on this process of closure, European nation states were able to exercise command over their actors and resources, necessary for the development of redistributive social policies. By creating explicit codes and forms of distinction between insiders and outsiders, nationals and non-nationals, European nation states developed culturally embedded systems of national citizenship, which rest, *inter alia*, on social rights. This institutionalised system of mutual rights and obligations, with great stability and social cooperation, can be regarded in fact as one of the most significant products of Western-style bounded structuring.[23] This makes Europeans not only feel proud of their nation's welfarist dimension, but also feel happy about the welfare state in which they live. In fact, with regards to health care, in a recent study which analysed how Europeans perceive their health care systems, one of the findings was that a vast majority of the population of the 14 countries under analysis supported the idea of an extensive role of the state in the field of health care.[24] Furthermore, health leads the list of values that Europeans consider most important for their happiness.[25] In the words of Davies,

> Citizens feel themselves to be, and are, inhabitants of a structure, and as such its walls and staircases become of great and common importance. Modern Europeans live within a state as much as they live within a nation, and sharing that state, and knowing that its existence depends on their collective participation, binds them to each other.
>
> This is a source of security, but also of self-respect. The welfare state is something that helps Europeans feel good about themselves, and about their country, because it is one of those happy institutions that apparently combines self-interest with compassion for others.[26]

Furthermore, it should not be forgotten that in a post-war context the development of European welfare states was also a way to recast patriotism in a less ethnic, militaristic and irrational form.[27]

Considering this process of closure upon which welfare state services were built, it is possible to argue that the provision of health care services was always viewed as a matter for the nation state's decision and competence. This link between the state territory and the provision of health services – also called the principle of territoriality – has always allowed EU Member States to use territorial elements

---

23 *Ibid.*, p.24.
24 WENDT, C., JÜRGEN KOHL, M.M. & PFEIFER, M. 2010. How do Europeans perceive their healthcare system? Patterns of satisfaction and preference for state involvement in the field of healthcare. *European Sociological Review*, 26(2): 177–92, p. 183.
25 EUROPEAN COMMISSION 2012. Standard Eurobarometer 77: The values of Europeans, p. 15.
26 DAVIES, G. 2006. The Process and Side-Effects of Harmonisation of European Welfare States. Jean Monnet Working Paper 02/06. Available at http://centers.law.nyu.edu/jeanmonnet/papers/06/060201.pdf [Accessed 14 December 2015].
27 *Ibid.*, p.46.

in defining the scope of their social security schemes and in determining the qualifying conditions for receiving benefits.[28]

Citizenship, the welfare state and the meaning of solidarity

Another important concept in the discussion of citizenship in contemporary welfare states is solidarity. The term itself is quite vague, and for a better definition of its meaning in the context of the welfare state it is necessary to look at the political dimension of solidarity. However, before this a brief overview of the different uses of solidarity will be provided.

The first normative use of the term solidarity dates back to the Roman law of obligations. The *obligation in solidum* was 'the liability of each individual member within a family or other community to pay common debts [. . .]'.[29] Since these times, the idea embedded in this concept has been that of mutual responsibility between the individual and the community in which he or she took part. Therefore, the core of solidarity is the idea that 'each individual vouches for the community and the community vouches for each individual [. . .]'.[30]

The normative use of the term was then expanded into the field of morality and politics. During the first half of the 19th century the term solidarity entered the political scene. In this context, it had a place alongside the term 'fraternity', which was highly diffused in the aftermath of the French Revolution, and meant the mutual attachment between individuals that implies mutual obligation to aid each other.[31]

In the modern world, the term did not lose its meaning as a tie binding a group of people. This group, however, became smaller in scope; it turned to become a community sharing a common history, language and culture. In this context, solidarity can be defined as the 'cement holding together a society'.[32] This political use of the term is the same found nowadays in the context of the welfare state. However, here it assumes a role closely connected to the language of citizenship: citizens of the same state, sharing the same background conditions related to history and culture, have obligations to help their needy fellow citizens. Therefore, solidarity in the context of the welfare state assumes a normative status which is used to justify redistributive social policies. Moreover, in the language of citizenship, it can be understood as a way of promoting social equality in order to allow all citizens the exercise of their full membership in the society.

Accordingly, the welfare state can be regarded as an institution that affects attitudes of solidarity and the willingness to help fellow citizens. Beer and Koster,

---

28 CORNELISSEN, R. 1996. The Principle of Territory and the Community Regulations on Social Security (Regulations 1408/71 and 574/72). *Common Market Law Review*, 33: 439–71, p. 441.

29 BAYERTZ, K. 1999. Four uses of "Solidarity". *In:* BAYERTZ, K. (ed.) *Solidarity*. Dordrecht; London: Kluwer Academic Publishers, p. 3.

30 *Ibid.*, p. 3.

31 *Ibid.*, p. 3.

32 *Ibid.*, p. 9.

for example, use Émile Durkhmeim's seminal work about the division of labour[33] to explain the relationship between the welfare state and solidarity. In the opinion of these authors, the interdependence between citizens in a society based on the division of labour is an important source of social solidarity. This mutual interdependence was intensified by the creation and expansion of the welfare state because in case of sickness, unemployment and old age, individuals are dependent on the support of their fellow citizens and this can create a feeling of solidarity towards them. Moreover, since the income transfers in the welfare state are mainly organised at the national level, the welfare state might also have contributed to creating a feeling of national identity. Before the existence of a national system of social security, there was little that connected a farmer to a wage labourer in a factory or to a civil servant. The welfare state, however, made them mutually dependent.[34]

It is, therefore, through this sense of belonging to nation states (welfare states) that citizens will develop the sentiments of solidarity and trust. The former makes them feel that they have certain obligations towards their fellow citizens and the latter gives them the idea of reciprocity, i.e. that one day others will do the same for them. These sentiments are especially important when it comes to the provision of social rights, because they prevent the temptation of free-riding or defecting from collective arrangements.[35] In this context, Stjernø proposes a definition of the concept of solidarity in the modern society that includes 'the preparedness to share resources with others, through personal contributions to those who are struggling and through taxation and redistribution organised by the state'.[36] Therefore, solidarity means willingness for collective action and its institutionalisation through the establishment of rights and citizenship.

Accordingly, with regard to the provision of social rights, especially health-related rights, it is possible to argue that these are a product of the welfare states by virtue of the combined ideas relating to citizenship and solidarity. As mentioned above, this explains why the notions of territory and membership to a community are important in this context; in the welfare state, the redistributive obligations originating from solidarity apply to citizens sharing the same territory, and most of the time, sharing a common history, language and culture, but not to the inhabitants of other states.

In relation to the provision of health services, and especially in the EU, solidarity is regarded as an overarching value of EU health systems. It is part of a set of values

33   DURKHEIM, É. 1932. *De la division du travail social, par Emile Durkheim, professeur à la Sorbonne. 6e édition*, Saint-Germain-lès-Corbeil, impr. Willaume Paris, libr. Félix Alcan, 108, Boulevard Saint-Germain.

34   BEER, P.D. & KOSTER, F. 2009. *Sticking together or falling apart: solidarity in an era of individualization and globalization*. Amsterdam: Amsterdam University Press, p. 50.

35   BELLAMY, R. 2008a. Evaluating Union citizenship: belonging, rights and participation within the EU. *Citizenship Studies*, 12: 597–611.

36   STJERNØ, S. 2005. *Solidarity in Europe: the history of an idea*, Cambridge: Cambridge University Press, p. 326.

– that also includes universality, access to good-quality care and equity – which is shared by health systems across Europe. In this context, solidarity is closely linked to the financial arrangement of national health systems and the need to ensure accessibility to all,[37] and can be defined as 'cross-subsidies from the rich to the poor and from the healthy to the sick'.[38]

However, this link between the provision of health care services and the state territory started to change by virtue of the creation and establishment of the EU, which, since 1958, has provided through the EC Treaty an exemption to the territoriality principle in order to encourage the free movement of people.[39] This process became more intensive in 'the early 70's and has worked to gradually thin out the national boundaries of citizenship, with specific and significant implications for social rights'.[40] The legislative framework, as well as the judicial decisions that contributed to these changes, will be analysed in Chapter 4. In this part, instead, the aim is to look at the concept of European social citizenship in order to see whether health care rights developed at the EU level can be comprised within this category, to observe how these rights are transposed to a supranational level and how they differ from social rights of citizenship developed at the national level.

European citizenship and social rights

The notion of European citizenship was not present when the Treaty of Rome was signed in 1957. It was only in the Treaty of Maastricht that the idea of European citizenship was introduced (Article 8).[41] The introduction of this new European status was, according to some authors, 'a legislative response to the growing concern of EU authorities about the democratic legitimacy of the European project'.[42] This 'supranational' citizenship is different from national citizenship and, indeed, is something that should be placed over and above national citizenship. It vested new rights in Europeans, *inter alia*, the right to circulate and reside freely in the Community; the right to vote and to stand as a candidate for European and municipal elections in the state in which he or she resides; the right to protection by the diplomatic or consular authorities of a Member State other than the citizen's Member State of origin on the territory

37 COUNCIL OF THE EUROPEAN UNION 2006. Council Conclusions on Common values and principles in European Union Health Systems. 2006/C 146/01.
38 KUTZIN, J. 2001. A descriptive framework for country-level analysis of health care financing arrangements. *Health Policy*, 56: 171–204.
39 MOSSIALOS, E., MCKEE, M., PALM, W. J., KARL, B. & MARHOLD, F. 2002. *EU law and the social character of health care*, Bern Oxford, P. Lang. P. 83.
40 FERRERA, M. 2005. *Op. cit.*, p. 49.
41 At the present moment, with the entry into force of the Lisbon Treaty, European citizenship is mentioned in Articles 9, 18 and 20 of the TFEU.
42 KOLB, A.-K. 1999. European social rights towards national welfare states: additional, substitute, illusory? *In:* BUSSEMAKER, J. (ed.) *Citizenship and welfare state reform in Europe.* London; New York: Routledge, p. 168.

of a third country in which the state of origin is not represented; and the right to petition the European Parliament and to submit a complaint to the Ombudsman.

Even while conferring rights on European citizens, Article 8 of the Treaty of Maastricht did not provide for any type of social rights. In fact, apart from the legislation necessary for the implementation of the Internal Market and the free movement of workers, social legislation had not been an issue for the EU until the mid-1980s.[43] The reason for this lack of social legislation at EU level lies in the fact that the project of the EU focused on economic policies rather than on redistributive social policies, which came about only as a consequence of the economic objectives of the Union. Furthermore, there has always been a lack of EU competence in legislating on social issues and little consensus among Member States about the character of a European social policy, since they have tried very often to protect their own national interests. As Kolb argues, 'whatever moral or ideological dimension social rights could have from a European citizenship perspective, they become bargaining chips in the political arena'.[44]

European social rights, thus, did not develop in the same way as national social rights, which, as the core of national welfare policies, are much more redistributive in nature. The social rights developed at the EU level have a more regulatory nature, since they were born as part of the Internal Market policies. In this regard, Majone proposes a distinction in relation to the social policies developed at the EU level, distinguishing them in policies of regulatory nature and those of non-regulatory nature.[45] The social policies of regulatory nature are limited to rule-making, although the ECJ also plays an important role by extending EU powers in this area. The regulatory social measures developed by the EU aim mainly at the formation of the Internal Market, such as the Regulations concerning Migrant Workers. In the words of Stuchlík and Kellermann, '[i]n the area of regulatory social policy European law sets minimum social standards and basic rights at the European level, and so creates uniform framework conditions for the Internal Market'.[46] Accordingly, they do not have a redistributive nature and are motivated by an efficiency criterion, having only indirect redistributive consequences.

The second category of social policies is represented by those policies which really have redistributive objectives. These policies aim at reducing inequalities between the different countries and regions, foment social cohesion within the Union and they are promoted through the different Structural and Cohesion

---

43 'Social issues became a more important issue during the mid-1980s. This is reflected in the Single European Act of 1985, particularly in Article 130 on economic and social cohesion, in the Charter of Fundamental Rights for Workers of 1989, and later in the Social Chapter of the Treaty of the European Union of 1992'. *Ibid.*, p. 168.

44 *Ibid.*, p.170.

45 MAJONE, G. 1996. *Regulating Europe*, London; New York, Routledge. P. 63.

46 STUCHLÍK, A. & KELLERMANN, C. 2009. Europe on the Way to a Social Union? The EU Social Agenda in the Context of European Welfarism. *International Policy Analysis*, Available at http://library.fes.de/pdf-files/id/ipa/06013.pdf [Accessed 14 December 2015], p. 11.

Funds of the EU. Rights promoted through these funds are much vaguer and, although redistributive in nature, they are minimal in comparison to national social policies.[47]

The majority of social policies resulting from EU action fall within the first category, i.e. policies of a regulatory nature. The rights originating from this type of EU policy were initially focused on workers and include, *inter alia*, the co-ordination of social security systems, rights that guarantee health and safety in the workplace, gender equality and non-discrimination for professional mobility. This initial focus on the labour market has changed over time by virtue of the expansion of the personal scope of mobility, and the rights deriving from free movement rules were extended to virtually the entire EU population and, in some cases, also to third-country or stateless persons/refugees residing in the territory of a Member State.[48]

Union citizenship, therefore, can be defined as a legal construction. In distinction to the traditional concept of citizenship, it does not have the element of commonness of history, polity and culture, and it does not relate to a specific territorial boundary.[49]

Access to health care rights at the EU level can be considered as a right falling into this category of regulatory social policies. The legislative framework of patient mobility will be explored in Chapter 4, where the legislation and case law related to this issue will be analysed. Here, however, it is important to mention that the right to access health care services in a cross-border context was created in order to guarantee the free movement of workers and was then extended to other categories of patients. This is to say that they have followed the same dynamics of other rights related to freedom of movement and the Internal Market project.

Although considered as an extension of national social rights and indirectly promoting some social benefits, the rights that originated from the process of European economic integration are different from national social rights, because, as already explained, they do not have the same redistributive scope of national rights. Due to their economic nature, some authors, e.g. Kandil, consider the rights that have been created by the process of economic integration, such as access to

---

47 The Structural Funds and the Cohesion Fund are the financial instruments of European Union (EU) regional policy, which is intended to narrow the development disparities among regions and Member States. The Funds participate fully, therefore, in pursuing the goal of economic, social and territorial cohesion. There are two Structural Funds: the European Regional Development Fund (ERDF), which is, at the moment, the largest, and the European Social Fund (ESF). Besides the structural funds, there is the Cohesion Fund which is intended for countries whose per capita GDP is below 90% of the Community average. The purpose of the Cohesion Fund is to grant financing to environment and transport infrastructure projects. Available at http://ec.europa.eu/regional_policy/en/funding/ [Accessed 24 November 2015].

48 Just to illustrate this change in personal scope, pensioners and students, who were not intended targets of free movement rules, have become their main beneficiaries. KOLB, A.-K. 1999. *Op. cit.*, p. 173.

49 REICH, N. 2001.Union Citizenship-Metaphor or Source of Rights? *European Law Journal*, 7: 4–23.

social benefits in a cross-border context, as part of the concept of European economic citizenship and not as part of European social citizenship.[50]

Therefore, it is possible to argue that the rights of access to social benefits in a cross-border EU context are a new category of rights created by the process of economic integration. As distinct from traditional social rights of citizenship attached to national states, these rights emerge from the specific set of actors, principles and dynamics that characterise European economic integration. Even if they have produced social benefits, and this is a reality especially with regard to transnational workers and their dependents, their final product has much more to do with the development of favourable conditions for the creation of the Internal Market than with the implementation of a social policy. As Goudappel explains,

> the ideal EU citizen is, apparently, a transnational worker. This means that for many legal inhabitants of a Member State, citizenship and the accompanying rights and duties depend on the rules and regulations of that particular Member State because they do not obtain any of the rights attached to the exercise of free movement rights until they decide to work in another Member State.[51]

The differences between social policy and rights deriving from the process of European integration, and social rights at the national level, lead to the conclusion that the concept of European social citizenship is different from the traditional notion of social citizenship. Rather than strengthening citizens' protection against socio-economic difficulties, they offer new conditions for various individual strategies and also open up the possibility of building on the status of the citizen as a consumer.[52] Accordingly, the concept of national social citizenship cannot be transposed to the EU level and the rights originating from the notion of a European social citizenship, instead of complementing or extending national social policies, create a new set of opportunities which are not directly related to social objectives, but are concerned with the market and citizens-consumers.[53]

This market citizenship draws on the idea of a mercantile form of citizenship designed to facilitate economic integration. Ideologically speaking, it can be regarded as a liberal conception of citizenship which works towards the self-interest of autonomous individuals who want to pursue their chosen forms of life.[54] The idea of market citizenship is also supported by the view of the EU's

50 KANDIL, F. 2004. European social citizenship and the requirement of European solidarity. *In:* MAGNUSSON, L. & STRÅTH, B. (eds) *A European social citizenship? Preconditions for future policies from a historical perspective.* Brussels; New York: P.I.E. – Peter Lang, p. 160.

51 GOUDAPPEL, F. 2010. *The Effects of EU Citizenship,* The Hague: TMC Asser, p. 37.

52 KOLB, A.-K. 1999. *Op. cit.,* p. 179.

53 CLARKE, J., NEWMAN, J., SMITH, N., VIDLER, E. & WESTMARLAND, L. 2007. *Creating Citizen-Consumers: changing publics and changing public services.* London: Sage.

54 KOSTAKOPOULOU, D. 2005. Ideas, Norms and European Citizenship: Explaining Institutional Change. *The Modern Law Review,* 68: 233–67. It must be noted, however, that this author, although describing different models for European citizenship, including the market model, does not support the idea that market citizenship is the model pursued by the EU.

constitutional asymmetry that privileges the economic through the Internal Market but provides limited legal bases for social policy.[55] Flear, for example, argues that the EU is not only concerned with governing the market, but also projects itself as thinking and behaving as a market actor[56] insofar as its political discourse is framed by a market rationality, and market concerns are found across all of its functions, including law.[57]

This idea of market citizenship was also spread to the field of health care through the litigation concerning patient mobility. As Erika Szyszczak contends, 'The *ad hoc* litigation has been driven by individual litigants using the opportunity of EU law to liberalise EU health care markets creating new ideas of a consumer-citizenship in health care services'.[58]

However, this market-oriented view is not the only way to look at EU citizenship. More recently, the ECJ had the opportunity of showing a different approach in relation to EU citizenship that is not concerned with a market citizen. In recent cases regarding rights that are not directly attached to free movement, such as the grant of the right of residence and work permit, the award of education/training grants and the recognition of surnames, the Court applied the EU Treaty provisions on citizenship in order to guarantee the exercise of rights originating from the status of Union citizen without the precondition of mobility. In this regard, in *Ruiz Zambrano*,[59] the Court decided that the right of residence and the grant of a work permit should not be refused by a Member State to third-country nationals when they are the ascendants of dependent minor children who are nationals of this Member State, where these children live and reside. The Court assumed that the refusal of granting the right of residence and work permit to the parents of Union children would deprive those children of the enjoyment of the substance of the rights attached to their status of Union citizens, as provided for in Article 20 TFEU.[60]

In a quite different situation, in *Grunkin and Paul*,[61] a case concerning the refusal of German authorities to recognise the surname of a German child who was born, lived and resided in Denmark and held a double-barrelled surname, given at birth according to Danish law, the Court concluded that the Treaty provisions on EU citizenship preclude the national authorities of a Member State from refusing to recognise a child's surname, as registered in a second Member State, in which the

---

55 FLEAR, M. 2007. Developing Euro-Biocitizens through Migration for Healthcare Services. *Maastricht Journal of European and Comparative Law (MJ)*, 14(3): 239–62.

56 FLEAR, M. 2009. The Open Method of Coordination on health care after the Lisbon Strategy II: Towards a neoliberal framing? *European Integration online Papers (EIoP)*, 13.

57 BROWN, W. 2005. *Edgework: critical essays on knowledge and politics*, Princeton, NJ: Princeton University Press, p. 42.

58 SZYSZCZAK, E. 2011. Patients' Rights: A Lost Cause or Missed Opportunity? *In:* GRONDEN, J.W.V.D., SZYSZCZAK, E., NEERGAARD, U. & KRAJEWSKI, M. (eds) *Health care and EU law*. The Hague: T.M.C. Asser, p. 109.

59 Case C-34/09, *Ruiz Zambrano* [2011] ECR I-01177.

60 *Ibid.*, para. 44.

61 Case C-353/06, *Grunkin and Paul* [2008] ECR I-07639.

child – who had only the nationality of the first Member State – was born and had been resident since birth.[62]

Although these cases on citizenship are not directly related to social rights and reveal a different aspect of citizenship that is not present in the cases of free movement, they can be helpful for the analysis of social rights of EU citizens who do not exercise their right to free movement. Even if, *a priori*, in the case of social rights, the rules applied to non-mobile EU citizens are national laws, it is possible to argue that the situation of EU citizens who opt to not exercise their right of free movement should not be worse than that of those citizens who have exercised this right.

A good way to understand this argument is by looking at another case regarding citizenship. In *Morgan*,[63] the issue at stake was the award of student/training grants by German authorities to German students who were pursuing their course of study in another Member State. By using the provisions on citizenship (ex Articles 17 and 18 EC, now Articles 20 and 21 TFEU), the ECJ took the view that the award of education/training grants by a Member State to student nationals of that same Member State who pursue studies in another Member State cannot be dependent on the condition that those studies are a continuation of education or training pursued for at least one year in their Member State of origin.

This decision is helpful in understanding the argument that EU citizens who opt not to exercise their right of free movement should not be worse off than citizens who exercised this right. As the Court argues in paragraph 26 of the judgement, the legislation of a Member State should not penalise their nationals for the mere fact that they use the opportunities offered by the Treaty in relation to free movement. Likewise, national legislation should not penalise those citizens who do not exercise their rights of free movement.

Using the case of health care, which is the core element of this book, it is easy to visualise this situation. Imagine, for example, the situation of a citizen of a given EU Member State who asks for authorisation to receive medical treatment in a city different from that in which he or she resides,[64] and this is denied by the local authorities. If this same citizen decided to go abroad, to have the treatment performed in another Member State, he or she would probably not find any problems, since there is EU legislation – Regulation 883/2004 and Directive 2011/24/EU – that provides for this right to receive treatment abroad. However, this citizen, in theory, should not be penalised just because he or she prefers not to go abroad. The decision of not crossing the frontier could be for several reasons: the person may not speak a foreign language and feel insecure about having health treatment in a foreign country; it can be extremely costly travelling abroad; and in his or her own country the person has the opportunity to be accompanied by family or colleagues during the performance of treatment and convalescence.

---

62 *Ibid.*, para. 39.
63 Joined cases C-11/06 and C-12/06, *Morgan* [2007] ECR I-9161.
64 In Italy, for example, it is easy to imagine an Italian citizen from Calabria who prefers to go to Milan because he or she knows that the medical treatment needed is performed better in Milan.

Indeed, this can be viewed as a question of reverse discrimination, which will be analysed in more depth in Chapter 6. Here, however, it suffices to say that in the same way that national rules should not penalise citizens for the mere fact that they exercise free movement, as is clear from the case law on cross-border health care and other cases on citizenship, such as *Morgan*,[65] these same rules should not likewise penalise those citizens who did not exercise their rights of free movement. While through the lens of EU law certain types of discrimination are allowed because they arise from purely internal situations and EU law is concerned with situations that bring forth mobility within the Union, these same situations may not be immune from the legislation and principles provided for by national legislation, such as non-discrimination, equality or equity. As will be explained at more length in Chapter 6, this 'permission' of discrimination under EU law can be problematic.

The different approach to EU citizenship taken by the ECJ in recent cases shows that a concept of European social citizenship cannot be attached exclusively to free movement rights – or the Internal Market – because this will serve only those citizens who are mobile. Accordingly, EU citizens who have stayed in their own Member State are not affected by the economic rights originating from the concept of European citizenship and only feel the effect of national law.[66] In this way, the rights that EU citizenship entitles will not be universal, such as national social rights, and will benefit only those who decide to exercise their free movement rights – usually those who possess the necessary resources required for intra-EU mobility, who will make use of their EU social rights.

Nevertheless, in relation to health care and social security benefits, the importance of rights attached to free movement must be pointed out because not all of these are a consequence of the notion of market citizenship. For example, the rules about the coordination of social security schemes (which will be analysed in more depth in Chapter 4) were necessary to guarantee decent welfare conditions to workers and citizens living in another Member State of the Union. In relation to health care, these rules initially guaranteed access to health care to migrant workers and their dependant families moving to or residing in the territory of another Member State, but subsequently this access was extended to virtually the entire EU population and, more recently, also to third countries or stateless persons/refugees residing in the territory of a Member State. Accordingly, they were important in guaranteeing access to health care to all these categories and worked as an extension of national social rights.

In effect, in spite of the fact that the achievement of the Internal Market is one of the main objectives of the Union, it should not be forgotten that there is an attempt to balance free movement rights, which are directly related to the formation of the market, against the policies deriving from the social sphere of the Union. Evidence of this are the references in EU legislation, such as Article 2 of the TEU, to social progress and social cohesion as objectives of the Union, having

---

65 Joined cases C-11/06 and C-12/06, para 26.
66 OUDAPPEL, F. 2010. *Op. cit.*, p. 154.

the same importance as the economic and market objectives. Following this same rationale, the ECJ has also highlighted in cases regarding free movement rights, such as in *Viking* and *Laval*,[67] the social objectives of the Union, stating, for example, that:

> Since the Community has thus not only an economic but also a social purpose, the rights under the provisions of the Treaty on the free movement of goods, persons, services and capital must be balanced against the objectives pursued by social policy, which include, as is clear from the first paragraph of Article 136 EC, inter alia, improved living and working conditions, so as to make possible their harmonisation while improvement is being maintained, proper social protection and dialogue between management and labour.[68]

In this regard, when I refer to the notion of market citizenship in relation to health care rights at the EU level I mean those rights which were born as a consequence of the jurisprudence of the ECJ, which are now included in Directive 2011/24/EU, providing citizens with a right to travel abroad in order to receive health care treatment in another Member State of the EU.[69] In effect, the Directive has the Internal Market provision as its legal basis (Article 114 TFEU), as will be shown in Chapter 4, and expressly states that 'the Treaty provisions on the freedom to provide services include the freedom for the recipients of healthcare [. . .]'.[70]

This is of special concern in the field of health care because privileging mobile citizens might have an impact on principles which traditionally have guided social rights at the national level as, for example, the principle of equity. In this regard, Flear argues that in relation to cross-border health care rights there is a risk of the 'circumvention of waiting lists by the middle classes. They are most likely and able to travel abroad, because of their greater confidence, their possession of foreign language skills unavailable to those from lower socio-economic groups, and, crucially, their ability to pay for travel and treatment upfront and wait for reimbursement'.[71] In a similar vein, Barnard points out that 'this may well have damaging consequences for the "citizenship" feelings experienced by non-mobile citizens wanting operations in their own countries'.[72] I will come back to this point

---

67 Case C-438/05, *International Transport Workers' Federation and Finnish Seamen's Union v Viking Line ABP, OÜ Viking Line Eesti*, [2007] ECR I -10779, and Case C-341/05, *Laval un Partneri*, [2007] ECR I-11767.

68 *Ibid.*, paras 79 and 105, respectively.

69 See, for example, *Decker*, Case C-120/95 [1998] ECR I-1831; *Kohll*, Case C-158/96 [1998] ECR I-1931; *Vanbraekel and others*, Case C-368/98 [2001] ECR I-5363;*Smits and Peerbooms*, Case C-157/99[2001]ECR I-5473;*Müller-Fauré and van Riet*, Case C-385/99 [2003] ECR I-4509; and *Watts*, Case C-372/04[2006] ECR I-4325.

70 Preamble, recitals 2 and 26.

71 FLEAR, M. 2009. *Op. cit.*, p. 2.

72 BARNARD, C. 2005. EU citizenship and the Principle of Solidarity. *In:* SPAVENTA, E. & DOUGAN, M. (eds) *Social welfare and EU law.* Oxford; Portland, OR: Hart, p. 179.

in the following chapters when analysing the meaning of equity in relation to health care and the case law on patient mobility.

Therefore, it is possible to conclude that social rights of citizenship, and especially health care rights, in a broader EU context, do not have the same meaning that they have at the national level. At the EU level, these rights are more attached to the notion of European integration and the exercise of free movement and, although conferred upon all EU citizens, they are more likely to be exercised by a minority of citizens who can afford the price of mobility. As Kolb argues, 'The free moving *Europe des elites* is also a reality in that sense. The potential legitimating power of EU social legislation could, thus, be diminished by its restricted scope and the social discrimination that it reveals'.[73] Even if recently the ECJ has shown a different approach in relation to citizenship, which is less attached to the idea of free movement, in relation to social rights of citizenship, especially health care related rights, the exercise of EU citizenship is still connected to the idea of free movement.

What about supranational (social) solidarity?

Another problem with social rights at the EU level is the establishment of a notion of supranational solidarity. As explained above, solidarity was essential for the development of social rights of citizenship; it is through the sentiments of trust and solidarity acquired by a common history, culture and a sense of belonging to a community that citizens accept they have certain obligations towards their fellow citizens. However, these elements are still organised at the national level. EU citizens have a sense of attachment and community in relation to their own member states, but not in relation to the Union. Besides that, as Lamping sustains, 'EU citizens are quite hesitant when it comes to transferring social policy competences to the supranational level, primarily because most of them expect the EU to decrease social standards rather than to preserve the existing level of social security'.[74]

Therefore, the development of supranational solidarity entails the creation of a new sense of social attachment to the Union, without giving up, however, the national systems of social sharing and belonging. But how should this post-national solidarity be created if social protection is still a matter decided at national level since the EU has limited powers in this area? Although the definition of post-national solidarity has not been sufficiently elaborated on, the idea embedded in this definition should depart from the preservation of the institutional and normative foundations of national welfare states, since these are the primary source of social protection in Europe. Accordingly, the EU could leave substantial scope for national social policy making, instead of intervening, and sometimes

---

73 KOLB, A.K. 1999. *Op. cit.*, p. 173.
74 LAMPING, W. 2010. Mission Impossible? Limits and Perils of Institutionalizing Post-National Social Policy. *In:* ROSS, M. & BORGMANN-PREBIL, Y. (eds) *Promoting solidarity in the European Union*. Oxford; New York: Oxford University Press, pp. 64–5.

undermining, the institutional arrangements of welfare states.[75] Moreover, solidarity should not lose its collective meaning when transposed to the EU level, because in the end it is also about fostering the interests of the collective and not of single individuals.[76]

Steffen Mau, for example, using Habermas' view about the process of Europeanisation, states that supranational solidarity 'implies that the solidarity previously reserved for the nation state needs to be extended to all citizens of the EU, so that Swedish and Portuguese people, for example, would take the responsibility for each other'.[77] Moreover, the process to achieve supranational solidarity should include the transformation of the segmentally differentiated deeper structures found at national level in an emerging European society.[78]

The Treaty on European Union (TEU) mentions the word solidarity on more than one occasion. The term is used in different contexts and with different meanings. It is, however, in its recital and in Article 1 that the use of solidarity refers to the idea of supranational solidarity among the peoples of the Union. In these two contexts it is possible to establish a link with the idea of social solidarity between the members of the Union. Nevertheless, in these two contexts the use of solidarity remains vague and not necessarily connected to social policies. In turn, the TFEU uses the term solidarity in the context of EU external policies, as in its recital and in Articles 67 and 80, with the meaning of solidarity among Member States in the cases of economic problems, such as lack of energy (Articles 122 and 194), terrorist attacks and natural or man-made disasters (Article 222). Therefore, in the TFEU, the uses of solidarity are not directly related to social policies.

Even if the meaning of solidarity in the EU Treaties is not clearly related to social policies, it is possible to identify institutionalised forms of transnational solidarity between the richer and poorer parts of the EU in some of the EU's regional policies, such as those which make investments – through the Regional and Structural Funds – in infrastructure and human capital in backward regions, or others with specific developmental problems, this is not exactly the type of solidarity found at the national level and which creates bonds between EU citizens. In fact, initially the Union recognised solidarity as a concept being national in kind: 'an organising principle that was perceived not to be its own'.[79] This approach, however, has changed throughout time and recently the Union seems to have absorbed the concept. Indeed, EU institutions have been promoting solidarity in a variety of ways. Steffen Mau identifies two ways in which solidarity is used in

75   *Ibid.*
76   BARNARD, C. 2010. Solidarity and the Commission's 'Renewed Social Agenda'. *In:* ROSS, M. & BORGMANN-PREBIL, Y. (eds) *Promoting solidarity in the European Union.* Oxford: Oxford University Press.
77   MAU, S. 2007. Forms and Prospects of European Solidarity. *In:* KARAGIANNIS, N. (ed.) *European solidarity.* Liverpool: Liverpool University Press, p. 133.
78   LAMPING, W. 2010. *Op. cit.*
79   SOMEK, A. 2007. Solidarity Decomposed: Being and time in European citizenship. *University of Iowa Legal Studies Research Paper,* Number 07–13, p. 4.

EU documents: the first refers to a 'quality that is ascribed to Europe as a kind of central virtue',[80] and the second regards 'specific policies designed to enhance the European solidarity'.[81] For example, in the Commission Communication 'Renewed social agenda: Opportunities, access and solidarity in 21st century Europe',[82] the word solidarity is used regularly with different meanings. Barnard identifies, for example, five of these:[83] (1) solidarity as a goal or an objective; (2) solidarity as an interpretative or guiding tool; (3) solidarity as a means; (4) solidarity as a process; and (5) solidarity as an instrument. The same author stresses,

> At a first glance, solidarity seems to be employed as much for its rhetorical value as its substance. On closer examination, it appears that solidarity helps to offer a social justice counterweight to the potentially neo-liberal direction that an agenda based purely on access and opportunities might lead the EU.[84]

Despite the attempt to give a more consistent meaning to the uses of solidarity, the Commission discourse is still vague and looks like a rhetorical way of fostering the idea of solidarity. This is explained, in part, by the limited legal bases for social policy for the Union to act in important social areas, such as health care and education, which in fact creates a gap between discourse and practice at the EU level.

In turn, the ECJ has also used solidarity in different contexts. In the field of competition law, for example, it has used the principle of solidarity in order to protect social welfare schemes from the application of the Treaty rules, as in the landmark case *Poucet and Pistre*,[85] in which the Court concluded that certain compulsory social schemes for self-employed persons were not to be considered as undertakings because they fulfilled an exclusive social function and their activities were based on the principle of solidarity. This same approach was applied in subsequent cases. In *Sodemare*,[86] both Advocate General Fennelly and the Court even tried to define social solidarity. The Advocate General provided a very short definition by explaining that '[s]ocial solidarity envisages the inherently uncommercial act of involuntary subsidization of one social group by another'.[87] The Court, by contrast, adopts a very long definition:

> it is designed as a matter of priority to assist those who are in a state of need owing to insufficient family income, total or partial lack of independence or

---

80　MAU, S. 2007. *Op. cit.*, p. 134.
81　*Ibid.*
82　COMMISSION OF THE EUROPEAN COMMUNITIES 2008b. Renewed social agenda: Opportunities, access and solidarity in 21st century Europe. *COM(2008) 412 final*.
83　BARNARD, C. 2010. *Op. cit.*, p. 94.
84　*Ibid.*, p. 74.
85　Joined cases C-159/91 and C-160/91, *Poucet and Pistre v AGF and Cancava* [1993] ECR, I-00637.
86　Case C-70/95, *Sodemare* [1997] ECR I-3395.
87　Opinion of Advocate General Fennelly in Case C-70/95, *Sodemare* [1997] ECR I-3395. Para 29.

the risk of being marginalized, and only then, within the limits imposed by the capacity of the establishments and resources available, to assist other persons who are, however, required to bear the costs thereof, to an extent commensurate with their financial means, in accordance with scales determined by reference to family income.[88]

More recently, in *FENIN*,[89] the Court held that the organisations running the Spanish National Health System (SNS) did not act as undertakings even when purchasing goods in a given market because they operate according to the principle of social solidarity.[90]

In the context of competition law, solidarity is recognised as a national concept and is used mostly to protect national systems against the application of the Treaty rules on competition. However, in the context of citizenship, the ECJ has made use of solidarity in a different way; the Court no longer refers to the nation aspect, but instead the EU aspect, i.e. solidarity between EU citizens. In fact, in *Grzelczyk*,[91] the Court used it to justify the payment of a minimum income guaranteed by the Belgian government to a French migrant student.

The problem with this approach, as pointed out by Barnard, is that it presents 'a paradox' within the solidarity debate, because if 'solidarity is in part about fostering the interest of the collective, allowing the individual to succeed runs the risk of undermining solidarity for the collective'.[92]

This same 'paradox' between the individual and the collective can be seen in judgements about cross-border health care.[93] These cases are only indirectly related to the question of solidarity, since the actual issue discussed by the Court is the freedom to receive services in another Member State, i.e. the cases are inserted in the context of the market freedoms. Some evidence of this fact is that, although health care is included in the chapter on solidarity (Chapter 4) of the Charter of Fundamental Rights of the European Union (Article 35), this provision is rarely, if ever, mentioned in any of the judgements on cross-border health care. It was invoked only once by Advocate General Ruiz-Jarabo Colomer, in *Stamatelaki*.[94] However, in these cases the question of individual rights prevailing over collective interests is also present. The Court, in applying the freedom to receive services in another Member State of the Union, recognised the right of individuals, under certain circumstances, to receive health treatment abroad and

---

88 Case C-70/95, *Sodemare* [1997] ECR I-3395. Para 29.
89 Case C-205/03, *FENIN v Commission* [2006] ECR I-6295.
90 KLEIS, M. & NICOLAIDES, P. 2006. The Concept of Undertaking in Education and Public Health Systems. *European State Aid Law Quarterly*, 505.
91 Case C-184/99, *Grzelczyk* [2001] ECR, I-6193.
92 BARNARD, C. 2010. *Op. cit.*, p. 77.
93 *Decker*, Case C-120/95 [1998] ECR I-1831; *Kohll*, Case C-158/96 [1998] ECR I-1931; *Vanbraekel and others*, Case C-368/98 [2001] ECR I-5363; *Smits and Peerbooms*, Case C-157/99[2001]ECR I-5473; *Müller-Fauré and van Riet*, Case C-385/99 [2003] ECR I-4509; and *Watts*, Case C-372/04 [2006] ECR I-4325.
94 Case C-444/05 *Stamatelaki* [2007] ECR I-3185.

obtain reimbursement from his or her health system of affiliation. Allowing individual economic rights to succeed in these situations can be interpreted as the superimposition of autonomous individuals upon the interests of the community, which are essential to the traditional (national) idea of solidarity. This approach risks undermining national social schemes, because what is being advanced is individual rights instead of solidarity for the collective.

It is important to note, however, that the Court did recognise in this case law 'the risk of seriously undermining the financial balance of a social security system to constitute an overriding reason in the general interest capable of justifying an obstacle to the freedom to provide services',[95] even if the exit of patients in all of these cases was not held as an overriding reason.

In the view of some authors, such as Rieder, the exit of patients does not represent a threat to solidarity insofar as 'the relationship between those who exit and those who stay is somehow one of organic solidarity [. . .]'.[96] Using Hirschman's theory of exit, voice and loyalty,[97] and Durkheim's division of labour, this author concludes that the group which can exit is contributing to the improvement of the quality of the home system, which, in turn, benefits the collective, and thereby the unequal access to exit would be justified and would not affect solidarity.

However, I do not think that the question is as simple as Rieder puts it. His view, in my opinion, does not take account of three facts. First, that the reasons for exit are not always related to the quality of the home system. Patients who go abroad to seek the best specialist in a certain health area, the most modern treatment, or who try to circumvent waiting lists at their home system, do not necessarily do that because the quality of their health system is low. After all, due to the scarcity of resources, public financed health systems cannot offer always, and in each specific health specialisation, the most modern treatment within a short time limit. Nevertheless, the fact that the system does not offer such treatments does not mean that those it does offer are of low quality. The truth is that when health is at stake, patients who can afford to, seek to do everything in their power to look after themselves.[98] Second, in the case that the quality of the system is really low, if the number of patients going abroad is small, as argued by the author,[99]

95 *Watts*, Case C-372/04[2006] ECR I-4325, para. 103; *Kohll*, Case C-158/96 [1998] ECR I-1931, para.41; *Smits and Peerbooms*, Case C-157/99 [2001] ECR I-5473, para.72; and *Müller-Fauré and van Riet*, Case C-385/99 [2003] ECR I-4509, para. 73.

96 RIEDER, C. M. 2010. When Patients Exit, What Happens to Solidarity? *In:* ROSS, M. & BORGMANN-PREBIL, Y. (eds) *Promoting solidarity in the European Union.* Oxford; New York: Oxford University Press.

97 To carry out his analysis, Reider does not use Hirschman's book (HIRSCHMAN, A.O. 1970. *Exit, voice, and loyalty: responses to decline in firms, organizations, and States.* Cambridge, MA; London: Harvard University Press.), but a review article from Brian Barry (BARRY, B. 1974. Review: [untitled]. *British Journal of Political Science,* 4: 79–107).

98 See opinion of Advocate General Colomer in Case C-385/99, *Müller-Fauré* [2003] ECR I-4509, paras 51 and 52.

99 'Certainly one could ask the question about why there is all this fuss about EU healthcare law when less than one per cent of German patients, for example, went abroad for treatment and in 2006 only 350 British patients did so'. RIEDER, C.M. 2010. *Op. Cit.*, p. 122.

then there is no reason for the home system to improve its quality and it will remain like this for those who do not have the financial 'option' to go abroad. Third, if equity is an overarching principle of EU health systems, recognising 'possible' unequal access to exit as a justified 'injustice' in name of the quality of the system does not seem compatible with one of the most important objectives of health systems in the EU. In effect, if health policy makers are constantly searching for the achievement of equity, as will be seen in the next chapter, the consequences of letting inequities arise in this delicate area could in practice compromise policy making at national level.

Despite the still confused and sometimes rhetorical way that solidarity has been used by EU institutions, these moves are important for the definition and development of EU social policy standards and rights. Especially in relation to the ECJ, it is possible to say that to date it has been the only actor capable of 'forcing national authorities to take the European dimension in social policy into consideration'.[100] Nevertheless, the recognition of economic individual rights (indirectly social rights) by the Court cannot be mistaken for supranational solidarity. This is more a process of individualisation rather than of fostering post-national solidarity. In the words of Lamping:

> Through its case law the ECJ is redefining in particular the *vertical* relation between the individual and the state by defining social rights and entitlements (which certainly can have distributive and redistributive effects *within* the national welfare state). But the ECJ jurisdiction is not redefining solidarity at the *horizontal* level, i.e. between states or between European citizens in terms of European solidarity spaces.[101]

In effect, the process of individualisation can have an impact on solidarity. Beer and Koster, analysing the consequences of individualisation over solidarity, concluded that the process of individualisation which takes place in this kind of situation, also called emancipation, is characterised by a declining influence of social institutions on individual attitudes and behaviour, that is, 'people's opinions and attitudes are decreasingly determined by the collectivity to which they belong and become more a choice of their own'.[102] Accordingly, this process of individualisation can harm not only voluntary solidarity but also compulsory solidarity, affecting people's expectations and their behaviour in relation to others in an original solidaristic environment.[103]

In a similar vein, Alexander Somek also maintains that individualism negatively affects national solidarity. He argues that individualism does not take account of the idea of membership of a community or a group and, thus, the obligations arising

---

100   LAMPING, W. 2010. *Op. cit.*, p. 66.
101   *Ibid.*, p. 70.
102   BEER, P.D. & KOSTER, F. 2009. *Op. cit.*, p. 80.
103   *Ibid.*, pp. 81–2.

from relationships stemming from this membership are of little or no avail. Extending these ideas to the case of the EU, he concludes that this 'explains the substance of European citizenship'.[104] Using the case law of the ECJ on cross-border health care, the author explains that the individualism present in the Union changed the perception of national health care systems; their essence as solidaristic mechanisms, which once nurtured the sense of belonging and bonds between individuals, came to be perceived as inflexible, outdated and defensive when they refused, under certain circumstances, to provide reimbursement for treatments undergone abroad. Therefore, 'with the prevalence of individualism national solidarity begins to appear both ugly and unkind'.[105]

It is possible to conclude, thus, that supranational solidarity is something very different from national solidarity. The ties and bonds present in the national version of this concept are not found in its supranational counterpart. Although some authors sustain, as does Barnard, that European solidarity is an extension of national solidarity, insofar as the difference would be in relation only to the degrees in which the first affects different groups, this book takes the view sustained by Alexander Somek, who argues that supranational and national solidarity are not only different but are also in opposition to each other: whereas national solidarity is about birth in a country, descent from other nationals, residence and enculturation, transnational solidarity – as the author calls supranational solidarity – is only about the simple presence in a Member State or, as he puts it, being and time.[106]

Conclusion

The objective of this chapter was to distinguish the traditional concept of citizenship from its European version in order to see how social rights of citizenship work in this context. Moreover, departing from the national concept of solidarity, which is intrinsically related to the concept of citizenship and the welfare state, this chapter explored, by using concrete actions of the EU and judgements of the ECJ, and especially the case law on cross-border health care, what is entailed by the supranational version of solidarity. This analysis of solidarity served not only to differ national from supranational solidarity, but also to show how the latter concept can harm the national version by following a somewhat individualist path.

It is important to note, in order to avoid any criticism related to the defence of a nationalist posture in relation to the provision of health care by EU Member States, that the ideas developed in this chapter aimed to show that the basis of citizenship rights related to health care were built at the national level, and at this level are considered as rights related to the social field. From the moment they are transposed to the supranational level, the social nature of these rights cannot be

104 SOMEK, A. 2007. *Op. cit.*, p. 54.
105 *Ibid.*, p. 55.
106 *Ibid.*, p. 39.

outweighed by market values. In doing so, the social rights of citizenship lose their essential nature and their inclusive perspective, becoming closer to the idea of a market citizenship. This can be attributed to the 'constitutional asymmetry' that exists within the EU, which gives rise to imbalance between EU policies designed to promote market efficiency and those to promote social protection.[107]

Therefore, the possibility of the transposition of the concepts of social rights of citizenship and solidarity to the supranational level is not denied. However, in order to do so, the EU must take into account the social values present at the national level, correcting part of the 'constitutional asymmetry' and thus turning the supranational versions of the concepts of social rights of citizenship and solidarity into a reality for all citizens and not only for mobile ones.

Since the basic concepts related to health care rights are thus established, the book now turns to explore the health care sector specifically.

107 SCHARPF, F.W. 2002. The European Social Model. *JCMS: Journal of Common Market Studies*, 40: 645–70.

3   The provision of health services at the national level

Models for the financing and delivery of health care, and their guiding principles

This chapter is devoted to a description of the historical development of welfare services in the field of health care in Europe that led to the emergence of EU health systems. This description is based on an analysis of western EU countries, since eastern countries were previously based on the Russian Semashko model. This health system model included a rigid referral system that excluded the possibility of a patient choosing their physician or medical facility. Although all post-soviet countries have recently undergone many changes in their health systems, the historical development of these systems was quite different from those of western EU countries.[1]

Following this, the main features of the forms of organisation and financing of Bismarckian and Beveridgean health systems will be analysed, as well as the principles governing the provision of health services at the national level.

The development of welfare services in the field of health care in Europe: a historic overview

As can be seen from the ideas regarding citizenship, solidarity and the welfare state developed in the previous chapter, European countries have typically become welfare states in which the social rights of citizenship are as important as civil and political rights. When it comes to the health field, it is possible to argue that '[h]ealth care constitutes an essential element in a typical European welfare state. A welfare state in Europe is originally a nation-state, where contributions to a national health care system normally are provided through taxation or by payments of premiums into an insurance scheme'.[2] However, despite the similarities between European

1   SHISHKIN, S., BURDYAK, A. & POTAPCHIK, E. 2013. Patient choice in the post-semashko health care system. Working Paper Series: Public Administration. WP BRP 09/PA/2013, National Research University: Higher School of Economics. Available at www.hse.ru/data/2013/12/24/1341565269/09PA2013.pdf [Accessed 5 November 2015].
2   NEERGAARD, U. 2011. EU Health Care Law in a Constitutional Light: Distribution of Competences, Notions of 'Solidarity', and 'Social Europe'. *In:* GRONDEN, J.W.V.D., SZYSZCZAK, E., NEERGAARD, U. & KRAJEWSKI, M. (eds) *Health care and EU law*. The Hague: T.M.C. Asser, p. 20.

welfare states, each European nation state – due to their particular historical and cultural backgrounds – followed its own process when building and structuring the basis of its welfare state, which resulted in differences in regard to the provision of welfare services, as in the case of health services. Therefore, in order to understand these differences, in this chapter I will explore the historical development of welfare services in the field of health in western EU countries, showing, then, the main models currently in existence for the organisation and provision of health services. After demonstrating these differences, the chapter will describe and explain the similarities that exist in relation to health services in the EU, that is, it will look at recognised common principles guiding EU health systems.

The most common typology used to distinguish the different models of welfare state is that proposed by Esping-Andersen.[3] He laid out three main regime-types of welfare states in which modern developed capitalist nations cluster. The differences between these models are centred on the relationship between the private and public sectors in the provision of social services, in the level of decommodification of social service goods and in the social structure. The first is the 'liberal' welfare state, in which means-tested assistance and modest social insurance plans predominate. The state has a reduced role in providing benefits, which are usually circumscribed to low-income citizens, whereas the market plays a strong role in the provision of welfare services and this role is constantly encouraged by the state, either passively or actively. The United States, Australia and New Zealand are examples of this type of welfare state. The second model is the 'corporatist' welfare state and it is based on the Bismarckian social insurance model, according to which social protection is defined according to professional categories or social status. This type of welfare state can be found in Germany, Austria, France and in the Benelux countries. The third and final type is the 'social-democrat' welfare state, in which benefits are provided according to universal premises, being equally distributed irrespectively of social, economic or occupational status. This model is the one developed in the Scandinavian countries and in the United Kingdom.

Although, in practice, welfare states and especially health systems are not exclusively designed according to this typology, and liberal elements are found in Scandinavian welfare types in the same way as redistributive elements can be found in liberal welfare types,[4] the use of Esping-Andersen's typology is useful to identify the patterns of evolution applied to each of these models. Therefore, although this work will not rely on Esping-Andersen's typology, his welfare state models will be used here for the purpose of describing the historical evolution of European welfare states.

Welfare schemes as we know them today were born in Europe between 1880 and 1920. However, it is possible to identify measures used to support disadvantaged people since the Middle Ages. These measures worked as a system of poor relief and the benefits were provided only when the person could prove

3   ESPING-ANDERSEN, G. 1990. *Op. cit.*
4   *Ibid.*, p. 28.

actual need and lack of resources.[5] The major role in providing these types of benefits was played by religious bodies,[6] such as local parishes, which granted outdoor relief to a wide class of persons, including able-bodied workers, and did so in many forms, including in-kind grants, cash and several forms of wage supplement.[7]

In England, for example, the first 'Poor Law' was introduced in 1388.[8] Almost two centuries later, in 1536, an act from Henry VIII made local officials responsible for poor relief.[9] In 1601, an Elizabethan Poor Law introduced taxes that could be levied on every inhabitant on a weekly or other basis for the support of the poor. This law formed the basis of poor law administration and funding in England.[10]

The turn of the 19th century marked some important changes in the development of poor relief policies. First, in some countries public institutions took the place of religious bodies in the role of providing poor relief. This change was, in part, due to the fact that poor relief was associated with the increase in begging and religious bodies were accused of spoiling and sheltering the poor by giving the beggars alms. Second, the system of poor relief turned out to be linked to the needs of the working class.[11] In England, the influence of liberal ideas, including those spread by T. R. Malthus' First Essay on Population, led to the adoption of a New Poor Law in 1834. This law aimed, *inter alia*, at reducing aid to vagrants by making sure that the non-working poor received less assistance than the labouring poor.

Despite these initial forms of poor relief, it was only between 1880 and the end of the First World War that welfare regimes were really introduced in different countries in Europe.[12] The adoption of welfare systems during this period is in

---

5 COUSINS, M. 2005. *European welfare states: comparative perspectives*. London; Thousand Oaks, CA: Sage, p. 78.

6 The administration of poor relief was almost entirely under the control of the Church and was thus administered by ecclesiastics. For a further discussion on this issue see LEONARD, E.M. 1900. *The early history of English poor relief (1900)*. Cambridge: Cambridge University Press Warehouse. Available at www.archive.org/stream/earlyhistoryofen00leonrich#page/n5/mode/2up [Accessed 14 December 2015].

7 OUIGLEY, T., COATE, S. & GUINNANE, T.W. 2001. Incentives, Information, and Welfare: England's New Poor Law and the Workhouse Test. Working Paper. Available at www.russellsage. org/sites/all/files/u4/Besley,%20Coate,%20%26%20Guinnane_Incentives,%20Information,% 20and%20Welfare.pdf [Accessed 18 December 2015].

8 This is known as *The Statute of Cambridge*.

9 The transfer of poor relief functions to the state is linked with the attempts of Henry VIII to outlaw begging. In 1536, Henry VIII dissolved the smaller religious houses of monks and nuns, and in 1539 the larger abbeys and monasteries were dissolved. QUIGLEY, W.P. 1996. Five hundred Years of English Poor Laws, 1349–1834: regulating the working and nonworking poor. *Akron Law Review*, 30: 1–63. Available at www.uakron.edu/dotAsset/726694.pdf [Accessed 18 December 2015].

10 *Ibid.*, p. 14.

11 'Because the poor and the proletariat were groups that overlapped during the initial development of the welfare state, social policy was linked with the needs of the working class'. DUPEYROUX, J.J. (1966) *Evolution et tendances des systèmes de sécurité sociale des pays membres des communautés européennes et de la Grande-Bretagne, apud* BALDWIN, P. 1990. *The politics of social solidarity: class bases of the European welfare state, 1875–1975*. Cambridge; New York: Cambridge University Press, p. 55.

12 COUSINS, M.P. 2005. *Op. cit.*, p. 79.

part due to the miserable living conditions, especially of the urban working class, caused by the multiple economic crises which came with rapid industrialisation. Moreover, in many countries the adoption of welfare regimes is also connected with political and military strategies. Therefore, the direction and grounds of welfare regimes followed by the different nations in Europe depended on the political context and the configuration of the working-class current at the time of the introduction of such regimes. Three factors in particular are of key importance for understanding welfare state developments: the nature of class mobilisation (especially of the working class); class–political coalition structures; and the historical legacy of regime institutionalisation.[13]

However, since the aim of this book is not an in-depth look at the development of the welfare state as a whole, only the historical aspects of the development of health systems and services will be described specifically. Special attention will be devoted to Germany and the United Kingdom, since each represents a different type of welfare state, according to Esping-Andersen's typology, and functions as a paradigm of one of the two general models of EU health systems: social health insurance (or Bismarckian model) and national health system (or Beveridgean model). These two models should be considered as ideal types and do not represent the exact reality of EU health systems. They correspond to the foundation of European social welfare systems, but nowadays 'no individual national public healthcare system conforms directly to either of the ideal types'.[14]

Finally, it is important to highlight that due to the economic crisis that occurred in 2008, some EU health systems experienced policy changes especially regarding public spending on health. These included, for example, measures such as cutting ministry of health budgets, reducing or freezing government budget transfers to health insurance schemes and introducing or tightening controls on growth rates of public spending on health. These changes, however, are more of a budgetary than an organisational nature and, hence, do not affect the analysis made in this chapter.[15]

Germany and the social insurance (or Bismarckian) model

Germany was the first nation to adopt a welfare programme, introducing in 1883 a disability social insurance scheme. However, social health insurance is approximately a 700-year-old historical process which dates back to the late

13　ESPING-ANDERSEN, G. 1990. *Op. cit.*, p. 29.
14　HERVEY, T.K. 2011b. If Only It Were So Simple: Public Health Services and EU Law *In:* CREMONA, M. (ed.) *Market integration and public services in the European Union.* Oxford: Oxford University Press, p. 184.
15　For an overview of the impact of the economic crisis over EU health systems, see THOMSON, S. *et al.* 2015. *Economic crisis, health systems and health in Europe: impact and implications for policy.* Policy Summary 12, WHO Regional Office for Europe and European Observatory on Health Systems and Policies. Available at www.euro.who.int/__data/assets/pdf_file/0008/257579/Economic-crisis-health-systems-Europe-impact-implications-policy.pdf [Accessed 5 November 2015].

medieval period with its roots in occupational associations. Since the beginning of the 14th century, small groups of workers created mutual assistance associations under the auspices of their craft guild. These associations generally only covered guild members while the rest of the population relied on charitable or religious organisations. It was only in the 19th century, with the banning of the guilds, that the state began to take on an active role in the provision of health services.[16]

In 1876 in Germany standards for minimum contributions and benefits were established by the Parliament, but these contributions were not made mandatory. In 1881 the Emperor's Charter declared that social welfare for the poor was essential for national survival in a hostile world. In this same year, motivated by military and economic concerns and worried about the Marxist influence over labour unions, the Prussian politician Otto von Bismarck – who later became chancellor of Germany – suggested a national health service-type system. Considering, however, that tax-based financial provisions were opposed by state governments as well as by liberal members of parliament from business, agriculture and the church, the legislation approved in 1883 (Health Insurance Act) reflected a compromise between these rival interests and was thus built upon existing local funds and occupation-based funds (miners, guilds and companies). In practice, the new legislation, besides making health insurance mandatory for workers of certain industries with hourly wages or up to a legally fixed income ceiling, regulated the sickness funds already in existence by placing their activities under state control. Accordingly, the role of the parliament and the central government was merely regulatory and limited to setting the framework and the legal standards for the self-administrated funds.[17]

In terms of benefits, the Health Insurance Act of 1883 defined a minimum benefit catalogue which the sickness funds could decide to extend. Therefore, just a 'minimum set of primary health care services, including medication, was to be provided while hospital care was left to the decision of the funds on a case-by-case basis'.[18] This type of regulation became widely used by many funds during the ensuing decades and was the motor for the gradual extension of the legal minimum catalogue.

The adoption of the Health Insurance Act in Germany, in 1883, was followed by the introduction of the Accident Insurance Law of 1884 and the Old Age Invalidity Act of 1889.[19] It was only in 1911 that a common regulatory framework for the different types of social insurance was adopted, through the enactment of

16 SALTMAN, R.B. & DUBOIS, H.F.W. 2004. The historical and social base of social health insurance systems. *In:* SALTMAN, R.B., BUSSE, R. & FIGUERAS, J. (eds) *Social health insurance systems in Western Europe.* Maidenhead, UK; New York: Open University, pp. 22–3.

17 *Ibid.,* pp. 13–14.

18 *Ibid.,* p. 14.

19 ALTENSTETTER, C. 1999. From solidarity to market competition? *In:* POWELL, F.D. & WESSEN, A.F. (eds) *Health care systems in transition: an international perspective.* Thousand Oaks, CA: Sage, p. 49.

the Imperial Insurance Regulation, which lasted, with some changes, until 1988, when many reforms were adopted.

The social security model inaugurated by Germany was followed by most of the European countries after 1883, which adopted similar legislation: Austria adopted it in 1887/1888, Sweden in 1891, Denmark in 1892, Belgium in 1894, France in 1898, and the United Kingdom in 1911. One of the last countries to adopt compulsory health insurance was Italy, in 1941.[20] However, during the 20th century and especially after the Second World War, many of these countries underwent reforms in their systems, moving from the social insurance model to a more universalistic model. This was the case, for example, of the United Kingdom, which adopted in 1946 the National Health Service Act, becoming then another paradigm for EU health systems. I will come back to this type of system in the following pages.

Despite all the political changes Germany has undergone throughout the years, which includes the period of National Socialism (1933–1945), the post-Second World War period and the reunification of the country during the 1990s, Germany has been able to maintain its social insurance model, which consolidated itself as a paradigm for EU health systems and has become known also as the Bismarckian model due to its origins. Nowadays, social health insurance is found in Germany, Austria, France, Belgium, the Netherlands and Luxembourg, and adapted models of social health insurance are also found, for example, in Hungary, Lithuania, the Czech Republic, Estonia, Latvia, Slovakia and Poland.[21]

Austria was the second country to adopt the social insurance model by introducing the industrial accident and health insurance scheme in 1887/1888. However, the development of the Austrian health system dates back to the period of the Austro-Hungarian monarchy and it is possible to find regulatory provisions concerning welfare services dating from 1810. These initial regulations obliged employers to pay for hospital stays and the care of sick employees. In 1867, the Associations Act enabled the creation of association-based funds which led to the establishment of the general workers' health insurance and invalidity relief funds in 1868. The insurance schemes introduced in 1887/1888 were the foundation of today's social security system. These schemes have evolved through time to incorporate other categories of workers, even after the collapse of the Austro-Hungarian monarchy. During the fascist period, the social security system underwent major cuts and it was only in the post-war period that improvements started to be made. In 1947/1948 the Social Insurance Act re-established an autonomously administered social security system and the Federation of Austrian Social Security Institutions was created. Between 1965 and 1967 major improvements were made by the adoption of the Farmers' Health Insurance Act

20   COUSINS, M.P. 2005. *Op. cit.*, p. 81.
21   SALTMAN, R.B. 2004. Social health insurance in perspective: the challenge of sustaining stability. *In:* SALTMAN, R.B., BUSSE, R. & FIGUERAS, J. (eds) *Social health insurance systems in Western Europe.* Maidenhead, UK; New York: Open University Press, p. 3.

and the Civil Servants' Health Insurance Act. Nowadays, almost the entire Austrian population has health insurance coverage (99.9% in 2011).[22]

In France, although a kind of social security model has existed since 1898, which was based on the mutual benefit movement, it was only in 1930 that the Act on Social Insurance was passed, providing compulsory protection for employees in industry and business whose earnings fell below a certain level. After the Second World War, with the aim of expanding coverage and transforming social security into a mandatory system for the whole population, new legislation was introduced. This process was, however, slow and was put in practice in stages: in 1945, the social security system officially came into being, focusing mainly on workers and their families; in 1966 and 1967 health insurance was extended to farmers and to self-employed non-agricultural workers; in 1974 a further step was adopted through the creation of a system of personal insurance for those who did not fall into any of the categories already covered. Nowadays in France there is no single unified system, but rather three main health insurance schemes are dominant: the general health insurance scheme, or *régime général*, which covers employees in commerce and industry and their families, and represents 95% of the population; the agricultural scheme, and the national insurance fund for the self-employed. The French health care system, thus, can be summarised as a mix of public and private providers and insurers. Public health insurance is compulsory and financed by both employees and employer contributions, and earmarked taxes, covering almost the whole population, while private health insurance is of a complementary type and voluntary.[23]

In Belgium, as in France, the health system also has its origins in the mutual benefit societies. Accordingly, before the introduction of the legislation which created the sickness funds in 1894, the voluntary 'mutualities' were organised according to employment type, and run as private initiatives, without state subsidies. After 1894, these sickness funds were not only recognised by the state, but were also able to receive state subsidies. Although recognised by the state, affiliation to the funds was voluntary until 1903, when the first type of compulsory insurance was created. However, it was only during the Second World War that steps towards the adoption of a compulsory social insurance system were taken. Thus, in 1944 the Social Security Act was passed, introducing universal access to social security and making all social insurance funds, including unemployment, health and disability insurance, compulsory for all salaried employees. In 1963, a further step was taken with the adoption of the Health Insurance Act and nowadays it is possible to say that the whole population is covered by the health system, either under the general scheme or the scheme for self-employed workers.[24]

22 HOFMARCHER, M. & QUENTIN, W. 2013. Austria: Health system review. *Health Systems in Transition*, 15(7): 1–291, p. 88.
23 CHEVREUL, K. *et al*. 2010. France: Health system review. *Health Systems in Transition*, 12(6): 1–291.
24 GERKENS, S. & MERKUR, S. 2010. Belgium: Health system review. *Health Systems in Transition*, 12(5): 1–266.

The Netherlands health insurance system has its origins in voluntary organisations which provided care on a charitable basis. The provision of care on a voluntary basis was the rule in the Netherlands until the Second World War. With the German occupation, pressure was put on to make health insurance compulsory. Thus, in 1941 the Sickness Fund Decree was adopted, splitting the health insurance market into three sub-markets: a compulsory social health insurance scheme for employed people (and their families), a voluntary social health insurance for self-employed people and private health insurance for the rest of the population. The division introduced by this legislation still exists in the Dutch health system. However, subsequent measures were adopted in order to increase the coverage by the health system, as for example, the Exceptional Medical Expenses Act adopted in 1967, which created an insurance scheme covering the whole population for serious medical risks. Over time, this insurance scheme has expanded to other population groups and it presently includes elderly people, the disabled and mentally ill patients with chronic problems. The Dutch health system nowadays is predominantly one of private ownership, although it is heavily regulated by the government.[25]

In Luxembourg, compulsory health insurance was introduced for the first time in 1901, following the same scheme proposed by Bismarck in Germany. In 1902 and 1911 respectively, accident and old age insurance were also introduced. Due to the rapid growth in the number of individual sickness funds, in 1925 legislation was introduced in order to codify the different types of insurance, which was amended in 1927 and 1933 to increase the benefits. Although it was a system of compulsory affiliation, until the Second World War many categories of workers were not covered by the health insurance system. It was only after the war that measures were adopted in order to increase coverage: in 1952 compulsory insurance was extended to civil servants and other categories of public employees; in 1958 to the independent professions (e.g. businessmen and craftsmen); in 1963 to farmers, and in 1964 to the independent intellectual professions (e.g. doctors, architects and lawyers). From 1973 onwards, the working population, their families, and all pensioners were covered by compulsory health insurance.[26]

Despite the different trajectories followed by the above-mentioned countries, they have all adopted a social model inspired by the one first introduced by Bismarck in Germany; therefore their health systems have similar organisational and financial characteristics.

In terms of organisational structure, the social insurance model is based upon three main actors: sickness funds, insured patients and providers. Sickness funds collect the premiums and use the revenues from members' premiums to fund

25 SCHÄFER, W. *et al.* 2010. The Netherlands: Health system review. Health Systems in Transition, 12(1): 1–229.
26 BERTHET, F. *et al.* 2015. Luxembourg: HiT in brief. *Health Systems in Transition.* Available at www.euro.who.int/__data/assets/pdf_file/0006/287943/Mini-HiT_Luxembourg-rev1.pdf [Accessed 24 November 2015].

collective contracts with providers for the provision of health care services for their members. These funds are usually private not-for-profit organisations with statutory recognition and responsibilities established by national legislation, although in some countries there are also public funds run by the state, as for example in France and Belgium.[27] The state, thus, is not seen as the owner of these social security structures, but rather their guardian and administrator. However, even if the state cannot be considered as the owner, social health insurance systems are part of the state's social income policies and, for this reason, have a redistributive nature. They are designed to achieve specific social objectives through a set of financial cross subsidies: from healthy to ill, from well-off to less well-off, from young to old and from individuals to families. This is, in effect, what makes social health insurance systems very different from standard commercial insurance. "Social health insurance requires individuals to contribute toward the best interest of the population generally through its structure of financial redistribution."[28] In fact, it is this idea of concern about the well-being of others expressed through the cross-subsidies mechanisms that links social insurance systems to the principle of solidarity. As Peter Baldwin points out:

> The novelty of social insurance was the extension of this confrontation of risk in community from a small circle, sometimes of self-selected to its advantage, sometimes isolated to its own peril, not only to a much larger group – possibly society as a whole – but even, through intergenerational transfers, to the still unborn. (. . .) Social insurance's advantage lay in the expanse of the community it embraced, the scope of the problem it resolved, the intervention allowed by the state's power and the justice of the redistribution that followed. The terms of misfortune's reapportionment were determined not privately, but by society as a whole in accordance with commonly accepted standards of equity.[29]

The number of funds, their size and their structure vary widely. In some countries, sickness funds are organised according to occupational status or on the basis of occupational groups. Austria, France and Luxembourg have a small and stable number of funds compared with Belgium, Germany and the Netherlands, which have competing funds with greatly varying numbers. In all countries except Germany, sickness funds are supplemented by a national umbrella organisation.[30]

With regard to insured members, social insurance systems use different criteria in order to define the group of individuals insured. Mandatory membership and

27 SALTMAN, R.B. 2004. *Op. cit.*, p. 7.
28 *Ibid.*, p. 5.
29 BALDWIN, P. 1990. *Op. cit.*, p. 2.
30 BUSSE, R., SALTMAN, R.B. & DUBOIS, H.F.W. 2004. Organization and financing of social health insurance systems: current status and recent policy developments. *In:* SALTMAN, R.B., BUSSE, R. & FIGUERAS, J. (eds) *Social health insurance systems in Western Europe.* Maidenhead, UK; New York: Open University Press, p. 34.

universal coverage is usually the rule and is established by law, although some countries provide for exceptions. For instance, in Belgium there is a special regime for the self-employed, in Germany self-employed people with an income over a state-determined ceiling have a choice between statutory and private health insurance, while in the Netherlands this category of high-income or self-employed individuals cannot enrol in the general regime.

In Austria, France and Luxembourg, membership is defined on the basis of occupational status or residence. Therefore, if a person belongs to a given professional category or works for a certain employer which has its own fund, he or she will be insured automatically by this fund. Otherwise, affiliation is based on the criterion of residence. This does not happen in Germany, Belgium or the Netherlands, where there is a certain degree of choice for members in regard to contributing to a sickness fund. These countries in turn have established a minimum interval for changing between funds.[31]

With regard to funding, contributions and premiums are the main source of financing for the health system.[32] These are usually income-related, that is, based on income from gainful employment, pensions or unemployment benefits, and not from savings or possessions, but there are some differences between countries regarding the contribution rates.[33] In Belgium, France, Luxembourg and the Netherlands the contribution rate is uniform for all persons, regardless of the sickness fund and employment status. By contrast, in both Austria and Germany this contribution rate varies, while in Austria rates vary according to employment status but not in relation to the sickness fund; in Germany the contribution rates differ among funds, but not according to employment status.[34]

Another rule regarding contributions and premiums is their mandatory status. Accordingly, every citizen whose earnings, including pensions and unemployment benefits, are below a certain threshold is compulsorily affiliated to the scheme. Exceptions apply to citizens whose salaries exceed the threshold and to some self-employed categories.

The health care benefits package usually comprises a wide range of services in all levels of care (primary, secondary and tertiary), including also long-term and specialist care such as rehabilitation, dental care and mental health services. Cost-sharing or co-payments are charged for some specific types of care or for pharmaceuticals. In the case of hospital care, contracts between the providers and

31 *Ibid.*, p. 42.
32 Other complementary sources of financing include contributions to other statutory insurance schemes, such as retirement, accidents and long-term care, as well as taxes, out-of-pocket payments and private health insurance. Taxation can be used either as a direct form of financing or in the form of subsidies. Indeed, the relation between financing through wage contributions and taxation will depend on how much income social insurance systems are able to generate through wage contributions and the percentage of overall health expenditure covered through these systems.
33 BUSSE, R. & BLÜMEL, M. 2014. Germany: Health system review. *Health Systems in Transition*, 16(2): 1–296.
34 *Ibid.*, p. 45.

the sickness funds guarantee the coverage of treatment costs although there is patient cost-sharing, which varies from country to country. In relation to ambulatory care, including physician visits, patients are free to choose the provider, but usually have to pay a cost-sharing percentage.

In relation to providers, it is possible to say that nowadays social insurance systems have a mix of public, private not-for-profit and private for-profit providers of health services.[35] The percentage of each of these categories of providers within the health system depends on the type of health care service. Hospitals, for example, are mainly public in most countries using social health insurance. There is, however, an important role played historically by private not-for-profit providers in this sector and a growing role played by the private for-profit sector, which is likely to increase with the process of privatisation in the health field that has taken place in some countries and is expected to continue in future years.[36] Moreover, the application of the Internal Market rules to health services may work also as a mechanism for fostering a new market for private health providers. I will come back to this point in the following chapters.

Finally, with regard to the way services are provided, social insurance systems can be further distinguished between those based on the principle of reimbursement and those based on the benefits-in-kind principle, according to which patients obtain medical benefits from practitioners or clinics that have a contract with social insurance funds and, thus, are not confronted with a medical bill. Belgium, Luxembourg and France operate on the basis of reimbursement whereas the Netherlands, Austria and Germany have a benefits-in-kind system.[37]

Britain and the tax-based (or Beveridgean) model

As mentioned above, the initial history of British welfare services follows the pattern adopted by Germany in 1883. In 1911 Britain introduced a national insurance fund for low-income workers. Nevertheless, Britain was the first country to change its social insurance system into a universal tax-financed health system. In 1946 it adopted the National Health Service Act and on 5 July 1948 the National Health Service (NHS) was formally introduced, on the occasion of the inauguration of Park Hospital in Manchester by the health secretary Aneurin Bevan.

The introduction of the NHS, as well as the social changes undergone by the British social security system during this period, were strongly influenced by the report produced by Sir William Beveridge, called *Social Insurance and Allied*

---

35 Another feature of these systems is that providers are separated from the funds, although historically many funds started as institutions combining the role of payers and providers.

36 See ANDRÉ, C. & HERMANN, C. 2008. The privatisation of health care in Europe. *PRESOM Newsletter, n. 5–6 (January/February).* Available at www.raumplanung.uni-dortmund.de/irpud/presom/fileadmin/docs/presom/external/Publications/WP5.pdf [Accessed 25 November 2015]; and MAARSE, H. 2006. The Privatization of Health Care in Europe: An Eight-Country Analysis. *Journal of Health Politics Policy and Law,* 31: 981–1014.

37 VAN DER MEI, A.P. 2003. *Op. cit.,* p. 224.

Services, published on 2 December 1942.[38] The report was generally concerned with basic conditions of equality and a better sense of community, and proposed a widespread reform of the British welfare system, including the universality of the social security regime, which should not be limited only to those in regular employment; an active labour market policy in order to combat unemployment; and the universality of health care. Although the report was not primarily about health care,[39] it treated these services as part of the 'allied services', which included a comprehensive scheme whose chief concern was the maintenance of employment and income. Moreover, according to the report, health care was important to that scheme as a means of protecting or restoring people's capacity to work.[40]

This atmosphere of social change was also influenced by the sentiments of the post-war period. The visions of a better future and the new sense of community were associated with the idea of a social system that could unite citizens and protect them equally against risk, regardless of their class, fate or biology.

The introduction of the NHS represented a radical change in the way welfare services, and especially health services, were to be provided in Britain: it established the principle of collective responsibility of the state for a comprehensive health service, which was to be available to the entire population free at the point of use. Freedom from user charges was thus a key feature of this approach, which placed heavy emphasis on equality of access.[41] Welfare policy turned to be informed by the idea that social rights should complete and not sidetrack the process of emancipation. Accordingly, the less fortunate were to be helped by treating all equally and poverty was no longer a status to exclude individuals from full membership in the community.[42]

Today the NHS is regarded as the paradigm of a tax-financed public health system, also known as the 'Beveridgean model' due to the inspiration it derived from the report of Sir William Beveridge. The main elements of the present-day organisational structure of the NHS were introduced by the National Health Service Act of 1973. However, in 2009 a new Health Act[43] was introduced – which came into force only on 9 January 2010 – providing for some changes within the NHS. Amongst these changes is the adoption of a Constitution[44] at the NHS level,

38 BEVERIDGE, W.H.B. 1969. *Social insurance and allied services.* New York: Agathon P.
39 As Baldwin argues, 'A National Health System (NHS) and universal family allowances were assumptions of his recommendations'. BALDWIN, P. 1990. *Op. cit.,* p. 117.
40 MUSGROVE, P. 2000. Health insurance: the influence of the Beveridge Report. *Bulletin of the World Health Organization,* 78: 845–6.
41 BOYLE, S. 2011. *Health Systems in Transition: United Kingdom.* Copenhagen Ø, Denmark: World Health Organization, on behalf of the European Observatory on Health Systems and Policies.
42 BALDWIN, P. 1990. *Op. cit.,* p. 108.
43 Health Act 2009. Available at www.opsi.gov.uk/acts/acts2009/ukpga_20090021_en_1# Legislation-Preamble [Accessed 26 November 2015].
44 UNITED KINGDOM DEPARTMENT OF HEALTH. *The NHS Constitution.* Available at www.nhs.uk/choiceintheNHS/Rightsandpledges/NHSConstitution/Documents/2013/the-nhs-constitution-for-england-2013.pdf [Accessed 24 November 2015].

which sets out the principles and values of the NHS, the rights and responsibilities of patients and staff, and the NHS pledges to patients and staff.[45]

The NHS is routinely contrasted with the 'Bismarckian model' of contribution-based, employment-related social security. The main difference between these types is the form of financing: while in social insurance systems financing comes basically from contributions and premiums, in taxed-based systems the main form of financing is public taxation.[46] In Europe, since 1960, many countries which had relied largely on the social insurance model have followed the same path as Britain, opting for a universal, tax-financed health system. This group includes, for example, Sweden, Norway, Denmark, Italy, Portugal, Spain and Greece.[47]

Sweden was the first country after Britain to introduce a tax-based system. However, even before the introduction of this universal tax-based system the country already had a long tradition of providing public care to its citizens, and since the 17th century physicians had been employed by the central government in order to provide basic medical care. In 1928, with the enactment of the Hospitals Act, inpatient hospital care became the responsibility of county councils but outpatient care remained excluded from the legislation. It was only after the Second World War that the first step towards the adoption of a universal system was taken, and in 1946 Parliament voted the National Health Insurance Act, which included coverage for physician consultations, prescription drugs and sickness compensation. Although the new legislation was adopted in 1946, the new health system was implemented only in 1955 due to budget constraints.[48]

Norway has a similar historical background of providing public care to its citizens from the early days of its health system. In the 18th century, municipalities and volunteer organisations played an important role as welfare and health care providers. In 1912, the Practitioners' Act was adopted, guaranteeing everyone equal access to physicians' services, regardless of income and settlement. However, it was only in 1967 that universal coverage of welfare services and expenses was adopted with the creation of the National Insurance Scheme (NIS), which is a public universal insurance scheme that assures the whole population universal coverage of welfare services, regardless of income. It is possible to say, thus, that currently the Norwegian health care system is built on the principle of equal access

45 BOYLE, S. 2011. *Op. cit.*, p. 118.

46 As Mossialos and Dixon explain, 'Taxation is heterogeneous – that is, there are different sources (direct or indirect), different levels (national or local) and different types of taxation (general or hypothecated)'. MOSSIALOS, E. & DIXON, A. 2002. Funding health care: an introduction. *In:* MOSSIALOS, E., DIXON, A., FIGUERAS, J. & KUTZIN, J. (eds) *Funding health care: options for Europe.* Buckingham, UK; Philadelphia, PA: Open University Press, p. 19.

47 WAGSTAFF, A. 2009. Social Health Insurance vs. Tax-Financed Health Systems – Evidence from the OECD. *Policy Research Working Paper 4821.* Washington, DC: The World Bank, p. 6. Available at www-wds.worldbank.org/external/default/WDSContentServer/IW3P/IB/2009/01/21/000158349_20090121101737/Rendered/PDF/WPS4821.pdf [Accessed 25 November 2015].

48 ANELL, A., GLENNGÅRD, A.H. & MERKUR, S. 2012. Sweden: Health system review. *Health Systems in Transition,* 14(5): 1–159.

to services for all inhabitants, regardless of their social or economic status and geographical location.[49]

Denmark has a different historical background compared to Sweden and Norway. Prior to the 18th century, the provision of care to workers was the responsibility of landlords or artisans' masters. By virtue of this initial connection between work and the provision of care, from the second half of the 19th century health insurance developed in Denmark. The system was organised according to professional categories: artisans, for example, organised their own aid funds as a continuation of the guilds' funds, and other groups organised health insurance funds for the poorer. These health insurance schemes were abolished only in 1973, when health care came to be financed by taxes.[50]

In Italy, during the 19th century several different arrangements for the provision of health care overlapped. Some were organisations sponsored by the Catholic Church, but there were also charitable organisations, a provincial network for preventive medicine and public health, autonomous mutual aid associations for artisans and workers, and independent not-for-profit structures. In the 20th century, health insurance funds were established and employers and employees became responsible for financing health care, by contributing a percentage of their monthly wage to the health insurance funds. During the fascist regime the system underwent some changes in order to expand the number of people covered by the health insurance scheme. Between 1974 and 1975 health insurance funds were abolished and a national health system was introduced, but it was only with the reform law of 1978 (Law 833/1978), which established human dignity, health needs and solidarity as the guiding principles of the health system, that universal coverage was guaranteed to all Italian citizens.[51]

In Portugal, until the 18th century health care was provided by religious bodies and only to the poor. In the 19th century the state took responsibility for part of the care by establishing hospitals aimed at supplementing the services provided by charitable institutions. During the 20th century new legislation in the field of public health was adopted, including the first social security law in 1946, which introduced a social security scheme inspired by the German model, for the provision of health care to the employed population and their dependants. The first step in the direction of universal public provision of health care came in 1971, with the adoption of legislation which sought to integrate health policy in the context of wider social policies, extending also the protection of the family and disabled persons. This legislation, however, has never been implemented and the actual establishment of the national health system occurred only after the revolution, in 1979.[52]

49   RINGARD, Å. *et al.* 2013. Norway: Health system review. *Health Systems in Transition*, 15(8): 1–162.
50   OLEJAZ, M. *et al.* 2012. Denmark: Health system review. *Health Systems in Transition*, 14(2): 1–192.
51   FERRÉ, F. *et al.* 2014. Italy: Health System Review. *Health Systems in Transition*, 16(4): 1–168.
52   BARROS, P., MACHADO, S. & SIMÕES, J. 2011. Portugal: Health system review. *Health Systems in Transition*, 13(4): 1–156.

The Spanish social security system dates back to the early 20th century. The National Institute of Social Insurance (Instituto Nacional de Previsión, IN) was created during the early 1900s in order to coordinate the design and implementation of the first social insurance policies. However, due to its means-tested basis, the health system achieved only low coverage until 1967 – 45% of the population was covered in 1960 – when the Basic Social Security Act was adopted. This law expanded the coverage to self-employed professionals and qualified civil servants. In addition, during this period there was also the expansion of a publicly owned network of centres and services for general medical care, and specialised outpatient and inpatient care. In 1978, in the transition to democracy, a new Constitution was adopted establishing the right to the protection of health for all Spaniards. However, it was only in 1982, when the Socialist Party obtained the majority of the seats in the central parliament, that the health system underwent a great reform which culminated in the approval of the General Health Care Act in 1986. This law refined the provisions of the 1978 Constitution, setting out the National Health System scheme and bringing all publicly administered health services under one roof.[53]

Greece was the last country to adopt a tax-based system. In the period between Greek independence and the first part of the 20th century, just a small proportion of the population had any type of health coverage. In 1934, the government introduced the Social Security Organisation (IKA) which focused only on health and pension coverage to blue- and white-collar workers in urban areas and in industries employing more than 70 workers. Following this trend, in 1953 there was an attempt to create a national health service but the law was never implemented. During the 1960s a great number of firms, especially from the financial sector, established their own social security schemes and there was a major expansion in numbers of private health providers. This type of system remained during the period of the dictatorship. It was with the re-establishment of democracy in 1974 and the election of members of the Socialist Party (PASOK) to Parliament in 1981 that the political situation allowed for the approval of legislation creating the National Health Service in 1983. Among the objectives of the new system was the establishment of universal coverage and equal access to health services, which became the responsibility of the state.[54]

Despite the different trajectories followed by each of these countries in the introduction of a national health service, they have all sought, sooner or later, to achieve the same goal, i.e. to create a more equitable and fair health system, based on the principles of universality and equity. The reasons why these countries decided to move from a social insurance to a tax-based model vary from country to country and are also related to their political trajectory. In fact, authors who

53 GARCÍA-ARMESTO, S. *et al.* 2010. Spain: Health system review. *Health Systems in Transition*, 12(4): 1–295.
54 ECONOMOU, C. 2010. Greece: Health system review. *Health Systems in Transition*, 12(7): 1–180.

tried to provide a political interpretation to the adoption of universal legislation after the Second World War argue that

> The universality of significant postwar legislation sprang not solely or even primarily from the strength of the left, but in fact followed equally immediate and direct interests developed by the bourgeoisie in all-inclusive social policy. It was not only the Social Democrats who cemented political support for solidaristic measures by including each citizen, but just as much as those who had traditionally been excluded from welfare who now saw their chance to be among the beneficiaries of the state's largesse. Conversely, the failure of apparent similar initiatives on the Continent was due not to the left's impotence, but to the radical redistributive ambitions that were here embodied in reform. Rather than benefiting middle-classes, French and German measures consciously aimed to help the poorest at the expense of the better-off, thereby provoking the resistance that led to their failure. In Britain and Scandinavia, it was the innocuous, indeed deliberately pro-bourgeois, aspects of reform that explain the ease of its success.[55]

The main features of tax-based systems, which differentiate them from social insurance systems, relate to their form of funding and organisational structure. With regard to funding, these systems are financed almost exclusively through taxes on income, purchases, property, capital gains and a variety of other items and activities. In effect, this model of financing mobilises funds from a much larger sector of the population, since citizens have to contribute regardless of their health status, income or occupation. Therefore, the scope for mobilising funds can be said to be wider than in social insurance systems. Moreover, tax-based systems may be more progressive than social insurance systems, since the capture of revenues will come from rents, capital gains and profits, instead of relying predominantly on a share of formal workers' salaries.[56]

Even if the use of taxes for financing the system is one of the major features of tax-based systems, among the countries which use this form of funding it is possible to find considerable differences in the type of taxes used. While some countries rely on national taxes, others rely on regional or local taxes. The first group includes, for example, the United Kingdom, Ireland and Portugal, and the second countries such as Denmark, Finland, Sweden, Italy and Spain.[57] Moreover, some countries earmark part of the tax revenue of certain products, such as cigarettes and alcoholic drinks, in order to finance their health system.[58] However, income

55 BALDWIN, P. 1990. *Op. cit.* P. 112.
56 SAVEDOFF, W. 2004. Tax-based financing for health systems: options and experiences. Geneva: World Health Organization, p. 4. Available at www.who.int/health_financing/taxed_based_financing_dp_04_4.pdf [Accessed 14 December 2015].
57 THOMSON, S., FOUBISTER, T. & MOSSIALOS, E. 2009. *Financing health care in the European Union: challenges and policy responses.* Denmark: World Health Organization on behalf of the European Observatory on Health Systems and Policies, pp. 33–4.
58 MOSSIALOS, E. & DIXON, A. 2002. *Op. cit.*

taxes are considered to be more progressive than consumption taxes, 'because the former can be structured to capture progressively larger shares of incomes, while the latter tend to capture similar shares of household income'.[59]

In relation to the organisation of the system, the rule is the centralisation of the provision of health services. This is, in fact, another important difference between tax-based systems and social insurance systems. As discussed above, in social insurance systems the sickness funds are institutions independent from the state that contract with public or private providers for the provision of health services for their members. Conversely, in tax-based systems there is no independent structure contracting with providers and very often the state operates its own health facilities directly. The state itself purchases or contracts health services through its health authorities or its department of health. Therefore, in terms of organisation and structure these systems can be said to be more centralised than social insurance systems.

In relation to providers, although primary and secondary care are normally provided at public facilities, some countries have introduced reforms, aiming at expanding patient choice, which allow health authorities to contract doctors from the private sector. For example, in Sweden, patients have the freedom to choose between first-contact care providers, which include primary care centres, hospital outpatient departments, private physicians or clinics.

In relation to the benefits package, tax-based systems, such as social insurance ones, offer a broad list of benefits comprising all levels of care (primary, secondary and tertiary), as well as long-term and specialist care, such as rehabilitation, dental care and mental health. The system coverage is also very broad. As distinct from social insurance systems, according to which affiliation to the scheme is the key to guarantee coverage, in tax-based systems usually all residents living lawfully in the country are entitled to benefits.

With regard to the provision of services, tax-based systems operate according to a benefits-in-kind mechanism and thus patients do not have to pay for medical visits and treatment in general. However, for some specific situations co-payments are required from users.[60] This is the case, for example, with pharmaceutical provision, some specialist care (such as dental care) and visits to private providers of some types of services – when there is this choice – since in this case visits are only partially subsidised by the public sector. Moreover, in contrast to social insurance systems,[61] in tax-based systems patients are subject to an initial visit to a general practitioner, who is considered as the point of entry into the health system.

Having described the evolution of the two models of systems for the provision of health services existing in the EU and established their main features, this book

59 SAVEDOFF, W. 2004. *Op. cit.*, p. 4.
60 In Italy, for example, there has been a steady increase in co-payments in the last decade, and it is now among the highest in the European Union (~30%). CALLAHAN, D. & WASUNNA, A.A. 2006. *Op. cit.*, p. 98.
61 The Netherlands constitutes an exception, where the GP visit is also obligatory.

turns now to the analysis of the common principles which guide these two different models.

Principles and values governing the provision of health care services in the EU

Following the analysis of the development of welfare services in the field of health in Europe, and the comparison between the two main models of health systems currently existing within the EU, this chapter moves now to the analysis of common principles and values shared by EU health systems. The point of departure for this analysis is the document from the Council of the European Union, 'Council Conclusions on Common values and principles in European Union Health Systems',[62] in which universality, access to good-quality care, equity and solidarity are stated as common values accepted by EU institutions and shared across Europe. The document also states common operational principles shared by EU health systems. These are: quality, safety, care that is based on evidence and ethics, patient involvement, redress, and privacy and confidentiality. Also explained in the document is the fact that these principles are shared across Europe, meaning that 'EU citizens would expect to find them, and structures to support them in a health system anywhere in the EU'.[63]

The Council document is important for this work because it recognises and states what can be considered as common guiding values and principles in all EU health systems. Even though it is possible to argue that principles vary from one society to another because they are systematically related to the moral concerns that have been built by each society and reflect the ideology which generated these concerns, it is possible to say that there is a common ideology followed by EU health systems that is reflected by those values and principles. This is the assumption made in this book.

Before entering the analysis itself, it is important to clarify three points. First, that this work will concentrate its analysis on the common values stated by the Council document, that is, universality, access to good-quality care, equity and solidarity. Moreover, the analysis will not follow exactly the order according to which the principles are stated in the document. The third point regards the terminology used in the document. Although I agree that universality, access to good-quality care, equity and solidarity can be viewed as values, since these reflect the features that EU Member States attribute and use to guide their health systems,[64] I am also of the opinion that these values can be regarded as principles

---

62 COUNCIL OF THE EUROPEAN UNION 2006. Council Conclusions on Common values and principles in European Union Health Systems. 2006/C 146/01.

63 *Ibid.*, p. 2.

64 According to the *Oxford Dictionary of Philosophy*, 'To acknowledge some feature of things as a value is to take it into account in decision making, or in other words to be inclined to advance it as a consideration in influencing choice and guiding oneself and others'. BLACKBURN, S. 2008. *The Oxford Dictionary of Philosophy. Oxford reference online.*

because they are used alike to shape health policies.[65] Therefore, universality, access to good-quality care, equity and solidarity are much more than just values. In the health services area, these attributes work not only as guidance to the development of health policy, but also as the ends or aims of this policy.[66] Furthermore, the Council, in a recent document on equity, entitled 'Council conclusions on Equity and Health in All Policies: Solidarity in Health', refers to equity as a principle, recalling that this 'is one of the key principles for EU health systems'.[67] In the same way, solidarity is often referred to as a principle.[68] For this reason, in this book I will refer to universality, access to good-quality care, equity and solidarity interchangeably as values or principles. These principles will be analysed in the following sections, but following a different order. I will start with solidarity because in my opinion it can be considered as a corollary of the other principles. As demonstrated in Chapter 2, solidarity is not only used in the field of health, but in all areas of social policy at the national level. In the same way, it is also very important at the EU level for different policy fields. Then I will look at equity, universality and, finally, at access to good-quality care.

Furthermore, it must be highlighted that the principle of access to good-quality care will be analysed in two parts. First, I will look at access as part of the principle of equity because, as will be shown, the definition of equity adopted in this book is that based on equal access to care. Then, I will analyse quality as a principle itself.

Finally, it is important to say that although the principles of equity, universality and access to good-quality care are analysed separately, they are indeed very much inter-related. This inter-relation will be pointed out in the analysis of each principle.

Solidarity

Even though the solidarity principle has already been analysed in Chapter 2, in this section this principle will be discussed from its operational side, that is, its meaning from a practical point of view and specifically related to health services.

---

65 A principle can be defined as a basic rule, law or doctrine that shapes judgments. Cf. BLACK, H.C. & GARNER, B.A. 2009. *Op. cit.*, p. 1.313.

66 LE GRAND, J. 2007. *Op. cit.*, p. 2.

67 COUNCIL OF THE EUROPEAN UNION 2010. Council conclusions on Equity and Health in All Policies: Solidarity in Health. Adopted by the Council of the European Union on 8 June 2010 at the *3019th Employment, Social Policy, Health and Consumer Affairs Council meeting*. Available at www.consilium.europa.eu/uedocs/cms_data/docs/pressdata/en/lsa/114994.pdf [Accessed 7 January 2016].

68 See, for example, RYLAND, D. 2007. Freedom, Solidarity and Health Care in the European Union. Paper submitted to the Conference 'The European Constitution and National Constitutions', held at Andrzej Frycz Modrzewski Kraków University, Krakow, Poland (21–24 October 2007). Available at http://eprints.lincoln.ac.uk/3051/1/Freedom_Solidarity_and_ Health_Care_in_the_European_Union_Krakow_October_2007.pdf [Accessed 14 December 2015].

Solidarity is a principle that is present in all areas of social services and policies. As Advocate General Fennelly synthesised in *Sodemare*[69], in general terms, solidarity operates as a form of cross-subsidisation of one social group by another. In the health field this can happen in different ways. In social insurance systems, for example, solidarity is present in the way that contributions are levied. The fact that contributions and premiums are based on salary and not on risk represents a mechanism of cross-subsidy between rich and poor members of the system. Moreover, it is also a form of distribution of health risks, since those individuals in a worse health condition do not pay a higher contribution, i.e. each individual contributes according to their ability (salary) but receives treatment according to need.[70] Another form of solidarity found in these systems is the inclusion of members' dependents in the system without additional costs. In this case the cross-subsidisation or redistribution is between single individuals and families. Similarly, in tax-based systems, solidarity mechanisms are also present. In the financing of the system, solidarity is found insofar as richer individuals pay higher taxes than those less well-off, but both groups receive treatment according to need.

These solidarity mechanisms become even clearer if we compare social insurance to private insurance. In the latter case no solidarity mechanisms are present. Therefore, not only are premiums based on risk, meaning that those individuals with a worse health status pay a higher premium, but also family dependents of the policy holder will pay additional premiums in order to become part of the scheme. In fact, the document 'Council Conclusions on Common values and principles in European Union Health Systems' mentions that 'solidarity is closely linked to the financial arrangement of our national health systems and the need to ensure accessibility to all [. . .]'.[71]

Therefore, it is possible to observe that solidarity plays an important role as an operational principle in publicly funded health systems. It not only works as a redistributive mechanism in terms of wealth, but it also promotes the sharing of health risks between young and old individuals as well as between those of varying health status. In fact, due to its crucial role in the health services field, the solidarity principle can be considered as a corollary of other principles applicable to the health services area, since its redistributive mechanisms are fundamental for the effective implementation of the principles of universality, equity and accessibility.

Equity

Defining the type of equity

Equity is an important principle in the context of health policies. Concerns about equity in health are present in almost all countries, since health inequalities are

---

69 Case C-70/95, *Sodemare* [1997] ECR I-3395.
70 CHERNICHOVSKY, D. 1995. Health System Reforms in Industrialized Democracies: An Emerging Paradigm. *The Milbank Quarterly*, 73: 339–72.
71 COUNCIL OF THE EUROPEAN UNION 2006. Council Conclusions on Common values and principles in European Union Health Systems. 2006/C 146/01.

directly related to economic development. For this reason, it is the subject of many world summits on health and many regional and international documents.[72] In Europe, for example, equity has become the object of a charter entitled the 'European Charter on Health Equity'.[73] However, as discussed in the first chapter, equity can be defined in a variety of ways. In the health care context, equity can also have different meanings. For example, it can be interpreted as equality of access to health care for those in equal need, equality of utilisation of health care for those in equal need, or equitable health outcomes.[74] In this book, equity will be regarded as equal access to health care for those in equal need. This choice is justified for two reasons. First, because most definitions of equity are 'concerned with the relationship between health care needs and access to health care for different groups in the population';[75] and second, because this is the type of equity that was agreed by international health authorities in two important international health summits as that which should be pursued by health systems around the world. The first summit was the International Forum on Common Access to Health Care Services,[76] held in Sweden in 2003, from which an evidence-sharing network was created to promote equitable health care access in all countries. The second was the 2005 Annual Conference of the Global Health Council[77], where health was discussed from a system's perspective, in which it was established that equal health care access is one of the most important issues in health policy in all societies today.[78] Therefore, the principle of access to health care for those in equal need is the most appropriate equity principle to be pursued by health policy makers, because it is specific to health care and it does not require discrimination between those who are already ill purely on the basis of factors that are exogenous to their

72　See, for example, PUBLIC HEALTH AGENCY OF CANADA AND WORLD HEALTH ORGANIZATION 2008. Health equity through intersectoral action: An analysis of 18 country case studies. World Health Organization (WHO) and Minister of Health (Canada). Available at www.who.int/social_determinants/resources/health_equity_isa_2008_en.pdf [Accessed 26 November 2015].

73　After being officially launched on 9 December 2010 by a number of stakeholders gathered in the European Parliament, the European Charter for Health Equity was open for signatures until the end of March 2011. Available at www.epha.org/IMG/pdf/European_Charter_Health_Equity_July_v.pdf [Accessed 26 November 2015].

74　OLIVER, A. & MOSSIALOS, E. 2004. *Op. cit.*

75　GULLIFORD, M. 2003. Equity and access to health care. *In:* GULLIFORD, M. & MORGAN, M. (eds) *Access to health care.* New York: Routledge, p. 36.

76　OLIVER, A. & MOSSIALOS, E. 2004. *Op. cit.*

77　'The Global Health Council, formerly the National Council of International Health, is a U.S.-based, nonprofit membership organization that was created in 1972 to identify priority world health problems and to report on them to the U.S. public, legislators, international and domestic government agencies, academic institutions and the global health community. In 1998, the organization changed its name to the Global Health Council and became a dynamic organization that puts global health squarely where it belongs – a priority for everyone, rich and poor alike. Jeffrey L. Sturchio has led the Council as its president and CEO since August 2009'. Available at www.globalmedicalresearch.org/index.php?option=com_content&view=article&id=246&Itemid=209 [Accessed 5 January 2016].

78　RUGER, J.P. 2010. *Health and social justice.* Oxford; New York: Oxford University Press, p. 133.

health, besides respecting acceptable reasons for differentials in health care utilisation by those in equal need.[79]

Having defined the type of equity with which this book is concerned, the analysis moves now to the discussion of the main aspects of equity in the access to health care for those in equal need. This includes the distinction between horizontal and vertical access, the meaning of access and barriers to it, and the concept of need.

Horizontal v. vertical equity

Although it has already been defined that the type of equity with which this book is concerned is equity of access to health care for those in equal need, it should be pointed out that equity of access comprises two dimensions: horizontal and vertical equity. Horizontal equity refers exactly to the type of equity defined above; vertical equity, however, requires that 'groups with unequal needs are treated in proportion to their inequality'.[80] This dimension is indeed the reverse side of horizontal equity and is particularly relevant when dealing with the needs of different socio-economic groups or those groups which need special attention, such as older people, people with mental health problems and disabled people. These groups require particular attention because, generally, there are fewer services and resources available for them.

Policies to address these special groups, and to achieve vertical equity, may include the idea of enhancing or restricting access to services to groups with different needs (priority setting and rationing) as well as removing barriers to access for those groups, as will be shown in the following sections.[81]

Therefore, even though this book is concerned with the idea of horizontal equity, it is important to acknowledge the importance that vertical equity plays when dealing with access to health care. In fact, even if the main objective of a health system is the achievement of horizontal equity, vertical equity will necessarily be part of the health policies developed by a certain health system.

The meaning of access: potential v. actual entry into the system

Even though access to health care services is a topic constantly discussed in the literature and by policy makers, there are no generally accepted definitions.[82] As Goddard and Smith argue:

> The precise formulation of the notion of 'access' is highly contingent on the context within which the analysis is taking place. Thus, in the US, access is

---

79 OLIVER, A. & MOSSIALOS, E. 2004. *Op. cit.*, p. 656.
80 GULLIFORD, M. 2003. *Op. cit*, p. 53.
81 *Ibid.*
82 OLIVER, A. & MOSSIALOS, E. 2004. *Op. cit.*, p. 656.

often considered to refer merely to whether or not the individual is insured, and nuances such as the level of insurance or the magnitude of copayments are secondary. In Europe, however, where almost all citizens are in principle insured, access can be quite a subtle concept. It might, at its most general level, refer to the ability to secure a specified range of services, at a specified level of quality, subject to a specified maximum level of personal inconvenience and cost, whilst in possession of a specified level of information.[83]

Other authors have recently proposed an analysis of access based on 'seven steps': population coverage, content of the benefits basket, cost-sharing arrangements, geographical factors, choice among available providers, organisational barriers and preferences.[84] Considering, however, that the intention of this work is not to define a concept of access, nor to develop an analysis of access focused on a specific health system, the understanding of basic aspects of access is sufficient for the purpose of this book. Therefore, only some aspects of access will be analysed here; they are those that are directly linked to the idea of equity of access within the EU context.

According to an earlier discussion on access proposed by Aday and Andersen in 1975,[85]access to the health system can be described either as the potential entry of the individual into the health system or as the actual process of utilising the services offered by the system. Therefore, the first dimension of access is concerned with the opportunity of obtaining services when it is needed, i.e. the availability of the services, while the second concerns the proof of the use of the service.

Although a number of authors on this topic use utilisation as a description of access,[86] considering that the mere availability of services does not mean that access will be realised,[87] other academic works have emphasised that utilisation may also be constrained by some 'barriers' to access, such as financial, geographical and personal factors that may influence the actual use of services.[88] Therefore, these barriers should also be taken into account when analysing access to health care.

83 GODDARD, M. & SMITH, P. 2001. Equity of access to health care services: Theory and evidence from the UK. *Social Science & Medicine*, 53: 1149–62.

84 BUSSE, R., GINNEKEN, E.V. & WO_RZ, M. 2011. Access to health care services within and between countries. *In:* WISMAR, M., PALM, W., FIGUERAS, J., ERNST, K. & GINNEKEN, E.V. (eds) *Cross-border health care in the European Union.* Copenhagen: World Health Organization, on Behalf of the European Observatory on Health Systems and Policies, p. 49.

85 ADAY, L.A. & ANDERSEN, R. 1975. *Development of indices of access to medical care.* Ann Arbor, MI: Health Administration Press. *Apud* GULLIFORD, M., FIGUEROA-MUÑOZ, J. & MORGAN, M. 2003. Introduction: meaning of 'access' in health care. *In:* GULLIFORD, M. & MORGAN, M. (eds) *Access to health care.* New York: Routledge.

86 Cf. OLIVER, A. & MOSSIALOS, E. 2004. *Op. cit.*, p. 656.

87 DONABEDIAN, A. 1972. Models for Organizing the Delivery of Personal Health Services and Criteria for Evaluating Them. *The Milbank Memorial Fund Quarterly*, 50(40): 103–54. *Apud* GULLIFORD, M., FIGUEROA-MUÑOZ, J. & MORGAN, M. 2003.*Op. cit.*

88 See, for instance, GODDARD, M. & SMITH, P. 2001. *Op. cit.*; OLIVER, A. & MOSSIALOS, E. 2004. *Op. cit.*; GULLIFORD, M., FIGUEROA-MUÑOZ, J. & MORGAN, M. 2003. *Op. cit.*

Barriers to access to health care

GEOGRAPHICAL BARRIERS

The achievement of a geographically uniform provision of health care, although desirable, is a difficult policy goal to meet. Location of health services and individual mobility are two factors that influence access not only in low-income countries but also in economically developed parts of the Western world.[89] As Haynes contends, '[s]ervices are more accessible to people who have cars than to people who do not, and where they can be reached by public transport compared to where they cannot'.[90] Therefore, people who have easy access to health services will tend to use services more than those who do not, and this can have an impact on equity. In fact, there is evidence that some health outcomes are worse where the location of health services or individual mobility is poor.[91]

So, how to overcome geography/geographical barriers and the mobility of individuals in order to facilitate and promote equal access to health services? Of course each country needs to evaluate its own problems regarding geographical barriers in order to face them and propose adequate policy measures. For example, countries which have more people living in rural areas will probably face more problems than those in which the majority of the population lives in urban areas. However, some general issues are involved in the development of policies for this specific area.

Policies to improve geographical access might focus, for example, on bringing people to services or on supplying services in areas where there is a lack of services. The first type of policies include measures such as the improvement of public transport between the areas where target groups live and the location of health facilities. It may also include financial aid in order to help individuals bear travel costs to the health facility and other costs involved in one's daily journey, such as unpaid work and childcare. This type of financial aid is especially important for low-income groups, since the costs involved to access services have a disproportionate effect on the poor.[92] On the other hand, policies to supply facilities in remote or poor areas will focus on the allocation of resources to specific regions or areas according to criteria defined by policy makers. Accordingly, first, health care resources must be distributed to regions according to population size, local GDP and per capita income, health care needs, etc., rather than any historical pattern of distribution towards relatively wealthy regions. Second, efforts should be made

89   HAYNES, R. 2003. Geographical access to health care. *In:* GULLIFORD, M. & MORGAN, M. (eds) *Access to health care.* New York: Routledge.

90   *Ibid.*, p. 13.

91   *Ibid.*, p. 15.

92   GIBSON, D.M., GOODIN, R.E. & GRAND, J.L. 1985. Come and get it: distributional biases in social service delivery systems. *Policy and Politics*, 13(2): 109–26; *Apud* HAYNES, R. 2003. Geographical access to health care. *In:* GULLIFORD, M. & MORGAN, M. (eds) *Access to health care.* New York: Routledge, p. 22.

to overcome any inequitable capacity constraints of poorer areas, to ensure that there are incentives for sufficient facilities and staff to locate and remain within these areas.[93]

FINANCIAL BARRIERS

Financial barriers refer to any financial difficulty that individuals may face when accessing health care. Survey data suggest that financial barriers to access are the largest single driver of unmet need in the EU.[94] The most common financial barrier found in EU health systems is co-payments for services or charges, but any other financial burden faced by patients when accessing health services can be regarded as a financial barrier. In the case of cross-border health care, for example, the burden of proving the type of care provided abroad, including the costs involved in the translation of health services' invoices from another Member State, are considered a type of financial barrier.[95] I will come back to this point later in this book.

In the EU, although health services are usually publicly provided and ability to pay is not a requirement for obtaining services, user chargers or co-payments have been increasingly imposed in many EU health systems in order to control the demand for services. As was shown in the first part of this chapter, this type of charge has been used equally in both tax-based and social insurance systems.

The problem is that charging for services, even when in the form of small contributions, may have a greater impact on low-income groups and consequently affect the use of health services by these groups. As Mossialos and Thomson maintain, although there is limited evidence of the impact of user charges on the utilisation of health care, they 'appear to have a higher impact on people in lower socio-economic groups and may affect the health of poorer people'.[96] Therefore, as discussed above in relation to the impact of travel expenses on access to services – which, in effect, can be also considered an indirect financial barrier – user charges also need some counterbalancing measures in order to be compatible with equity of access. Accordingly, some countries, for example, use means testing to waive the payments of these charges for certain individuals.[97]

---

93 OLIVER, A. & MOSSIALOS, E. 2004. *Op. cit.*, p. 657.

94 EXPERT PANEL ON EFFECTIVE WAYS OF INVESTING IN HEALTH 175 (EXPH) 2015. Preliminary Report on Access to Health Services in the European Union. Available at http://ec.europa.eu/health/expert_panel/opinions/docs/010_access_healthcare_en.pdf [Accessed 14 December 2015].

95 JELFS, E. & BAETEN, R. 2012. *Simulation on the EU Cross-Border Care Directive (Final Report)*. Brussels: European Social Observatory (Ose), European Health Management Association (EHMA), Association Internationale de la Mutualité (AIM), p. 18.

96 MOSSIALOS, E. & THOMSON, S. 2003. Access to health care in the European Union: the impact of user charges and voluntary health insurance. *In:* GULLIFORD, M. & MORGAN, M. (eds) *Access to health care*. New York: Routledge.

97 OLIVER, A. & MOSSIALOS, E. 2004. *Op. cit.*

PERSONAL BARRIERS

The utilisation of health services is also influenced, for example, by cultural beliefs, information knowledge and previous experiences. Individuals may not use services if they do not identify a need or are not willing to become service users. For example, individuals from certain ethnical groups may not make use of preventive health services because they do not believe that they are necessary. Similarly, people with lower educational levels may not use services as often as those with higher educational levels. In addition, those who have had previous bad experiences with the use of services may decide not to use them again.

In the case of cross-border health care, difficulties in finding information about health care provision in other Member States, or the mere fact of not speaking another language, can be regarded as a personal barrier in accessing health services.[98] I will come back to this point later in this book.

Therefore, considering that these barriers have an impact on equity of access, health systems need to develop policies in order to address them. Policies in this area can focus on the attempt to change patients' behaviour, but more recently the tendency has been to acknowledge patients' perceptions of their needs and manage their demands 'by developing a graduated service to reduce demands on general practitioners and on hospital staff in accident or emergency departments'.[99]

Need

Another concept that plays an important role in the comprehension of the principle of equity is need. Nevertheless, as stated in Chapter 1, it is not easy to define need. For example, clinicians and health economists usually use different definitions for need. While the former sustain that what counts as need is the pre-treatment state of the individual's health, with greater ill health equating to greater need, the latter hold that the individual's capacity to benefit from health care determines the size of their need.[100] According to Gulliford, this second definition is widely accepted because it 'encompasses not just the existence of a health problem but the possibility of intervening so as to improve health'.[101] The same author argues, however, that in practical terms, 'needs are more often measured in terms of health status'.[102]

Considering the difficulties in defining need, what is important to acknowledge for the purposes of this book is that need must be considered objectively because subjective evaluations of need may lead to confusion with people's wants, rather than needs. Secondly, for the purpose of establishing the relationship between need

98 BAETEN, R. 2012. *Europeanization of national health systems: national impact and EU codification of the patient mobility case law*. Report in the context of the EPSU Project. Belgium: European Social Observatory (OSE), p. 27.

99 GULLIFORD, M., FIGUEROA-MUÑOZ, J. & MORGAN, M. 2003. *Op. cit.*, p. 6.

100 OLIVER, A. & MOSSIALOS, E. 2004. *Op. cit.*

101 GULLIFORD, M. 2003. *Op. cit.*, p. 38.

102 *Ibid.*

and the utilisation of services, the idea is that utilisation of services should reflect actual needs for care.[103]

In terms of health policies, the assessment of need is important to identify the health issues facing a certain group or population. The identification of health needs permits the setting of priorities and resource allocation. In the UK, for example, the National Institute for Health and Clinical Excellence (NICE) developed a practical guide for health needs assessment. This guide works as a systematic method for reviewing the health issues facing a population, leading to agreed priorities and resource allocation that will improve health and reduce inequalities.[104]

From the elements presented in this section regarding the principle of equity, it is possible to conclude that equity and access are intrinsically related. Equity can be said to be not just a principle, but an objective of all EU health systems. It contributes to social cohesion and is a corollary of the principle of solidarity, insofar it aims at diminishing the differences in access to health services between the richer and the poorer.

Quality

Quality in health care can be defined in several ways. This is due to historical reasons related to the medical profession, such as whether doctors are state employees or view themselves as liberal professionals,[105]and is also due to the different meanings and approaches taken in the literature in relation to quality.[106] Harteloh suggests, for example, that when defining quality it is possible to focus on different aspects, such as the degree to which expectations are met; the structure, process and outcomes of medical interventions; the competence of doctors and efficacy of medical interventions; the attitude of health care personnel; the conformity to requirements, guidelines or law; and the ratio of 'possibilities realised' (which can refer to actual medical care, health, disabilities, handicaps, mortality or patients' experiences) and a 'framework of norms and values' (which contains implicit or explicit medical criteria, scientific knowledge, individual expectations

---

103 GULLIFORD, M., FIGUEROA-MUÑOZ, J., MORGAN, M., HUGHES, D., GIBSON, B., BEECH, R. & HUDSON, M. 2002. *Op. cit.*

104 CAVANAGH, S. & CHADWICK, K. 2005. Health needs assessment: A practical guide. Cambridge: National Institute for Health and Clinical Excellence (NICE). Available at www.nice. org.uk/proxy/?sourceUrl=http%3A%2F%2Fwww.nice.org.uk%2Fnicemedia%2Fdocuments% 2FHealth_Needs_Assessment_A_Practical_Guide.pdf [Accessed 29 November 2015].

105 LEGIDO-QUIGLEY, H., MCKEE, M., WALSHE, K., SUÑOL, R., NOLTE, E. & KLAZINGA, N. 2008. How can quality of health care be safeguarded across the European Union? *British Medical Journal*, 336: 920.

106 For an overview of the most important definitions of quality of care in the literature, see LEGIDO-QUIGLEY, H., MCKEE, M., NOLTE, E. & GLINOS, I.A. 2008. *Assuring the quality of healthcare in the European Union: A case for action*, Copenhagen: World Health Organization, on behalf of the European Observatory on Health Systems and Policies.

or desires, social utility or values).[107] Moreover, initiatives on the quality of health care can be top down, consisting of legislation or regulations from governments and official bodies, or bottom up, which are usually initiated by health professionals and other providers.[108]

At the EU level, quality in health care includes, for example: (1) the obligation of continuous training of health care staff based on national standards; (2) the use of best practices in quality; (3) stimulation of innovation and good practice; (4) development of systems to ensure good clinical governance; and (5) monitoring quality in the health system.[109]

Moreover, great attention is also devoted to safety, which is considered to be part of the agenda on quality in health care and refers to the 'monitoring of risk factors and adequate training for health professionals, and protection against misleading advertising of health products and treatments'.[110]

There is, in fact, an assumption that national health services in any EU Member State will be of quality, in the sense that EU citizens would expect to find medical services and goods of quality anywhere in the EU. This is not only stated in EU documents, such as in the 'Council Conclusions on Common values and principles in European Union Health Systems', but also confirmed by some ECJ rulings. In *Kohll*,[111] for example, the Court took the view that the quality of medical services could not be used as a public health reason to create an obstacle to the freedom to receive services in another Member State, because 'doctors and dentists established in other Member States must be afforded all guarantees equivalent to those accorded to doctors and dentists established on national territory, for the purposes of freedom to provide services'.[112] In *Decker*, the Court arrived at the same conclusion in relation to the purchase of a medicinal product (pair of spectacles) in another Member State.[113]

Indeed, the guarantee of good-quality services and goods is part of EU policy on the functioning of the Internal Market. Therefore, apart from documents and rulings related to health services, there are also pieces of EU law on this topic. The Directive on the recognition of professional qualifications[114] is an example of this.

107 HARTELOH, P.P.M. 2003. The Meaning of Quality in Health Care: A Conceptual Analysis. *Health Care Analysis*, 11, 259–67, p. 262.
108 LEGIDO-QUIGLEY, H., MCKEE, M., NOLTE, E. & GLINOS, I.A. 2008. *Op. cit.*
109 COUNCIL OF THE EUROPEAN UNION 2006. Council Conclusions on Common values and principles in European Union Health Systems. 2006/C 146/01.
110 *Ibid.*
111 *Kohll*, Case C-158/96 [1998] ECR I-1931.
112 *Ibid.*, para. 48. See also paras 43 and 49.
113 *Decker*, Case C-120/95 [1998] ECR I-1831, paras 41, 43 and 45. In relation to the purchase of medicinal products, the Court also cites Case 215/87, *Schumacher v Hauptzollamt Frankfurt am Main-Ost* [1989] ECR 617, para. 20, and Case C-62/90 *Commission v Germany* [1992] ECR I-2575, para. 18.
114 EUROPEAN PARLIAMENT AND THE COUNCIL OF THE EUROPEAN UNION 2005. Directive 2005/36/EC on the recognition of professional qualifications.

In relation to health professionals, the Directive provides for an entire section dedicated to the recognition of doctors (Section 2).

Despite the assumption that quality in health care will be the same in all EU Member States, the approach to quality still varies considerably within the EU. Legido-Quigley and colleagues,[115] for example, identified seven broad categories of initiatives in the area of quality in health care: (1) approval of drugs and medical devices; (2) training of health professionals; (3) registration, licensing and accreditation of health facilities; (4) patient safety; (5) clinical guidelines; (6) peer review; and (7) quality indicators. Of these seven initiatives only two – approval of drugs and medical devices, and training of health professionals – are common approaches to quality in the EU. Furthermore, this is due to the fact that in these areas there is either the harmonisation of laws,[116] as in the case of the former, or there is mutual recognition, as in the case of health professionals.

Different approaches to quality can become a problem for issues regarding cross-border health care, because patients who go abroad to receive medical care expect to find at least the same quality levels that are offered by their health system of affiliation. Problems regarding the quality of providers of health services can lead to the question of liability. In Chapter 6 I will come back to this issue. It suffices to say here that the question of liability becomes even worse when treatments undergone abroad are done at the expense of the patient's Member State of affiliation, insofar as in this case there will be doubts regarding who is liable: the provider that performed the treatment or the health system/Member State that paid for the service.

Universality

Universality in terms of health care can be defined as access of all residents to affordable health coverage for a defined set of benefits.[117] This is a reality in almost all EU health systems, irrespectively of the way in which services are organised. In national health systems, this is clear insofar as all residents lawfully living in the country have access to the benefits package. In social insurance systems, although contributions are based on salary and, thus, affiliation to the scheme is the key to guaranteeing coverage, there are mechanisms to guarantee affiliation for those earning below a certain threshold or without a formal job. Germany, for example, managed to integrate into the statutory scheme certain social groups that are covered by public agencies in some other EU countries, such as

115 LEGIDO-QUIGLEY, H., MCKEE, M., NOLTE, E. & GLINOS, I.A. 2008. *Op. cit.*

116 PERMANAND, G., MOSSIALOS, E. & MCKEE, M. 2006. Regulating medicines in Europe: the European Medicines Agency, marketing authorisation, transparency and pharmaco vigilance. *Clinical Medicine*, 6(1): 87–90.

117 AMERICAN COLLEGE OF PHYSICIANS 2008. Achieving a High-Performance Health Care System with Universal Access: What the United States Can Learn from Other Countries. *Annals of Internal Medicine*, 148(1).

the unemployed, non-working dependants, people incapable of gainful employment, pensioners, students and the disabled.[118]

Therefore, universality in health care also means that access is not based on the ability to pay. In fact, according to the Council of the EU, '[u]niversality means that no-one is barred access to health care'.[119] Therefore, it can be said that universality is directly related to the principles of equity and accessibility; a universal health system not only facilitates access, but also promotes a more equitable health system insofar as access does not rely on ability to pay and, thus, the better-off and the worse-off have the same potential access to the system. Moreover, universality is a corollary of the principle of solidarity since promoting a universal health system also works as a redistributive mechanism.

Conclusion

The aim of this chapter was to develop the elements that explain the evolution of welfare services in the field of health care at the national level. The description of the historical evolution of national health systems was intended to aid the comprehension of the present features of the different models of EU health systems. The organisational and financial characteristics of these different models explain, *inter alia*, the relation established between patients and the health systems and thus the health benefits available to patients. The second part of the chapter then showed that although there are considerable differences in the organisation and financing of EU health systems, they all share common principles and values that are used to shape health policies. At least three of these principles – solidarity, equity and universality – are concerned with the achievement of social justice and social cohesion, as already stated by the Council of the EU in the document 'Council Conclusions on Common values and principles in European Union Health Systems'. This concern about social values can be said to reflect the egalitarian ideology with regards to health care. In spite of the fact that EU health systems have introduced market mechanisms in recent decades, the commitment to solidarity, equity and universality is still a reality in the EU. Evidence of this is the fact that the participation of the private sector in EU health systems is still minimal. In terms of health expenditure, the participation of private health insurance in the total health expenditure in EU countries ranges between zero and 15.2%. Likewise, the percentage of the population covered by private health insurance is low.[120] Even in countries where there is a higher number of people covered by private health insurance, as in the Netherlands, the role of this form

118 BUSSE, R., & BLÜMEL, M. 2014. *Op. cit.*
119 COUNCIL OF THE EUROPEAN UNION 2006. Council Conclusions on Common values and principles in European Union Health Systems. 2006/C 146/01.
120 ORGANISATION FOR ECONOMIC CO-OPERATION AND DEVELOPMENT (OECD) 2004. The OECD Health Project. *Private Health Insurance in OECD Countries*. Available at www.keepeek.com/Digital-Asset-Management/oecd/social-issues-migration-health/private-health-insurance-in-oecd-countries_9789264007451-en#page2 [Accessed 27 November 2015].

of insurance is usually in supplementing or complementing the statutory social insurance.[121] Comparing these figures to those from countries that follow a more libertarian ideology, such as the United States, shows a considerable higher participation of the private sector in total health expenditure: in the US, the participation of private health insurance in total health expenditure is around 35.1%, and approximately 72% of the population has some form of private health insurance that works mainly as the primary source of health coverage.

Therefore, the topics developed in this chapter will aid the discussion in Chapter 6 about how the EU approach to health care may affect the common principles shared by EU health systems. However, before starting this discussion, it is important to explain what this book means by 'the EU approach to health care'. Thereby, the following chapter is devoted to the explanation of the framework of health service provision at the EU level.

121 As the OECD Policy Brief explains, 'Private health insurance is used at different levels, and for different reasons, in individual OECD countries. In some countries it is the primary source of health coverage for at least part of the populations; in others it duplicates the public system, offering a private alternative; and finally it acts as a complement or supplement to public programmes'. *Ibid.*

4 The framework of health services provision at the EU level

This chapter analyses primary and secondary EU legislation regarding health care relating specifically to cross-border provision of services. In relation to primary legislation, this analysis includes Treaty provisions regarding public health as well as those on competition law and services of general interest. In relation to secondary legislation, it includes former regulation 1408/71 (now 883/2004) and Directive 2011/24. The chapter also looks at the jurisprudence of the ECJ, describing the most important cases concerning patient mobility and then compares the approach of the Court in these cases to the one it took in cases concerning competition law in the field of health care.

Applicable legislation

The Treaty rules: the provision on Public Health

There are many ways in which the health field intersects with EU law. Article 168 of TFEU provides that '[a] high level of human protection shall be ensured in the definition and implementation of all Union policies and activities'. Therefore, it is possible to argue that different EU policies and actions affect the health field and vice versa. Thinking in terms of competences, the EU has powers to complement Member States' action on health and, according to the European Commission, this consists mainly of three objectives: protecting people from health threats, promoting healthy lifestyles and helping national authorities in the EU cooperate on health issues. These three main objectives entail different types of action which are presented in the Health Strategy[1] and implemented through the Health Programme.[2] In order to reach these objectives the EU develops specific policies. Some of these are directly related to health objectives. This is the case,

---

1 COMMISSION OF THE EUROPEAN COMMUNITIES 2007. White Paper – Together for Health: A Strategic Approach for the EU 2008–2013. COM(2007) 630 final.
2 Regulation (EU) 282/2014 of the European Parliament and of the Council of 11 March 2014 on the establishment of a third Programme for the Union's action in the field of health (2014–2020) and repealing Decision No 1350/2007/EC (Text with EEA relevance).

for example, with the tobacco and pharmaceuticals policies. Nevertheless, there are other policies not directly related to health objectives but that still affect the field of health, such as environmental policies, the mobility of health professionals and the coordination of social security schemes. In effect, some authors argue that these policies are in reality a shadow of the Internal Market.[3]

Although there is a vast dimension of issues related to health in the context of EU law and policies, this work concentrates on the provision of health services, analysing specifically the case of cross-border health care in terms of patient mobility, which is considered the '[s]ignature issue of EU health-care services law'.[4] It is, therefore, this specific issue of EU law and policy that is used as an example to demonstrate how EU health systems can be affected by EU law and libertarian ideas.

Originally, the health field was not perceived as a policy area in which EU competence could develop. The Treaty of Rome did not provide for health as a separate issue; health was addressed as a policy area related to the more general field of health and safety in the workplace, referred to in its Articles 36, 48 (3) and 56 (1) EEC. Moreover, 'references to public health issues were found as derogations for the Member States in relation to the free movement principle in the old Article 36 and Article 46 EC'.[5] The first European legal powers in the field of health were introduced by the Treaty of Maastricht, which dedicated its Title X to Public Health and, under Article 129 EC, empowered the Community to take action in the field of health. This Treaty provision established 'a high level of health protection' as an objective of the Community, and explicitly recognised that 'Health protection requirements shall form a constituent part of the Community's other policies'. The means provided for in the Article to achieve this objective were actions 'encouraging co-operation between the Member States, and if necessary, lending support to their action'.

In spite of the creation of a specific legal basis for Community competence in the field of health, the main role of the Community established by Article 129 EC was that of coordination, with the adoption of incentive measures or recommendations, expressly excluding the possibility of any Community action regarding 'harmonisation of the laws or regulations of the Member States'.[6] The wording of this Article appears as a clear application of the principle of subsidiarity and was a way to guarantee that the health field would continue to be the exclusive and rightful domain of domestic policy making[7] in which only persuasive methods, such as financial support and measures of soft law, could be adopted by the Community.

3 GREER, S. & JARMAN, H. 2012. Managing risks in EU health services policy: Spot markets, legal certainty and bureaucratic resistance. *Journal of European Social Policy*, 22: 259–72.
4 *Ibid.*
5 SZYSZCZAK, E. 2011. *Op. cit.*, p. 105.
6 Article 129 (4) Maastricht Treaty.
7 WISMAR, M. 2001. ECJ in the driving seat on health policy. But what's the destination? *Eurohealth*, 7(4).

Following the introduction of this Treaty provision in the field of health, in 1993 both the Council and the Commission started to make use of this new legal basis to develop action in this area. The Council adopted a Resolution on future action in the field of public health,[8] and the Commission presented a formal Communication on the Framework for Action in the Field of Public Health as an initial strategy document to develop work on public health. Based on this communication eight action programmes were agreed: health promotion, cancer, drug dependence, AIDS and other communicable diseases, health monitoring, rare diseases, accidents and injuries, and pollution-related diseases.[9]

The new Treaty provision dedicated to health did not, however, provide a complete framework for the development of an EU policy, since many essential elements for policy initiatives in the area were lacking. For example, Article 129 EC only provided powers for actions concerning the protection of human health, whereas health policies usually deal with actions concerning not only the protection but also the promotion of health, including, for example, the provision of health care, regulation of health professionals and producers of medicinal products, and individual entitlements to provision of medical treatment.[10] Moreover, the development of a health policy requires a clear vision and a statement of aims, priorities, limitations, responsibilities, methods and resource implications[11] – issues that were not covered by the new Article. Nevertheless, it is possible to say that Article 129 EC was an initial attempt to set health policy on the road to be established as an EU policy and that it filled a gap for a legal basis in this field, providing a specific legal basis for Community action, which had previously been unclear.[12]

In 1996, at the time of the Inter-Governmental Council which culminated in the Treaty of Amsterdam, the amendment of Article 129 EC was not initially intended. However, according to Hervey, some health threats, including the BSE crisis,[13] 'galvanized the governments of the Member States into taking some

8   COUNCIL AND THE MINISTERS FOR HEALTH 1993. Resolution of the Council and the Ministers for Health, meeting within the Council of 27 May 1993 on future action in the field of public health. OJ C 174, 25/06/1993 P. 0001 – 0003.

9   See http://ec.europa.eu/health/programme/policy/eight_programmes/index_en.htm [Accessed 29 November 2015].

10 HERVEY, T.K. 2002b. Mapping the contours of European Union health law and policy. *European Public Law*, 8(1): 69–105, p. 70.

11 MOSSIALOS, E. & MCKEE, M. 2002. The theoretical basis and historical evolution of health policy in the European Union. *In:* ELIAS MOSSIALOS, M.M., PALM, W., KARL, B. & MARHOLD, F. (eds) *EU Law and the social character of health care.* Brussels: Presses Interuniversitaires Européenes – Peter Lang, p. 63.

12 According to Hervey and Machale, there has been EU-level activity in the field since the late 1970s under Article 2 and the general legal basis of Article 235 EEC. An example of Community action in the 1980s is Decision 88/351/EEC of the Council and Representatives of the Governments of the Member States meeting within Council. HERVEY, T.K. & MCHALE, J.V. 2004. *Op. cit.*, p. 73.

13 Or 'mad cow disease'. For further details, see WORLD HEALTH ORGANIZATION 2002. *Understanding the BSE threat.* Available at www.who.int/csr/resources/publications/bse/BSEthreat. pdf [Accessed 6 January 2016].

action in that respect'[14] leading to the changes incorporated into the new Article 152 EC.

By comparing Articles 129 and 152 EC it is possible to identify a number of changes. The first and probably most important is the relationship between health policies and other Community policies and activities. With this new provision, the Community's obligation is no longer simply to contribute to ensuring a high level of health protection in other Community policies, but to 'ensure' a high level of health protection 'in the definition and implementation of all Community policies and activities'.[15] As Hervey argues, '[o]n a broad reading, Article 152 EC might require extra weight to be given to health goals, or indeed might render measures in other areas unlawful if a "high level of human health protection" cannot be guaranteed'.[16]

The second important change concerns the general aim of Community action in the field of health, which is now also focused on the promotion of health; this suggests that the new legal basis provides for the development of a real European Health Policy. The third change can be identified in Article 152 (4) EC, which not only specifies the measures that shall be adopted by the Council, but also describes the respective areas in which those measures are to be adopted. Thus, in the area of organs and substances of human origin, blood and blood derivatives, such measures aim at 'setting high standards of quality and safety' (Article 152 (4) a), while in the veterinary and phytosanitary fields the objective is the protection of public health (Article 152 (4) b).

The last important change is found in Article 152 (5) EC, which provides for the application of the principle of subsidiarity, explicitly preserving Member States' competence in the organisation and delivery of health services and medical care. Although Article 129 EC also provided for the same principle, there was no explicit reference to the area of health services and medical care; this may suggest that Member States wanted to preserve their competence over the financing of national health systems.[17]

Therefore, the content of Article 152 EC enabled the setting of a more specific legal basis and framework for the development of a European Health Policy to be carried out on a collective basis rather than on an individual basis. This permitted some policy areas to remain, in principle, within the competence of Member States. Therefore, areas concerning individual health entitlements, such as the responsibility for health care and relationships between individual recipients of health care, remained within Member States' competence.[18]

14   HERVEY, T.K. 2002a. The Legal Basis of European Community Public Health Policy. *In:* MCKEE, M., MOSSIALOS, E. & BAETEN, R. (eds) *The impact of EU Law on Health Care Systems.* Brussels: Presses Interuniversitaires Européenes – Peter Lang, p. 28.
15   First sub-paragraph of Article 152 EC.
16   HERVEY, T.K. 2002b. *Op. cit.,* p. 30.
17   HERVEY, T.K. 2002b. *Op. cit.,* p. 32.
18   HERVEY, T.K. & MCHALE, J.V. 2004. *Op. cit.,* p. 74.

With the entry into force of the Treaty of Lisbon, public health is now under Title XIV and the former Article 152 EC was renumbered Article 168 TFEU. This new Article is not substantially different from Article 152 EC. The first part of the new public health provision also points out the need to ensure a high level of health protection in the definition and implementation of all Union policies and activities. In terms of competences, the Union's role continues to be subsidiary and mainly involves complementing national policies in public health policy areas, such as physical and mental illness and diseases, major health scourges, drugs-related health damage and cross-border threats to health (Article 168 (1)). Moreover, the Union's role also includes encouraging cooperation between Member States in those policy areas and promoting coordination of Member States' activities, 'in particular initiatives aiming at the establishment of guidelines and indicators, the organisation of exchange of best practice, and the preparation of the necessary elements for periodic monitoring and evaluation'.[19]

Apart from the role of complementing and cooperating with Member States in the policy areas mentioned above, the European Parliament and the Council may adopt measures – through the ordinary legislative procedure – in order to meet common quality and safety concerns in the veterinary and phytosanitary fields and in the relation to organs and substances of human origin, including blood and blood derivatives, medicinal products and devices for medical use (Article 168 (4)).

Other incentive measures aimed at protecting and improving human health can also be adopted by the Parliament and the Council. This applies especially to cross-border health scourges, serious cross-border threats to health and to the protection of public health regarding tobacco and the abuse of alcohol. The adoption of measures in these areas excludes, however, any harmonisation of the laws and regulations of the Member States (Article 168 (5)).

The powers of the Union to act provided in Article 168 are in fact in line with Article 4(2) of the TFEU, which provides that in the area of common safety concerns in public health matters the Union and Member States share competences.

Another area covered in Article 168 is the organisation and delivery of health services and medical care. In this area, the Union, in principle, does not hold shared competences. According to the Treaty provision (Article 168 (7)), 'Union action shall respect the responsibilities of the Member States for the definition of their health policy and for the organisation and delivery of health services and medical care'. These responsibilities include the management of health services and medical care and the allocation of resources. As will be shown in the following sections, the organisation and delivery of health services is a sensitive and disputed field within the health area.

Therefore, according to the new provision on public health, shared competences between the Union and Member States are now dominant in the field of health. However, in relation to health services, the role of the Union continues to be subsidiary. Other provisions that are part of the European framework regarding health services are also in line with the principle of subsidiarity, such as Article 35 of the Charter of Fundamental Rights and Article 2 of the Protocol on Services of General Interest. These two provisions will be commented on later in this book.

Apart from these differences regarding the division of competences in the various fields comprised by the larger area of health, the relationship between the Internal Market and health issues and the powers of the Union to adopt harmonising measures in this area, as provided for in Article 114 TFEU, gives the impression of a 'blurred line between Member States and the EU in the area of the regulation of health care'.[20] The following section better explains this blurred line.

The question of competence

The lack of exclusive competence of the Union in the area of health in general, and especially in the field of health services, did not leave health out of the scope of the Treaty rules. Indeed, since the introduction of the first European legal powers in the field of health by the Treaty of Maastricht, EU institutions and Member States have tried to find their way toward developing an EU health policy and establishing the types of actions that can be adopted at the EU level. As Neergaard states, 'over the time span of the existence of the EEC/EC/EU, health care has increasingly become an area of interest to this level of governance, having the unavoidable consequence of erosion of national competences'.[21] In this regard, a major and important contribution has been made by the ECJ, which through its rulings better defined the scope and application of the Treaty provisions in the field of health, as well as clarifying the interaction between health and other EU policies. In fact, the jurisprudence of the Court has shown that the Union's powers in the health area are perfectly possible insofar there is an intersection between health and other policy areas, such as the Internal Market. A good example of this is the Tobacco Advertising Case.[22] This case concerned the application for annulment of Directive 98/43/EC of the European Parliament and of the Council on the approximation of the laws, regulations and administrative provisions of the Member States relating to the advertising and sponsorship of tobacco products. The applicant (the German government) put forward two broad arguments: the first was that the Directive was adopted under an incorrect legal basis (thus Article 100a, now Article 114 TFEU), because the 'centre of gravity' of the measure was found in health protection rather than in the Internal Market, and harmonising measures in the field of health are expressly prohibited by the Treaty provision (thus Article 129, now Article 168 TFEU); the second was that the Directive, although choosing Internal Market provisions as its legal basis, did not comply

---

20 NEERGAARD, U. 2011. *Op. cit.*, pp. 24–5.
21 *Ibid.*, p. 25.
22 Case C-376/98, *Germany v Parliament and Council (Tobacco Advertising)* [2000] ECR I-8419.

with the conditions imposed by them. As a result, the Court decided to annul the Directive, upholding Germany's pleas alleging that Article 100a was not an appropriate legal basis for the Directive.

Although the lack of Community competence to adopt harmonising measures in the field of health was a secondary question in the judgement,[23] when analysing the reliance on the Internal Market provision for the adoption of the Directive, the Court had to examine that argument, and it was the first time that the Court ruled that the Community lacks competence to adopt a health protection measure.[24] Besides recognising the lack of Community competence in the field of health, the ECJ held other important questions that help to clarify the competences in the field of health, such as the fact that other Treaty provisions may not be used as a legal basis to circumvent the prohibition of harmonisation established by the public health Article.[25] This is to say that in the analysis of the validity of a measure, the Court must verify whether the measure in fact pursues the objectives stated by the Community, rather than considering only its material subject matter. Thus, in the Tobacco Case, even if the Directive used Internal Market provisions as its legal basis, the Court recognised that the national measures affected by the Directive were to a large extent inspired by public health policy objectives.[26]

Other important issues concerning the relationship between health and Internal Market policies were examined by the ECJ. One finding was that the possibility of parallel pursuit of health protection and Internal Market aims by a measure does exist, and this flows from the Treaty itself when it establishes that health requirements are to be ensured in other Community policies.[27] Consequently, the provision on public health 'does not mean that harmonising measures adopted on the basis of other provisions of the treaty cannot have any impact on the protection of human health'.[28] Indeed, Advocate General Fennelly pointed out in his opinion that the Internal Market and the public health provisions are not inconsistent with each other, and that the competence restriction on public health cannot be interpreted as also meaning a restriction in other policy fields just because it sometimes has a bearing on health.[29]

In spite of the clarification and recognition by the Court that the Union lacks competence to adopt measures in the field of health protection, the Tobacco Case was undoubtedly much more an issue of the sustainable legal basis of the Internal Market provisions. Furthermore, the case also seems to demonstrate that when health protection and Internal Market provisions are possible legal bases for the

---

23   In fact, Advocate General Fennelly states that he considers 'Article 129 of the Treaty to be irrelevant to the debate on legal basis with which these cases are concerned'. (Para. 73 of the Opinion of Advocate General Fenelly in Case C-376/98, *Germany v Parliament and Council (Tobacco Advertising)* [2000] ECR I-8419.)

24   Case C-376/98, para. 77.

25   *Ibid.*, para. 79.

26   *Ibid.*, para. 76.

27   Para. 58 of the Opinion of Advocate General Fennelly in Case C-376/98.

28   Case C-376/98, para. 78.

29   Para. 71 of the Opinion of Advocate General Fennelly in Case C-376/98.

adoption of a measure, the measure can be held valid and the issue of competence will be favourably resolved, provided that the conditions of the Internal Market are fulfilled, that is to say, if it is proved that the objective of the measure is the improvement of the Internal Market (its establishment or functioning), the Union is competent to adopt an harmonising measure, even if health protection is a decisive factor in the content of the legislation concerned.[30]

It is clear, therefore, that the limitations on direct Union competence over public health protection are to some extent offset by Internal Market competences.[31] It seems from the Court's ruling on the Tobacco Advertising Case that when the Internal Market policy intersects with health policy, the latter tends to be considered as part of the former, or better, as one of its objectives as stated by Article 114 (then Article 100a), and once proved that the conditions of Article 114 are fulfilled, the Internal Market legal basis is naturally the choice for the EU.[32] Accordingly, it is possible that measures with an element of health protection may be lawfully enacted on the basis of other more specific provisions and, where the Internal Market can be a proper legal basis for such measures, it must be used.[33]

As the question of competence shows, health may intersect with other EU policy areas and this also applies to health services. Considering that the analysis of these services is one of the core elements of this book, it is important to analyse how these other policy areas and respective Treaty provisions interrelate with health services. Accordingly, in the next section I will analyse other policy areas and Treaty provisions that intersect with health services. This analysis will include the relevant case law of the ECJ in relation to each of the policy areas and Treaty provisions.

The Treaty rules: other Treaty provisions

The Internal Market and provisions on services

As already mentioned, Article 168 (7) TFEU deals specifically with the organisation and delivery of health services and medical care and recognises Member States' competence regarding these health activities. However, the organisation and delivery of health services have become a disputed area arising from two different and interrelated issues. The first is the question of competence, analysed above,

---

30 See para. 88 of the judgement and paras 69 and 73 of the Opinion of Advocate General Fennelly.

31 WYATT, D. 2005. Community Competence to regulate Medical Services. *In:* SPAVENTA, E. & DOUGAN, M. (eds) *Social welfare and EU law.* Oxford: Hart, p. 132.

32 For instance, in the subsequent Tobacco Case (Case C-491/01, *British American Tobacco* [2002] ECR I-11453) concerning a challenge to another Directive adopted by the Community (Directive 2001/37/EC) under an internal market legal basis, the Court held that the internal market conditions were fulfilled since the measure aimed at improving the conditions of the internal market, because there were in fact differences between national laws on the manufacture, presentation and sale of tobacco products. See HOUDRY, V. 2015. La France et l'action de l'Union en matièere de santé. *In:* BROSSET, E. (ed.) *Droit européen et protection de la santé: bilan et perspectives.* Brussels: Bruylant, pp. 79–82, p.80.

33 HERVEY, T.K. & MCHALE, J.V. 2004. *Op. cit.,* p. 105.

and the second concerns the nature of health services. In relation to competence, although the Union does not have direct powers to act in this area, since 'Member States are, in principle, responsible for the provision of health services on their territory',[34] the provision of health services in a cross-border context is regulated also by EU law (e.g. Regulation 883/2004 and Directive 2011/24/EU). Therefore, the provision of cross-border health services has weakened the responsibility of Member States over their health systems, which was challenged before by the ECJ in recent years. In fact, the principles developed by the Court in cross-border health care cases show that the special nature of health services as a social security benefit does not render it beyond the scope of the Union's competence, and hence that national regulation of the social security system should be consistent with EU law.[35] This can be viewed, in a way, as the 'superiority' of free movement principles over Member States' competences to organise their health systems. In this regard, Neergaard suggests that:

> a legislative competence in a given area may be thought of as 'vertical' in character, whereas free movement principles may be thought of as 'horizontal' as these principles often will function as cutting across all kinds of areas, and Member States are not protected there from, 'just' because they have a legislative competence in a given area pursuant to the Treaty.[36]

With regard to the nature of health services, while at the national level the delivery of these services has for a long time been viewed as a social matter, at the EU level it is viewed as an economic subject. In effect, it is this economic approach[37] regarding health services that rendered possible a more active role of the Union in this area. The ECJ made this assumption when deciding cross-border health care cases. By assuming that the provision of medical services comprises services normally provided for remuneration, the Court included health services within the meaning of the Treaty provision on services (ex Article 49, now Article 56 TFEU), as will be shown below. It is important to emphasise that I will not analyse all the cases regarding cross-border health care, since this is not the only focus of this book. The cases selected for analysis are those which I consider important to demonstrate the evolution of the Court's approach in relation to health services in a cross-border dimension. The understanding of this evolution is relevant because Directive 2011/24/EU – which will be also examined in this chapter – reflects the principles developed by the ECJ in the case law concerning cross-border health care.[38]

---

34 KANAVOS, P. & MACKEE, M. 2000. Cross-border issues in the provision of health services. *Journal of Health Services Research & Policy*, 5(4): 231–6.

35 KOUTRAKOS, P. 2005. Healthcare as an Economic Service under EU law. *In:* SPAVENTA, E. & DOUGAN, M. (eds) *Social welfare and EU law.* Oxford: Hart, p. 107.

36 NEERGAARD, U. 2011. *Op. cit.*, p. 26.

37 This economic approach towards health services is supported by the idea of the primacy of the economic integration project. JOERGES, C. 2009. A renaissance of the European Constitution? *In:* NEERGAARD, U.B., NIELSEN, R. & ROSEBERRY, L.M. (eds) *Integrating welfare functions into EU law: from Rome to Lisbon.* Copenhagen: DJØF.

38 See the Preamble of Directive 2011/24/EU, para. 8.

THE FIRST CASES ON CROSS-BORDER HEALTH CARE: KOHLL[39] AND DECKER[40]

Prior to these first two rulings on cross-border health care, treatment received by EU citizens in another Member State was limited.[41] According to the rules established by Regulation 1408/71, it was restricted to migrant workers, through the S1 form (previously form E106)[42], emergency care for people temporarily abroad, through the European Health Insurance Card (ex-form E111),[43] and to those seeking planned care abroad, but pre-authorised by their Member State of origin, through the S2 form (previously form E112).[44] However, the rulings in *Kohll* and *Decker*, both concerning citizens affiliated to the Luxembourg health insurance system and judged on the same day (28 April 1998), established the first precedents 'by which patients going abroad for treatment would not need prior authorisation and would be reimbursed in line with rates applied in their home country'.[45] Therefore, these rulings concerned patients who went abroad to seek health care and not those consuming health care because they were abroad at the time they needed care.[46]

In *Kohll* the dispute regarded the request for prior authorisation before the Luxembourg health insurance fund for orthodontic treatment to be provided

---

39 Case C-158/96, *Kohll* [1998] ECR I-1931.

40 Case C-120/95, *Decker* [1998] ECR I-1831.

41 KANAVOS, P. & MACKEE, M. 2000. *Op. cit.*, p. 231.

42 Certificate of entitlement to health care in case you do not live in the country where you are insured. Useful for cross-border workers, pensioners or civil servants and their dependants. Available at http://ec.europa.eu/youreurope/citizens/work/e-forms/eu-index_en.htm#s1 [Accessed 1 December 2015].

43 The European Health Insurance Card ensures that EU citizens have the same access to public sector health care (e.g. a doctor, a pharmacy, a hospital or a health care centre) as nationals of the country they are visiting. It makes it easier for people from the European Union's 28 Member States plus Iceland, Liechtenstein, Norway and Switzerland to access health care services during temporary visits abroad. See information available at http://ec.europa.eu/social/main.jsp?catId=559&langId=en [Accessed 1 December 2015].

44 Authorisation to obtain a planned health treatment in another EU or EFTA country. 'You should be treated in the same way as residents of that country – you may have to pay a percentage of the costs up front'. The scheme enables citizens to make an application to their local health authority for authorisation to travel to another Member State of the European Union to receive medical treatment there. It provides that authorisation must be granted by the health authority where the treatment is not available in the home Member State or where the treatment cannot be provided in the home state without undue delay. See information available at http://ec.europa.eu/youreurope/citizens/work/e-forms/eu-index_en.htm#s1 [Accessed 1 December 2015].

45 KANAVOS, P. & MACKEE, M. 2000. *Op. cit.*, p. 231.

46 According to Glinos and Baeten, there are two main types of patient who make use of cross-border health care. The first group includes long-term residents, students, travelling professionals and tourists, that is patients consuming cross-border health care because 'they are abroad at the time when the need for health care arises'; and the second group refers specifically to patients who seek health care abroad, 'either because they live in a border-region where cross-border is more convenient, or because they perceive a relative weakness in their national health care system, which pushes them to go abroad (such as waiting lists, lack of suitable treatment, or prohibitive prices)'; GLINOS, I.A. & BAETEN, R. 2006. A Literature Review of Cross-Border Patient Mobility in the European Union. Brussels: Observatoire Social Européen. Available at www.ose.be/files/publication/health/WP12_lit_review_final.pdf [Accessed 3 December 2015].

to the daughter of Mr. Raymond Kohll in Trier, Germany. After receiving a refusal of the authorisation requested, on the grounds that the treatment was not urgent and that it was available and adequate in Luxembourg, Mr. Kholl initiated proceedings against the *Union des Caisses de Maladie* before the competent administrative bodies. Both decisions at the administrative level dismissed Mr. Kohll's plea. He then appealed to the Luxembourg *Cour de Cassation*, which decided to stay the proceedings and to refer the case to the ECJ for a preliminary ruling on the interpretation of Articles 59 and 60 of the Treaty establishing the EEC (now Articles 56 and 57 TFEU).

The arguments raised by the Luxembourg social security scheme and other Member States' governments were basically that: (1) the situation at issue does not fall within the scope of the Community provisions on freedom to provide services, because the issue concerns social security and should be examined from the point of view of Article 22 of Regulation 1408/71; and (2) the risk of upsetting the financial balance of the social security scheme, which aims to ensure a balanced medical and hospital service available to all its insured, constitutes an overriding reason in the general interest capable of justifying restrictions on freedom to provide services, that is, the requirement of prior authorisation.[47]

The ECJ decided that the provision of orthodontic treatment should be regarded as a service within the meaning of Article 60 of the Treaty establishing the EEC. Moreover, although recognising that Member States have discretion in organising their health systems, the Court asserted that in doing that they should respect EU law. Once it was recognised that EU law applied to the situation in question, the ECJ went on to apply the two-stage test, i.e. first to determine whether there was any restriction on the free movement of goods or services and, if this answer was positive, whether this restriction was justified.[48] In applying this test, the ECJ concluded that the request for prior authorisation constituted a restriction on free movement. Then, the ECJ analysed the three justifications presented by the Luxembourg government: (1) that prior authorisation constitutes the only effective and least restrictive means of controlling expenditure on health and balancing the budget of the social security system; (2) that authorisation is necessary on grounds of the protection of public health in order to guarantee the quality of medical services, which in the case of persons going to another Member State can be ascertained only at the time of the request for authorisation; and (3) that prior authorisation is justified on grounds of the protection of public health, insofar as it is necessary to maintain a balanced medical and hospital service open to all.[49]

The ECJ rejected all the justifications presented. First, although recognising that the risk of seriously undermining the financial balance of the social security system may constitute an overriding reason in the general interest capable of justifying a barrier of that kind, the ECJ concluded that the reimbursement of the costs in accordance with the tariff of the State of insurance has no significant effect on the

47 Case C-158/96 [1998] ECR I-1931, paras. 16, 37 and 38
48 NICKLESS, J. 2002. *Op. cit.*, p. 59.
49 Case C-158/96 [1998] ECR I-1931, paras 37, 38 and 43.

financing of the social security system.[50] Second, in relation to the quality of services, the Court concluded that doctors and dentists established in other Member States must be afforded all guarantees equivalent to those accorded to doctors and dentists established in the national territory.[51] Finally, the Court explained that neither the Luxembourg social security scheme nor the governments of Member States submitting observations proved that the rules at issue were necessary to provide a balanced medical and hospital service accessible to all.[52] Therefore, on the basis of all these circumstances, the ECJ decided that the requirement of prior authorisation constituted a restriction on free movement and thus violated the Treaty rules.[53]

In *Decker*, the questions submitted to the ECJ were similar to those in *Kohll*. The difference was that the situation regarded the reimbursement of a pair of spectacles purchased by Mr. Decker in another Member State and so the Treaty provision in question was Article 30 of the Treaty establishing the EEC, on the free movement of goods (now Article 34 TFEU). Here, once more, the Court decided that the refusal to reimburse a pair of spectacles purchased in another Member State, on the grounds that prior authorisation was required, constituted a restriction on the free movement of goods.

These two cases represented the first steps of the ECJ in the direction of an economic view of health services, resulting in the application of the Treaty provisions on services and goods to the field of health services and goods. As Kanavos and Mackee argue, '[f]or the first time, the Court's ruling has made health services subject to two of the fundamental principles on which the EU was constructed: freedom in the movement of goods and freedom in the movement of services'.[54] The application of the rules on free movement to cross-border health care services created an alternative method for obtaining non-emergency health treatment abroad that would coexist with the procedure contained in Regulation 1408/71.[55]

In this regard, as Baquero Cruz explains:

> Read today, these judgments may appear to be timid exploratory judgments, but in 1998 they were catalytic decisions which, like *Luisi and Carbone*, pointed to new and unforeseen doors that would soon be opened. They introduced the important distinction between hospital and non-hospital treatment. They are also important in that they do not dwell upon the issue of the economic nature of the service provided; it is almost taken for granted.[56]

---

50 *Ibid.*, para. 42.
51 *Ibid.*, para. 48.
52 *Ibid.*, para. 52.
53 *Ibid.*, para. 54.
54 KANAVOS, P. & MACKEE, M. 2000. *Op. cit.*, p. 232.
55 NICKLESS, J. 2002. *Op. cit.*, p. 61.
56 CRUZ, J.B. 2011. The Case Law of the European Court of Justice on the Mobility of Patients: An Assessment. *In:* GRONDEN, J.W.V.D., SZYSZCZAK, E., NEERGAARD, U. & KRAJEWSKI, M. (eds) *Health care and EU law*. The Hague: T.M.C. Asser, p. 83.

The reactions of Member States to these judgements reflected mixed feelings. While some countries, such as Germany, sustained that the decisions threatened the equilibrium of health systems and needed to be contested, others believed that the decisions would not affect their own health systems, either because they already provided for the possibility of a patient being treated by foreign-based providers, as in the case of the Netherlands, or because they did not see their system as an enterprise offering services within the meaning of the Treaty rules, as in the case of the UK.[57]

Nevertheless, some successive cases surprised the feelings and beliefs of Member States regarding their own health systems. Although the situation in *Kohll* regarded non-hospital services and the affiliation to a social insurance system, the ECJ went on to expand its economic approach to health services, applying this reasoning to hospital treatments and to health systems operating on a benefits-in-kind basis.

HOSPITAL TREATMENT PROVIDED BY A HEALTH INSURANCE SYSTEM OPERATING ON
A BENEFITS-IN-KIND BASIS: *SMITS (EPOUSE GERAETS) AND PEERBOOMS*[58]

Three years after the decisions on *Kohll* and *Decker*, the ECJ had to deal again with the question of cross-border health services. This time the dispute concerned hospital treatment for Parkinson's disease and intensive neurostimulation therapy provided to two citizens affiliated to the Netherlands' health insurance scheme, which operates on a benefits-in-kind basis. Indeed, the case concerned two different proceedings submitted by the Netherlands national court. The first concerned the treatment for Parkinson's disease received by Mrs. Geraets-Smits, in Kassel, Germany. The multidisciplinary treatment received involved, *inter alia*, examinations, physiotherapy, ergotherapy and socio-psychological support. She then applied for reimbursement of the hospital treatment costs incurred in Germany and was informed by the Dutch health insurance authorities that the costs of the treatment would not be refunded because there was satisfactory and adequate treatment for Parkinson's disease available in the Netherlands, and the specific clinical treatment provided in Germany offered no additional advantage.

The second proceeding concerned the case of Mr. Peerbooms, a 36-year-old man, who, after falling into a coma, was transferred in a vegetative state from a hospital in the Netherlands to a clinic in Austria. The special intensive neurostimulation therapy he received in Austria was in use only experimentally in the Netherlands and patients over the age of 25 years were not allowed to undergo

---

57 KANAVOS, P. & MACKEE, M. 2000. *Op. cit.*, p. 234.
58 Case C-*157/99* [2001] ECR I-5473. In the same day as this judgement, another case on cross-border health care was judged by the ECJ: *Vanbraekel and others*, Case C-368/98 [2001] ECR I-5363. Although in *Vanbraekel* cross-border hospital treatment was also part of the facts, the main issue discussed in that case was the limits of reimbursement, that is, whether the treatment should be reimbursed in accordance with the scheme of the patient's state of affiliation or in accordance with that organised by the state where the treatment had taken place. For this reason, I will not include this case in the discussion.

this therapy. Therefore, in the Netherlands Mr. Peerbooms would not have been allowed to receive this treatment. Then, Mr. Peerbooms' neurologist sought for reimbursement of the costs incurred by the therapy in Austria. The Dutch health insurance authority refused the request for reimbursement, arguing that the treatment was considered experimental in the Netherlands and there was no scientific evidence of its effectiveness. Therefore, that type of treatment was not regarded as normal within the professional circles concerned and, consequently, as a benefit qualifying for reimbursement under Dutch law. Moreover, it was also argued that, should the treatment was held to be normal, the refusal was based therefore on the consideration that satisfactory and adequate treatment was available without undue delay in the Netherlands at an establishment with which the sickness insurance fund had contractual arrangements.

Both Mrs. Geraets-Smits and Mr. Peerbooms lodged appeals against the refusal of reimbursement before the respective Dutch national courts, which decided to stay proceedings and to refer the cases to the ECJ for a preliminary ruling. The Court basically had to decide on two issues: first, whether the Treaty provisions on free movement applied to health care provided in hospitals; then, as in *Kohll* and *Decker*, it had to apply the two-stage test – first to determine whether the requirement of prior authorisation for receiving hospital treatment in another Member State represented a restriction on free movement and, in case this answer was positive, whether this restriction could be justified. In relation to the first issue, the ECJ decided that the provision of hospital services fell within the scope of the Treaty rules on the freedom to provide services. The Court argued that the fact that hospital medical treatment is financed directly by the sickness insurance funds on the basis of agreements and pre-set scales of fees does not remove this treatment from the sphere of services within the meaning of the Treaty. It was also emphasised that the essential characteristic of remuneration – consideration for the service in question – was present in the cases since the payments made by the Dutch sickness insurance funds, though set at a flat rate, were indeed the consideration for the hospital services and unquestionably represented remuneration for the hospital that received them, which, in turn, was engaged in an activity of an economic character.[59]

It is important to point out that this view was, nevertheless, contrary to that expressed by Advocate General Colomer in his opinion. He was of the view that in a health system such as that of the Netherlands, according to which 'the funds operate by concluding with health-care institutions and independent medical practitioners agreements in which they determine in advance the extent and quality of the benefits to be provided, and the financial contribution the fund will make, which, for practitioners, consists in the payment of a fixed flat-rate amount, and, for each hospital, in the payment of an attendance charge intended to finance the institution rather than to cover the real cost of hospital accommodation',[60] hospital

59   Case C-157/99 [2001] ECR I-5473, paras 56, 58 and 59.
60   Opinion of Advocate General Colomer in Case C-157/99 [2001] ECR I-5473, paras 29 and 32.

treatment could not be considered as a service within the meaning of the Treaty provisions on free movement because it lacked the element of remuneration. To support his arguments he used the Court's decision in *Humbel*.[61]

The ECJ then went on to determine the authorisation procedure required by the Dutch health authorities in order to determine whether they were fair and proportional. It conducted this analysis by looking at the two tests used to decide whether authorisation should be given or not, that is, (1) whether the treatment was regarded as normal in the professional circles concerned, and (2) whether the treatment was available in sufficient time from a contracted provider in the Netherlands.[62]

In applying these tests, the ECJ concluded that the requirement and grant of prior authorisation can be subject to the conditions that (1) the treatment must be regarded as 'normal in the professional circles concerned', a criterion also applied in determining whether hospital treatment provided in the national territory is covered, and (2) the insured person's medical condition requires that treatment. However, the Court also concluded that the 'normality' of the treatment could not be considered only by the professional circles in the Netherlands and, in order to be regarded as normal, the treatment should be tried and tested by international medical science. In relation to the second condition, the ECJ concluded that 'authorisation can be refused on the ground of lack of medical necessity only if the same or equally effective treatment can be obtained without undue delay at an establishment having a contractual arrangement with the insured person's sickness insurance fund'.[63]

This second part of the judgement also shows contrasting views between the Court and Advocate General Colomer, who determined the question of prior authorisation as a restriction to free movement concluding that:

> It is my view that, in those circumstances, the requirement of authorisation constitutes not only a necessary and proportionate means of attaining the objective of maintaining the financial equilibrium of the system, but also the only means available to sickness funds for controlling payments to a non-contracted provider for health care which they have already paid the contracted providers to dispense, since this represents an additional financial burden. It seems clear to me that, under a social security system where health-care resources, practitioners and institutions are pre-established, sickness funds must be able to expect that, barring rare exceptions subject to their consent, any health care which insured persons require will actually be provided by the practitioners and institutions contracted, regardless of whether they are situated on national territory or abroad.[64]

61   Case 263/86 *Belgian State v Humbel* [1988] ECR I-5365.
62   NICKLESS, J. 2002. *Op. cit.*, p. 72.
63   Case C-157/99 [2001] ECR I-5473, para. 108.
64   Opinion of Advocate General Colomer in Case C-157/99 [2001] ECR I-5473, para. 55.

The novelty of this case was the recognition that hospital treatment in a system operating on a benefits-in-kind basis also fell within the scope of the Treaty rules on free movement. Moreover, the judgement was also innovative from the point of view of providing some 'technical' definitions about what should be considered as normal in terms of medical treatment, and how to evaluate an equally effective treatment.

CLARIFYING AND CONFIRMING THE PRINCIPLES ESTABLISHED BY THE PREVIOUS CASE LAW: *MULLER-FAURÉ AND VAN RIET*[65]

After *Smits and Peerbooms* the Court judged the *Müller-Fauré and van Riet* case in 2003. The case was not so different from the previous ones on cross-border health care. As in *Smits and Peerbooms*, it concerned two citizens affiliated to the Netherlands health insurance scheme. The first was Ms. Müller-Fauré, who, while on holiday in Germany, underwent dental treatment involving the fitting of six crowns and a fixed prosthesis on the upper jaw. After her return she asked for reimbursement of the expenses incurred, which was refused by the Dutch fund since no exceptional circumstances were present in her case. The other was Ms. Van Riet, whose doctor requested that the Amsterdam Fund's medical adviser grant authorisation for his patient to have an arthroscopy performed in a hospital in Belgium where that examination could be carried out much sooner than in the Netherlands. The fund rejected the doctor's application, and in the meantime Ms. Van Riet had the arthroscopy carried out in Belgium. After this examination, she was submitted for an ulnar reduction to relieve the pain, which was also carried out in Belgium, partly in hospital and partly elsewhere. However, the Dutch funding authorities refused to reimburse the total of the costs incurred by Ms. Van Riet in Belgium by arguing that (1) there was neither an emergency nor any medical necessity to justify Ms. Van Riet receiving treatment abroad, and (2) there was appropriate treatment available in the Netherlands within a reasonable period.

In this case, once more, the ECJ applied the same principles used in the previous case law on cross-border health care. First, the Court took for granted that health services are economic activities and fall within the scope of the Treaty rules, repeating that there is 'no need to distinguish in that regard between care provided in a hospital environment and care provided outside such an environment'.[66] Indeed, to reach this conclusion the Court focused on the fact that the treatment provided abroad was paid directly by the patient to the doctor or the establishment providing the service.[67] Therefore, as Spaventa points out, 'There is no mention in this ruling of the relationship between the patient and the sickness fund, nor of the relationship between sickness funds and health care

---

65 Case C-385/99, *Müller-Fauré and van Riet* [2003] ECR I-4509.
66 *Ibid.*, para. 38.
67 *Ibid.*, para. 39.

providers, thus suggesting that that case was of general application'.[68] It shows that the criterion used by the Court in order to classify a service as economic is remuneration in relation to the foreign health provider, i.e. the amount of payment paid by the patient abroad. However, this reasoning is not satisfactory to categorise health services as economic services because the remuneration factor will be present only until the moment the patient asks for reimbursement from his or her health system of affiliation. From the moment when the patient is reimbursed, the element of remuneration is cancelled out and the service becomes free of charge. Therefore, remuneration cannot be used as a criterion because it is present only in the relationship between the patient and the foreign health care provider, but not in the relationship between the patient and his or her system of affiliation, which is the one subject to scrutiny before the Court.

Following this, the Court then concluded that the rules on prior authorisation established by the Dutch health care funds constituted a barrier to free movement. In considering the justifications for the imposition of barriers, the Court concluded that the risk of undermining the financial balance of the health system can constitute an overriding reason justifying the imposition of a barrier, such as the requirement of prior authorisation. However, this would apply only in relation to hospital services and provided that the order for prior authorisation is based 'on objective, non-discriminatory criteria which are known in advance, in such a way as to circumscribe the exercise of the national authorities' discretion, so that it is not used arbitrarily'.[69] In relation to non-hospital services, the Court found no evidence that the liberty to have treatment in another Member State without prior authorisation would undermine the financial balance of the health system.[70] The final issue analysed by the ECJ was the essential characteristics of the Netherlands sickness insurance scheme, which had already been subject to analysis in *Smits and Peerbooms*. Again, the conclusion was that the evidence and arguments submitted to the Court did not show that removal of the prior authorisation requirement for treatment received in another Member State, in particular other than in a hospital, would undermine the essential characteristics of the Netherlands' sickness insurance scheme.[71] This view, however, was contrary to that of Advocate General Colomer, who was of the opinion that the requirement of prior authorisation for cross-border health care, even for non-hospital treatment, would be justified in the type of health system such as that of the Netherlands, which works by providing benefits-in-kind services.[72] In this regard, it is worth citing part of his argumentation:

> Although it is true that, when organising their social security systems, the Member States must comply with Community law, that obligation cannot

68 SPAVENTA, E. 2007. *Free movement of persons in the European Union: barriers to movement in their constitutional context.* Leiden, Netherlands: Kluwer Law International, p. 53.

69 *Ibid.*, para. 85.

70 *Ibid.*, para. 93.

71 *Ibid*, para. 108.

72 Opinion of Advocate General Colomer in Case C-385/99, *Müller-Fauré and van Riet* [2003] ECR I-4509, para. 62.

require them to abandon the principles and philosophy which has traditionally governed their sickness insurance, nor require them to undergo restructuring on a scale such as to enable them to reimburse those of their insured persons who choose to go to the doctor in another Member State.[73]

Although the facts of this case and its decision were similar to the previous case law on cross-border health care, the importance of *Müller-Fauré and van Riet* was to confirm and show that the main principles created by the Court regarding this issue were already well consolidated. Furthermore, as Baquero Cruz argues, the case also guarantees 'a common solution and a level playing field [. . .]' for systems operating under reimbursement and those under benefits-in-kind.[74]

HOSPITAL TREATMENT PROVIDED BY A NATIONAL HEALTH SYSTEM OPERATING ON A
BENEFITS-IN-KIND BASIS: *WATTS*[75]

Five years later, the ECJ had to deal with another case concerning hospital treatment. This time, however, the health system in question was that of the UK (NHS), that is, a system publicly funded through taxation and providing services free at the point of delivery (operating on a benefits-in-kind basis), as already explained in the previous chapter. The case concerned Mrs. Yvonne Watts, who suffered from arthritis and needed to undergo orthopaedic surgery for hip replacement. Within the British health system her case was classified as 'routine' and thus she would have to wait 12 months for the surgery. For this reason, she asked for an authorisation to undergo the surgery abroad. This authorisation was denied by the competent health body on the ground that 12 months could not be considered as 'undue delay', and therefore that the condition set out in Article 22 of Regulation No 1408/71 was not satisfied. Following legal proceedings before the Administrative Court, Mrs. Watts had the waiting time for the surgery reduced to 3 or 4 months. Nevertheless she decided to undergo the hip replacement operation in France, bearing the expenses of the surgery. Mrs. Watts continued the legal proceedings started before the Administrative Court in order to include the reimbursement for the expenses of the treatment she had in France. The case was dismissed at first instance. She then appealed to the Court of Appeal, which referred several questions to the ECJ regarding the interpretation of ex Article 49 EC (now Article 56 TFEU).

As in the previous case law on cross-border health care, here the ECJ also took for granted that the hospital treatment provided to Mrs. Watts should be considered an economic activity falling within the Treaty rules. In the view of the Court, the fact that the service in question was a hospital treatment and the health system was completely public made no difference to the categorisation of the service as an economic service. According to the Court, the Treaty provision should apply

---

73 *Ibid.*, para. 58.
74 CRUZ, J.B. 2011. *Op. cit.*, p. 87.
75 Case C-372/04, *Watts* [2006] ECR I-4325.

'regardless of the way in which the national system with which that person [the patient] is registered and from which reimbursement of the cost of those services is subsequently sought operates'.[76] Here again the Court confirmed the argumentation adopted in *Müller-Fauré and van Riet*: what mattered for the ECJ in order to classify the health service as an economic service was the fact that Mrs. Watts paid a foreign supplier for the treatment she received. Therefore, the fact that she subsequently sought the reimbursement from a national health system providing services free of charge made no difference.[77] In this regard, it is important to note that one of the questions asked by the referring Court was whether NHS bodies providing hospital treatment were service providers within Articles 49 EC and 50 EC. However, this question was not clearly answered by the ECJ. In fact:

> This question put the Court in a difficult situation for hermeneutic and practical reasons. For hermeneutic reasons, since Article 50 EC states that in order to fall within the scope of Article 49 EC the service needs to be provided for 'remuneration', which is clearly not the case in the relation to public health systems when the treatment is free at the point of delivery. For practical reasons, because if the Court had held that the NHS treatment is a service within the scope of Article 49 EC, then Member States would have been in a position of having to justify denial of such service to non-residents. Maybe not surprisingly then, the Court decided that it was not necessary to answer such question: rather, as in *Müller-Fauré*, it focused on the relationship between patient and foreign service provider to bring the situation within the scope of Article 49 EC.[78]

Although it seems strange that the ECJ did not take account of the particularities of a completely public health system such as the NHS, deciding to focus on the relationship between the patient and the foreign provider, it was probably the only way that the ECJ could maintain its previous line of argumentation applied in the other cases on patient mobility. From the moment that it decided not to exclude other public health systems from the economic logic, it would be difficult for the ECJ to justify the exclusion of the NHS, that is, having admitted that the benefits-in-kind Belgian and Dutch systems were economic in nature, it would be hard to say that the treatments received by persons affiliated to national health systems in another Member State were not economic, thus insulating these particular systems from all others because of their specific nature.[79]

By applying this reasoning, the ECJ then concluded that the system of prior authorisation for cross-border health services established by the NHS constituted an obstacle to the freedom to provide services because patients treated within the

76   *Ibid.*, para. 90.
77   *Ibid.*, paras 88 and 89.
78   SPAVENTA, E. 2007. *Op. cit.*, pp. 53–4.
79   CRUZ, J.B. 2011. *Op. cit.*, p. 88.

NHS did not need prior authorisation, whereas for the NHS to assume the costs of hospital treatment in another Member State the patient would need this authorisation. Thus, according to the Court, this mechanism 'deters, or even prevents, the patients concerned from applying to providers of hospital services established in another Member State [. . .]'.[80]

Following this, the ECJ went on to decide whether this obstacle could be justified on the basis of overriding reasons of public health, as the maintenance of a public health system open to all. To decide this question, the Court applied the same 'necessity-proportionality test' applied to previous case law on this issue.

In applying this test the ECJ concluded, as in the previous case law, that the UK system of prior authorisation was incompatible with the Treaty rules. According to the Court's view:

> A refusal to grant prior authorisation cannot be based merely on the existence of waiting lists intended to enable the supply of hospital care to be planned and managed on the basis of predetermined general clinical priorities, without carrying out an objective medical assessment of the patient's medical condition, the history and probable course of his illness, the degree of pain he is in and/or the nature of his disability at the time when the request for authorisation was made or renewed.[81]

The ECJ also decided on the calculation of the costs to be reimbursed to the patient. In this regard, an interesting point concerning the special features of the NHS decided by the Court was that even if within the NHS there is no set tariff for reimbursement of treatments, the health authority must objectively quantify an equivalent treatment in a hospital covering the service in question within the NHS in order to calculate the amount to be reimbursed to the patient. This seems to be a measure that would require substantial changes in the organisation of services within the health system concerned. The reason for not having a quantified tariff was due to the fact that, most of the time, secondary care including hospital care was provided in state facilities. Therefore, introducing prices for services previously not priced implies many changes to the health system.

Finally, another important question decided by the ECJ in this case concerned the compatibility of the obligation to reimburse the costs of treatment abroad with the rule provided for in Article 152(5) EC (now Article 168 (7)). Again, at this point the Court was not so clear in its answer. At the same time it recognised that 'the requirements arising from Article 49 EC and Article 22 of Regulation 1408/71 are not to be interpreted as imposing on the Member States an obligation to reimburse the cost of hospital treatment in other Member States without reference to any budgetary consideration', and that 'Community action in the field of public health is to fully respect the responsibilities of the Member States for the

---

80   *Ibid.*, para. 98.
81   *Ibid.*, para. 123.

organisation and delivery of health services and medical care', it concluded that Member States may be required to adjust their national systems of social security on the basis of Treaty provisions or other Community rules and that this does not contravene Article 152 (5) EC.

In my view, the problem with this interpretation of the Court is that the discretion attributed to Member States by Article 152 (5) – now Article 168 (7) – regarding this specific field of social policy completely loses its sense. The adjustments that may be required to adapt a social system to this kind of interpretation of the Treaty and other Community rules may not be so simple or superficial as the Court presupposes. Some changes can have significant practical effects on the organisation and delivery of health services, and this was not discussed by the ECJ. In fact, these adaptations can be more difficult for 'national health systems' than for 'social insurance systems', since the former show a higher degree of institutional misfit to EU obligations than the latter. A simple absorption of EU obligations is not possible for national health systems without changes in their core institutions.[82] Therefore, this idea that adjustments to the health system do not have further implications in the organisation and delivery of services shows 'that the ECJ has not fully understood the sociological component of medical decision-making'.[83]

The cases discussed above were those which settled the principles regarding the relationship between health services and free movement law. In fact, two years after the judgement in *Watts*, the European Commission launched the proposal for a directive on patients' rights[84] that consolidated all of the principles defined by the ECJ, codified now by Directive 2011/24/EU, and which will be analysed in a further section of this chapter. Apart from these cases, the Court has decided during the last 15 years a number of other cases that deal with patient mobility. They are less well-known and do not concern the specific application of free movement law, but they are useful to determine the scope of free movement in relation to Regulation 883/2004. However, discussing all of these would go beyond the scope of this book. Therefore, the option was to summarise these cases in Table 4.1 below, presenting the main issues discussed and the main conclusions of the Court.

A DIFFERENT APPROACH: *COMMISSION V. FRANCE*[85]

More recently the ECJ seems to have taken a different approach in relation to some aspects of cross-border health care. The Court has backtracked on its activist role, moving to a more conservative approach. In October 2010, when judging

---

82   KOSTERA, T. 2008. *Op. cit.*, p. 29.
83   NEWDICK, C. 2008. *Op. cit.*, p. 862.
84   COMMISSION OF THE EUROPEAN COMMUNITIES 2008a. Proposal for a directive of the European parliament and of the Council on the application of patients' rights in cross-border healthcare. 2008/0142 (COD).
85   Case C-512/08, *Commission v France* [2010] ECR I – 08833.

Table 4.1 Other cases concerning patient mobility and the coordination of social security schemes

Case and year of judgement	Summary of the relevant facts	ECJ's main conclusions
Vanbraekel C-368/98 (2001)	Amount to be paid to a Belgian national of hospital treatment costs incurred in France.	When prior authorisation is granted based on Regulation 1408/71, the person is entitled to be reimbursed by an amount equivalent to that which would have been borne by the institution of the place of treatment and if this amount is less than the one which is applicable in the Member State of affiliation, additional reimbursement covering that difference must be granted to the insured person by the competent institution.
Inizan C-56/01 (2003)	French insured person who had a refusal from a French insurer to reimburse the cost of hospital treatment that the claimant intended to undergo in Germany.	Prior authorisation under Article 22 of Regulation 1408/71 may not be refused where it is apparent, first, that the treatment in question is among the benefits provided for by the legislation of the Member State of residence, and, second, that treatment cannot be obtained without undue delay in that Member State. Articles 49 EC and 50 EC do not preclude legislation of a Member State that makes reimbursement of the cost of cross-border hospital care conditional upon prior authorisation and makes the grant of that authorisation subject to the condition that appropriate treatment could not be received within the territory of the Member State of residence. However, authorisation may be refused on that ground only if treatment, which is the same or equally effective for the patient, can be obtained without undue delay in the Member State of residence.
Van der Duin C-156/01 (2003)	Dutch citizen resident in France, but entitled to Dutch pension benefits, who wished to receive medical treatment in the Netherlands.	The requirement of prior authorisation (Article 22 of Regulation 1408/71) applies to pensioners and members of their families who reside in a Member State other than the one which is liable for payment of that pension when those socially insured persons wish to go to the Member State liable for payment of the pension in order to receive medical treatment there. In such a situation, the institution competent to issue prior authorisation and responsible for the costs of the medical treatment concerned is the one of the place of residence.
Leichtle C-8/02 (2004)	German insured person who had a refusal from his sickness insurance fund to reimburse expenditure on board, lodging, travel, visitors' tax and a final medical report connected with a health cure to be taken in Italy.	Articles 49 EC and 50 EC preclude legislation of a Member State that makes reimbursement of expenditure in connection with a health cure taken in another Member State conditional on obtaining prior recognition of eligibility that the proposed cure is absolutely necessary owing to the greatly increased prospects of success in that other Member State. Articles 49 EC and 50 EC do not in principle preclude rules of a Member State that makes reimbursement of expenditure in connection with a health cure taken in another Member State conditional on the fact that the SPA in question is listed in the Register of Health Spas. However, it was left for the national court to ensure if the use of this list was discriminatory.

Table 4.1 continued

Case and year of judgement	Summary of the relevant facts	ECJ's main conclusions
Keller C-145/03 (2005)	Spanish insured person who had a refusal from her Spanish health insurer to reimburse the costs of hospital treatment received in a hospital in Switzerland, since prior authorisation was first given to treatment to be taken in Germany.	Where prior authorisation is given under Article 22 of Regulation 1408/71, it is up to the Member State of treatment to decide whether it is necessary to transfer the patient to a hospital in another State to take a superior treatment even if that State is a non-member country of the EU. In such a situation, the cost of the treatment is initially borne by the Member State of treatment and must be subsequently reimbursed by the competent institution of the Member State of affiliation if it is within the list of benefits covered by the competent health insurance scheme.
Herrera C-466/04 (2006)	Refusal of the public health service of the Autonomous Community of Cantabria to pay the travel, accommodation and subsistence costs incurred by a Spanish resident for hospital treatment received in France, and the costs incurred by a member of his family who accompanied him.	Authorisation given under Article 22 of Regulation 1408/71 by the competent institution for an insured person to go to another Member State in order to receive hospital treatment appropriate to his medical condition does not confer on such a person the right to be reimbursed by the competent institution for the costs of travel, accommodation and subsistence, which that person and any person accompanying him incurred in the territory of the Member State of treatment, with the exception of the costs of accommodation and meals in hospital for the insured person himself. However, Article 56 TFEU confers the possibility of reimbursement of such costs, provided that similar costs would have been reimbursed if treatment was undergone in the Member State of affiliation.
Stamatelaki C-444/05 (2007)	Greek insured and resident person who wished to obtain the reimbursement of costs incurred in a private hospital in the United Kingdom.	Article 49 EC precludes legislation of a Member State which excludes all reimbursement by a national social security institution of the costs occasioned by treatment of persons insured with it in private hospitals in another Member State.

Case	Facts	Ruling
Chamier-Glisczinski C-208/07 (2009)	German citizen, resident in Austria, who had a refusal from the German employee sickness insurance fund to pay certain costs relating to care received in a specialised establishment of long-term care in Austria, where such type of care was not covered.	Where, unlike the social security system of the Member State of affiliation, that of the Member State of residence of a person reliant on care, insured as a member of the family of an employed or self-employed person, does not provide for the provision of benefits in kind in situations of reliance on care, Articles 19 or 22(1)(b) of Regulation 1408/71 do not require the provision of such benefits outside the competent State by or on behalf of the competent institution. Moreover, if the Member State of residence does not confer the provision of benefits in kind in given situations of reliance on care, Regulation 1408/71 does not preclude the possibility of the Member State of affiliation to cover the costs linked to a stay in a care home situated in the Member State of residence up to an amount equal to the benefits to which that person would have been entitled if he had received the same care in a care home – party to a service agreement – situated in the Member State of affiliation.
Elchinov C-173/09 (2010)	Bulgarian insured person who had a refusal from his health insurer to reimburse the costs of hospital treatment received in Germany.	Articles 49 EC and 22 of Regulation 1408/71 preclude a rule of a Member State which is interpreted as excluding, in all cases, payment for hospital treatment given in another Member State without prior authorisation. With regard to medical treatment that cannot be given in the Member State where the patient resides and is insured, Article 22 of Regulation 1408/71 must be interpreted as meaning that the authorisation required under this Article cannot be refused: (1) if, where the list of benefits for which the national legislation provides does not expressly and precisely specify the treatment method applied but defines types of treatment reimbursed by the competent institution, it is established that the treatment method in question corresponds to types of treatment included in that list, and (2) if no alternative treatment which is equally effective can be given without undue delay in the Member State where the patient resides and is insured. Moreover, with regards to reimbursement, the amount is equal to that determined in the Member State of treatment. If that amount is less than the one applicable in the Member State of residence, complementary reimbursement corresponding to the difference between those two amounts must in addition be paid.
Petru C-268/13 (2014)	Romanian insured and resident person who wished to obtain the reimbursement of costs incurred with open heart surgery received in Germany.	Authorisation necessary under Article 22 of Regulation 1408/71 cannot be refused where it is because of a lack of medication, basic medical supplies and infrastructure that the hospital care concerned cannot be provided in good time in the insured person's Member State of residence. The question of whether that is impossible must be determined by reference to all the hospital establishments in that Member State that are capable of providing the treatment in question and by reference to the period within which the treatment could be obtained in good time.

the case *Commission v. France*, the Court presented a different view about cross-border health care. It concerned an action brought by the European Commission against France under Article 226 EC for failure to fulfil obligations regarding cross-border health care, which constituted infringements of Article 49 EC and of the Court's previous rulings on this subject. The action was preceded by letters sent by the Commission to the French Republic alleging that Article R. 332–4 of the French Social Security Code was incompatible with Article 49 EC. This allegation was based on three specific complaints: first, the requirement of prior authorisation for reimbursement of certain non-hospital treatments which use major medical equipment; second, the lack of any provision requiring acknowledgement of receipt to be sent to persons seeking prior authorisation of payment for hospital treatment given in another Member State; and third, the lack of any provision enabling a person insured under the French system to receive an additional reimbursement in the circumstances laid down in paragraph 53 of *Vanbraekel and Others*.[86] The Commission then communicated to the French Republic that it was withdrawing the second complaint. Therefore, the action was brought based on the first and third complaints. The Court dismissed the action in its entirety, rejecting both claims. With regard to the first, which is of more importance for the present discussion, the Court concluded that the prior authorisation required by the legislation of the French Republic for treatment planned in another Member State and involving the use of major medical equipment outside hospital infrastructures constituted a restriction of the freedom to provide services for both persons insured under the French system and the providers of those services.[87] However, the ECJ then decided that the prior authorisation in the case of treatments using major medical equipment was a justified restriction under EU law because:

> If persons insured under the French system could, freely and in any circumstances, obtain at the expense of the competent institution, from service providers established in other Member States, treatment involving the use of major medical equipment corresponding to that listed exhaustively in the Public Health Code, the planning endeavours of the national authorities and the financial balance of the supply of up-to-date treatment would as a result be jeopardised.[88]

In its reasoning the Court explained that the use of these types of medical equipment created important considerations relating to planning requirements:

> with particular regard to quantity and geographical distribution, in order to help ensure throughout national territory a rationalised, stable, balanced and

---

86   *Ibid.*, para. 10.
87   *Ibid.*, para. 32.
88   *Ibid.*, para. 40.

accessible supply of up-to-date treatment, and also to avoid, so far as possible, any waste of financial, technical and human resources.[89]

In effect, Advocate General Sharpston in her opinion seems to understand clearly the importance of prior authorisation for the health planning strategy, including the allocation of resources. As she explains:

As I understand it, prior authorisation is not being used in this instance solely as a tool to regulate patient migration, although that may be part of its function. Rather, its core purpose seems to be one that is fundamental to health care strategy. It is to enable the competent authorities to plan how to use their available resources to finance health services at the initial stage where resources, demographics, infrastructure, the deployment of equipment and personnel are assessed. Thus, the prior authorisation procedure enables the French authorities better to address the general question of allocating resources to the health service, as well as to manage a particular aspect of that service (namely, the effects of patient migrant on the financial sustainability of the health and social security system).

The overriding considerations capable of justifying a restriction like a requirement of prior authorisation are based on the need for national authorities to plan the use of their resources for social security and health care in order to attain a high level of public health protection. It is that that is crucial to the assessment of whether prior authorisation is justified, rather than whether the treatment using major medical equipment is provided inside or outside a hospital.[90]

In relation to the other claim, the Court decided that the Commission had not established that the French legal order brought about a situation capable of depriving persons insured under the French system of the right to an additional reimbursement as decided in *Vanbraekel and Others*.[91]

This case shows a different approach from the Court in relation to cross-border health care and the use of authorisation. It is the first time that the Court had analysed in more detail the importance of planning for health care strategy and the use of prior authorisation in this context. There are some possible explanations for this different approach. First, as Advocate General Sharpstone explained, in her opinion 'the Court has not yet considered the equivalent issues in relation to medical services provided outside a hospital setting ('non-hospital medical services)'.[92] Another explanation is the fact that the case concerns an infringement action and, as distinct from the cases stated above, does not deal directly with the

89 *Ibid.*, para. 37.
90 Opinion of Advocate General Sharpston in Case C-512/08, paras 65 and 66.
91 Case C-512/08, para. 69.
92 Opinion of Advocate General Sharpston in Case C-512/08, para. 61.

actual situation of an individual patient searching for medical treatment. It is my opinion that judges tend to be more sensitive when dealing with real situations that involve individuals' lives and their state of health. A third explanation is the fact that this case was judged after the entry into force of the Lisbon Treaty, which established a compromise between market and non-market values by including in the foundational provisions of the Treaty on European Union (TEU) wording that indirectly refers to welfare, attempting to rebalance these values.[93] Accordingly, the view taken by the Court aimed at protecting the organisation and financial balance of the health system and can be seen as a way to protect welfare services from market forces, in this case the Internal Market rules. In effect, since the entry into force of the Lisbon Treaty and the reaching of an agreement for a final text of the Directive on Patients' Rights, the Court has been taking into account and explicitly recognising important aspects of EU health systems. For example, in *Commission v. Spain*,[94] which concerned scheduled treatment and the failure of Spain to fulfil its obligations under Article 49 EC, the Court takes into account national arrangements regarding the regulation of social security schemes, asserting that disregarding these arrangements 'would ultimately undermine the very fabric of the system which Regulation No 1408/71 sought to establish'.[95]

In this regard, the possibility raised by Hatzopoulos and Hervey is that

> the Court acts as a 'broker', arousing the EU legislature and/or curbing member states' resistance. Once, however, the member states and the EU political institutions have come to grips with the issue raised by the Court, and have reached a clear position, the Court readily steps down from its proactive stance and aligns its own position with that of the political institutions. The revolution is over.[96]

The analysis provided in this section was of a descriptive nature. A more critical analysis of the ECJ's reasoning will be carried out in Chapter 6, where this will be linked to the possible impact of the EU approach to health services on the principles that govern national EU health systems.

Services of General Interest (SGI) and rules on competition applying to undertakings

Having analysed the relationship between health services and the Internal Market, the next step is to analyse the relationship between these services and other policy

93 DAMJANOVIC, D. & WITTE, B.D. 2008. Welfare Integration through EU Law: The Overall Picture in the Light of the Lisbon Treaty *EUI Working Papers LAW N. 2008/34*. Available at http://ssrn.com/abstract=1326827 or http://dx.doi.org/10.2139/ssrn.1326827 [Accessed 14 December 2015].
94 Case C-211/08, *Commission v Spain* [2010] ECR I-5267.
95 *Ibid.*, para. 79.
96 HATZOPOULOS, V. & HERVEY, T. 2013. Coming into line: the EU's Court softens on cross-border health care. *Health Economics, Policy and Law*, 8: 1–5.

areas governed by the Treaty. Another policy area which intersects with health services is that of SGI. Indeed, as will be shown, health care intersects not only with SGI, it is also part of these services. As Erika Szyszczak states: 'Health care is closely linked to social services and social protection in the EU Member States and viewed as part of the services provided in the [national] general interest'.[97] In this context, however, the issues do not concern recipients of health services, as in the case of free movement, but providers of health services. Taking this into consideration, in this section I will provide an overview of the relationship between health services and SGI. Then, I will analyse the Treaty rules and some case law of the ECJ concerning providers of health services.

HEALTH SERVICES AND SGI: A BRIEF HISTORICAL OVERVIEW

The reality of SGI includes both general economic and non-economic interest services, covering a broad range of types of activity, from the large network industries to health, education and social services.[98] The concept is related to the term public service, but they are not always identical since the legal traditions concerning public services are quite different in each Member State. Nor is there a precise definition of services of general interest. According to the Green Paper, 'terminological differences, semantic confusion and different traditions in the Member States have led to many misunderstandings in the discussion at European level'.[99] The fact that the European Treaties do not provide a definition of services of general interest makes the situation even more confusing. Therefore, SGI is a very broad and vague concept that only becomes more concrete when one looks at its content; it is broader than the definition of services of general economic interest (SGEI) – provided for in Article 14 and 106 TFEU, in the Services Directive[100] and in Article 36 of the Charter of Fundamental Rights – and covers both market and non-market services classed by the public authorities as being of general interest and subject to specific obligations.[101] According to the Commission, universality, transparency, continuity and accessibility are elements that can be used as a traditional criterion to determine the general interest of a service.

Services of general economic interest are, on the other hand, more concrete since they are expressly mentioned in EU law documents. Although none of these legal texts provides for a definition of SGEI, from the text of the Services Directive, as well as the Commission's documents, it may be understood that SGEI consist of services provided by the large network industries, such as the postal sector, the electricity sector, the gas sector, water distribution and supply services, and the

---

97 SZYSZCZAK, E. 2011. *Op. cit.*, p. 106.
98 COMMISSION OF THE EUROPEAN COMMUNITIES 2003. Green paper on services of general interest. *COM (2003) 270*.
99 *Ibid.*, p. 6.
100 EUROPEAN PARLIAMENT AND COUNCIL OF THE EUROPEAN UNION 2006. Directive 2006/123/EC on services in the internal market.
101 *Ibid.*, p. 7.

treatment of waste.[102] Nonetheless, the concept is a fluid one and the lists provided in those documents are just examples. Considering that economic activities are those that consist in offering a good in a certain market, the concept will also be applied to other sectors where economic activities are developed.[103] It is possible to say, thus, that neither the examples provided in EU legal documents, nor the concept of economic activity, are enough to define services of general economic interest. Therefore, once more, what really makes the concept less fluid and more coherent are the common elements applicable to these services, namely: universal service, continuity, quality of service, affordability, as well as user and consumer protection.[104]

The other subgroup included in services of general interest consists of the so-called non-economic services of general interest. This can be viewed as a 'younger' concept than services of general economic interest. In the Green Paper, non-economic services are addressed as being those which are prerogatives of the State, such as national education and compulsory basic social security schemes. However, the Commission makes clear that there is an evolving and dynamic character in the distinction between economic and non-economic services and that in recent decades more and more services have become of economic relevance.[105] In the White Paper,[106] however, the term 'non-economic services' is no longer used, being substituted by the term 'social services of general interest', which includes both social and health services of general interest. The same notion of flexibility and evolution applicable to services of non-economic interest applies to social services and, thus, their content is not static, changing according to social and technological evolution.

In 2006, as a follow-up to the White Paper, the Commission put forward a document dealing specifically with social services of general interest.[107] Although listing two categories of social services, the communication does not cover health services, which could apparently mean that, in the view of the Commission, health services are not included in the subgroup of social services of general interest.[108]

102 NEERGAARD, U.B. 2008. Services of General (Economic) Interest and the Services Directive – What is left out, why and where to go? *In:* NEERGAARD, U.B., NIELSEN, R. & ROSEBERRY, L.M. (eds) *The Services Directive: consequences for the welfare state and the European social model.* Copenhagen: DJØF, p. 77.

103 COLLECTIF SSIG-FR. 2006. *Les services sociaux et de santé d'intérêt général: droits fondamentaux versus marché intérieur? Une contribution au débat communautaire,* Brussels: Bruylant, p. 17.

104 COMMISSION OF THE EUROPEAN COMMUNITIES 2003. Green paper on services of general interest. *COM (2003) 270.* P. 15.

105 *Ibid.,* p.14.

106 COMMISSION OF THE EUROPEAN COMMUNITIES 2004b. White Paper on services of general interest. *COM (2004) 374.*

107 COMMISSION OF THE EUROPEAN COMMUNITIES 2006b. Implementing the Community Lisbon programme. Social services of general interest in the European Union. *COM (2006) 177.*

108 NEERGAARD, U.B. 2009. Services of General Economic Interest: the Nature of the Beast. *In:* KRAJEWSKI, M., NEERGAARD, U.B. & VAN DE GRONDEN, J. (eds) *The changing legal framework for services of general interest in Europe: between competition and solidarity.* The Hague: T.M.C. Asser.

Following the communication on social services of general interest and after the exclusion of health services provisions from the Services Directive,[109] again in 2006, the Commission launched a consultation regarding health services.[110] In this document, the Commission states the need 'to develop a systematic approach in order to identify and recognize the specific characteristics of social and health services of general interest and to clarify the framework in which they operate'.[111] In effect, the consultation on health services, together with the case law of the ECJ on patient mobility, were the background foundations for the proposal for a Directive on patients' rights, which attributes an economic approach to health services, submitting them to the free movement rules.

The idea that health services are non-economic activities or purely social has been changing since the 1980s, when most Member States adopted health reforms, as explained in the first chapter of this book. The introduction of market elements in the provision of health services associated with the diversity of services that integrate the health sector creates a high level of uncertainty in this area. Health services are, thus, a special group of services of general interest that have to be addressed on a case-by-case basis, because only a concrete evaluation of the activities involved in the health sector makes it possible to determine whether they belong to the services group of economic, non-economic or social, or even to a third group of services of general interest referred to by some authors as being a grey area.[112]

Although the Commission has already recognised that health services have undergone a modernisation process that requires more clarity and predictability at the EU level in order to ensure a smooth evolution of these services and to assist Member States that already use market-based systems to deliver social and health services,[113] insofar as it is possible to make a conclusion, the relationship between health services and services of general interest seems still to be dominated by legal uncertainty. This is so also because the central concepts – services of economic and non-economic interest – are themselves not well-defined. In this regard, Sauter, for instance, proposes that it makes sense to leave open the definition of services of general economic interest because the EC Treaty gives the Member States considerable freedom to define missions and to establish the organisational principles of these services.[114] However, more clarity in this field is important and

---

109 One of the main criticisms concerning the inclusion of health services in the services directive was that the core concept of the proposal was a simple relationship between a consumer and a provider and health services, however, form part of a complex system, also involving a third party, which pays the majority of the bill. BAETEN, R. 2005. The potential impact of the services directive on health services. *In:* NIHOUL, P. & SIMON, A.-C. (eds) *L'Europe et les soins de santé: marché intérieur, sécurité sociale, concurrence.* Brussels: Larcier.

110 COMMISSION OF THE EUROPEAN COMMUNITIES 2006a. Communication from the Commission. Consultation regarding community action on health services. SEC (2006) 1195/4.

111 *Ibid.,* p. 2.

112 NEERGAARD, U.B. 2008. *Op. cit.,* p. 91.

113 COMMISSION OF THE EUROPEAN COMMUNITIES 2004b. White Paper on services of general interest. *COM (2004) 374,* p. 16.

114 SAUTER, W. 2008. Services of General economic Interest and Universal Service in EU Law. *Services of general economic interest in the single market: what a role for Europe?* Conference held in the European University Institute: Robert Schuman Centre for Advanced Studies.

desirable since the legal consequences vary considerably depending on which concept – economic or non-economic interest – is involved, even in terms of competences.[115]

Therefore, there is still a lack of clarity in this specific area and it is not an easy task to categorise health services as economic, non-economic or a purely social activity. This becomes even harder considering that health activities can be mixed in nature and that Member States and EU institutions might have different perceptions about the provision of health services. In this regard, Hatzopoulos argues that Member States

> are not running mere services (health care, educational, etc.), but systems. The shift of attention from systems (at national level) to services (at the EU level) without any effort to integrate the latter into the former may prove a powerful means of deconstructing national systems. By itself this is not a catastrophic consequence, as long as the faltering national systems are gradually replaced by a supra- or infra-national framework for the provision of well-articulated services of general interest. But will such a replacement take place?[116]

This shows that the borderline between economic and non-economic services in the health field is at the moment blurred, risky and uncertain.[117] However, a correct categorisation of health services is both desirable and necessary, even on a case-by-case analysis, because when they operate as a social or welfare activity they relate to a set of specific objectives, such as solidarity, social and territorial cohesion, non-discrimination, the attainment of fundamental rights (right to health and social inclusion), prevention against social exclusion, and fighting against vulnerability.[118] Moreover, health services have some particularities, for example, in the way they are provided and financed, which certainly make them different from other SGI such as energy, postal and transportation services. Governments still regulate and subsidise the health care sector, and in many Member States insurance for medical care is mandatory and health care facilities are provided by State institutions.[119]

In this regard, it is important to note that even with the health reforms undertaken by most EU health systems and the introduction of market mechanisms in the health sector, the outcomes resulting from these reforms have not changed the nature of the welfare state and have not implied the loss of social rights or the diminution of the universal social protection guaranteed by EU health systems.[120] Health policy continues to be made at the national level, accompanied by tight

---

115 NEERGAARD, U.B. 2008. *Op. cit.*, p. 94.
116 HATZOPOULOS, V. 2012. *Regulating services in the European Union.* Oxford: Oxford University Press [Electronic version], p. 55.
117 NEERGAARD, U.B. 2009. *Op. cit.*, p. 39.
118 COLLECTIF SSIG-FR. 2006. *Op.cit.*, p. 21.
119 VAN DER MEI, A.P. 2003. *Op. cit.*, p. 223.
120 ESPING-ANDERSEN, G. 1999. *Op. cit.*

aggregate expenditure, and strong government control still prevails in all instances of the health system – financing, organisation and delivery.[121]Therefore, it is possible to argue that EU health systems remain under government domination and focused on the goal of solidarity and universal access, even if entrepreneurial activities are accepted or encouraged.

Accordingly, an incorrect categorisation of health services and the application of a purely economic approach to this sector might lead to the undesirable outcome of undermining the model of solidarity upon which European welfare states were established. In effect, the entry into force of the Lisbon Treaty offers a new and clearer framework to health services, especially in a national context. Apart from the general attempt made in the Treaty to overcome the decoupling of the EU economic agenda from national social market traditions,[122] what can be seen in the wording of the Treaty on European Union by the reference to a 'highly competitive social market economy' (Article 3 (3) TEU),[123] in the area of SGI, Protocol n. 26 can bring new hope for a more consistent approach in relation to health services.

In this vein, there are five points in the Protocol which, in my opinion, are important in the field of health services insofar as they can provide new elements and concepts which could be used in the construction of a clearer framework for health services. The first point is that for the first time the term 'SGI' is mentioned in a Treaty. Considering that health services can be of either an economic or non-economic nature (or even a mixed one) and that SGI comprise both types of activities, the Protocol is applicable to the whole field of health services. Second, the fact that the Protocol considers SGEI separately from services of non-economic interest (Article 2) can work as a helpful tool for a better categorisation of health services, especially in determining when they are not playing an economic role. Moreover, even when these services are regarded as economic in nature, as for example in the case law on cross-border health care, Article 1 establishes essential values attached to SGEI which can protect them from a purely economic approach and also from the question of competence creep. Thus, in applying this provision to the field of health services, it is possible to reinforce important elements that must be taken into account when dealing with these services. With regard to elements provided for in Article 1, the reference to the essential role and wide discretion of national authorities can be viewed as a reference to the principles of solidarity and subsidiarity. In the field of health services, Article 1 can indeed be regarded as a reinforcement of the discretion of Member States provided for in Article 168 (7) TFEU.

---

121 SALTMAN, R.B. 2002. *Op. cit.*

122 NEERGAARD, U.B., NIELSEN, R. & ROSEBERRY, L.M. 2009. *Integrating welfare functions into EU law: from Rome to Lisbon.* Copenhagen: DJØF, p. 10.

123 As Neergaard argues, the term 'social market economy' can be seen as an important expression of a compromise 'between the forces aiming for liberalization and the forces aiming at keeping a kind of status quo, which in any case may be viewed as a compromise of the more socially concerned forces'. NEERGAARD, U.B. 2009. *Op. cit.*, p. 48.

Another important element provided for in Article 1 is the reference to diversity. Besides the fact that this expression assumes now a legal status, in the field of health it is essential to recognise the diversity among Member States in the organisation and provision of health services. Apart from the distinction between health insurance systems and national health systems, some Member States allow market forces to work more freely than others within the health services area. For instance, these differences were not fully discussed by the ECJ in the case law on cross-border health care. In my view, if the Court had really taken into consideration the differences existent between EU health systems, it could have arrived at different resolutions in those disputes.

The last relevant point in Article 1 is the reference to the principles of equality and universality. This is extremely important in the field of health, and especially in the EU, because this means that equal access to health care services must be guaranteed to all residents of a Member State. These principles work not only as the basis for the development of health care policies in the EU, but, in effect, can be regarded as a corollary of the principle of solidarity.

Finally, apart from the Protocol on SGI, the entry into force of the Lisbon Treaty brings another helpful instrument into the area of health services and SGI. The Charter of Fundamental Rights, which now has a binding effect and is considered as having the same legal value as the Treaties, recognises in its Articles 35 and 36, respectively, the access to health care and to SGEI as fundamental rights. Although it is still too early to know how the EU institutions will make use of it, the simple recognition of these services as fundamental rights opens the possibility of establishing a new framework in this area. Furthermore, in relation to the nature of health services, the Charter also brings an important contribution by giving a clear indication that the Charter's drafters did not consider health care (nor social security and social assistance) to be economic and, hence, to qualify as SGEIs under Article 36, since those services are protected by a different provision (Article 35).[124]

It is therefore possible to argue that the elements introduced by the new Protocol provide the possibility of giving a clearer framework when dealing with SGI and especially in the field of health services. This not only permits the application of a more consistent view when looking at the nature of these services (economic or non-economic), but it also works as a shield for those health services that need a high degree of protection. In effect, it could also work, for example, to reinforce the derogations provided for by Article 106 (2) TFEU, which could in turn be read across to provide a derogation from the application of the free movement rules in relation to health care, since the Court seems to grant Member States a wider margin of operation when justifying a SGEI using Article 106 (2).[125]

---

124 HATZOPOULOS, V. 2012. *Op. cit.*, p. 10.
125 SZYSZCZAK, E. 2009. Modernising Healthcare: Pilgrimage for the Holy Grail? *In:* KRAJEWSKI, M., NEERGAARD, U.B. & VAN DE GRONDEN, J. (eds) *The changing legal framework for services of general interest in Europe: between competition and solidarity.* The Hague: T.M.C. Asser, p. 201. This kind of derogation was in fact already recognised by the Court in disputes regarding the application of ex Article 49 EC to other SGEI, such as in Case C-266/96, *Corsica Ferries.*

Considering the changes introduced by Protocol n. 26, the Commission launched a Communication entitled 'A Quality Framework for Services of General Interest in Europe', in which it explains the changes it already adopted in relation to health services. With regard to state aids, for example, the document explains that a larger number of social services in the future will likely be exempted from the *ex ante* notification and assessment process by the Commission, irrespective of the amount of compensation, if they fulfil some basic conditions of transparency, correct definition and absence of overcompensation. They include, in addition to hospitals and social housing, services of general economic interest meeting social needs as regards health and long-term care, childcare, access to and reintegration into the labour market, and the care and social inclusion of vulnerable groups.[126] Likewise, the document also provides for special treatment for social and health services in the area of public procurement and concessions. It states that these services will be 'subject to a lighter regime which takes into account their specific role and characteristics. They will be subject to higher thresholds and will have to comply only with transparency and equal treatment obligations'.[127]

After this brief overview about the relationship between health services and SGI, in the next section I will analyse the Treaty provisions that might apply to providers of health services in the context of SGI.

HEALTH SERVICES, SGI AND THE PROVISIONS ON COMPETITION LAW

The Treaty provisions of competition law are considered an essential tool to ensure that undertakings compete on a level playing field throughout the EU. It 'endeavours to make markets open to all firms that should have the opportunity to attract business based on factors such as price and quality, rather than unfair market distortions'.[128] In relation to health services, in a context where these services are exclusively publicly provided, competition law will normally not be applied. However, the reforms of health systems have brought an increasing presence of market mechanisms in the financing and delivery of services, creating thus a mixed context of markets and solidarity-based provision of health services. Accordingly, competitive health markets create the possibility of application of the Treaty provisions on competition law (Articles 101 and 102 TFEU).

On the other hand, there is the need to protect those services that fulfil basic needs and play a social role from the application of competition law provisions. Those services, as explained before, are included in the definition of SGI. The Treaty provisions that deal specifically with SGEI are Articles 14 and 106 (2) TFEU. The former is a general provision which explains the role and mission of

---

126 COMMISSION OF THE EUROPEAN COMMUNITIES 2011. Communication from the Commission to the European Parliament, the Council, the European Economic and Social Committee and the Committee of the Regions – A Quality Framework for Services of General Interest in Europe. *COM(2011)*, p. 6.

127 *Ibid.*, p. 7.

128 MOSSIALOS, E. & LEAR, J. 2012. Balancing economic freedom against social policy principles: EC competition law and national health systems. *Health Policy*, 106: 127–37.

SGEI within the context of the EU, and defines the rules according to which EU institutions may act in order to establish principles and conditions concerning the provision, commission and funding of SGEI that will enable these services to fulfil their role and mission. In contrast, Article 106 (2) is a provision concerning competition law. It establishes that:

> Undertakings entrusted with the operation of services of general economic interest or having the character of a revenue-producing monopoly shall be subject to the rules contained in the Treaties, in particular to the rules on competition, in so far as the application of such rules does not obstruct the performance, in law or in fact, of the particular tasks assigned to them. The development of trade must not be affected to such an extent as would be contrary to the interests of the Union.

This provision is, therefore, an exception to the application of competition rules to services that have the special nature of general interest. It may be used to justify restrictions on competition caused by some market-correction policies adopted by Member States in specific sectors, as in the case of the health care sector.

Other provisions concerning SGI that may apply to health services are the interpretative clauses provided by Protocol n. 26. Although at this moment it is still difficult to predict what the implications of the Protocol for the field of health services would be, it is possible to state that the Protocol opens the door for a more case-by-case analysis of health services insofar as it addresses the question of national discretion and provides for the situation of non-economic services of general interest, which can be very important in the field of health services.

Furthermore, the other provisions on competition law, namely, Articles 101 and 102, also apply to health services. In fact, it is these Articles that have been more commonly discussed by the ECJ when deciding cases involving the providers of health services. Therefore, in order to provide a clearer view of how the aforementioned provisions are applied in the field of health services, it is important to look at the case law of the ECJ that deals with providers of these services.

COMPETITION LAW AND HEALTH SERVICES: CASES CONCERNING NATIONAL BODIES
MANAGING HEALTH CARE SCHEMES AND THE CONCEPT OF UNDERTAKING

The idea of this section is to analyse the approach applied by the ECJ to cases involving competition law and providers/managers of health care services/schemes. In the field of competition law, the test applied by the Court to determine whether the provisions of the Treaty prohibit a measure, provision or practice within a given health care system basically comprises three stages. First, the Court analyses whether the body in question is an undertaking. This first stage of analysis works as a filter and, *per se*, can remove many measures or provisions of public health care systems from the scope of EU competition law. The second stage aims to determine whether the service works in the general interest. If the answer is affirmative, an exemption from the Treaty provisions may apply. The final stage of the test concerns the proportionality test. Here, the objective is to determine, in the case of a *prima facie* restriction on competition, whether this restriction is justified.[129]

As will be seen in following, although the analysis of the Court in these cases departs from the premise of market competition, the outcomes are usually favourable to the protection of the organisations entrusted with the task of providing health services, be it because they are not considered as undertakings or because the SGEI exception applies, justifying, thus, the anti-competitive mechanism employed to achieve a public interest objective.

The cases that will be used in this section to illustrate the Court's approach are *FENIN*[130] and *AOK*.[131] Although not analysed in detail, other cases such as *Ambulanz Glöckner*[132] and *AG2R Prévoyance*[133] will be also taken into consideration in the analysis. Following that, the comparison between the free movement and the competition case laws regarding health care will concentrate on the application of the principle of solidarity and the nature of health services, i.e. whether they are an economic activity or not.

FENIN   FENIN (Federación Nacional de Empresas de Instrumentación Científica Médica y Dental) is an association of the majority of the undertakings marketing medical goods and equipment to Spanish hospitals. In 1997 it submitted a complaint to the European Commission, under ex Article 82 EC (now Article 102 TFEU), alleging that the organisations that run the Spanish Health System (SNS) were abusing a dominant position in the Spanish market for medical goods and equipment, insofar as they were taking an average of 300 days to pay their debts to members of FENIN, whereas they settled their debts to other suppliers in a more reasonable time.

In August 1999, the Commission absolutely rejected FENIN's complaint[134] on the grounds that the conditions necessary to apply Article 82 EC were not present in this case because the organisations running the SNS were not acting as undertakings when they purchased medical goods and equipment from the members of FENIN, and this condition was necessary for applying this Treaty provision to the case.

FENIN then brought an action before the Court of First Instance (CFI)[135] alleging, amongst other things, that the Commission had erred when assessing the

129   HERVEY, T.K. 2011a. Cooperation between Health Care Authorities in the Proposed Directive on Patients' Rights in Cross-Border Healthcare. *In:* GRONDEN, J.W.V.D., SZYSZCZAK, E., NEERGAARD, U. & KRAJEWSKI, M. (eds) *Health care and EU law*. The Hague: T.M.C. Asser, pp. 188–9.

130   Case C-205/03, *FENIN v Commission* [2006] ECR I-6295.

131   Joined Cases C-264/01, C-306/01, C-354/01 and C-355/01 *AOK Bundesverband and Others* [2004] ECR I-2493.

132   Case C-475/99, *Ambulanz Glöckner* [2001] ECR I-8089.

133   Case C-437/09, *AG2R Prévoyance* [2011] ECR I-00973.

134   Fenin contested the Commission's first rejection to the complaint, which occurred in December 1998.

135   With the entry into force of the Lisbon Treaty, the former Court of First Instance is now called 'General Court'.

application of Articles 82 and 86 EC to the case, inasmuch as it concluded that the organisations running the SNS were not acting as undertakings.

In its reasoning to determine whether the organisations of the SNS were acting as undertakings, the Court began by stating that 'in Community competition law the concept of an undertaking covers any entity engaged in an economic activity, regardless of its legal status and the way in which it is financed'.[136] It then went on to say that it is the activity of offering goods and services in a given market that characterises an economic activity and not the business of purchasing itself.[137]

Accordingly, the Court argued that, when an organisation purchases goods not for the purpose of offering them as part of an economic activity, but to use these goods in the context of a purely social activity, this organisation is not acting as an undertaking. Therefore, in applying these assumptions to the organisations running the SNS, the Court concluded that they do not act as undertakings because they operate according to the principle of solidarity, which means that the SNS is funded from social security contributions and provides universal services free of charge to its members. In this sense, even when purchasing goods, the SNS entities do not operate as undertakings because they do that in order to provide free services to its members and it would be incorrect to dissociate the purchase of goods from this subsequent free provision of health services.[138]

Based on that, the CFI rejected this and the other pleas formulated by FENIN, dismissing its application. In the appeal, the ECJ reached the same conclusions as the CFI and dismissed FENIN's appeal. However, it is worth noting that Advocate General Maduro, although reaching almost the same conclusions as the CFI, developed a different approach from that sustained by the Commission and the CFI in relation to the types of activity performed by the SNS.[139] His reasoning is interesting for the scope of this book because, besides explaining the criteria used by the ECJ in order to categorise an activity as non-economic, he distinguished the economic and non-economic activities that can be developed by the same health provider and drew a parallel with the free movement rules and case law. In this regard, there are three points of his reasoning that deserve to be commented on here.

First, AG Maduro explained that in order to classify a given activity as non-economic the Court 'will look to the nature, the aim and the rules which govern an activity'.[140] In regard to the health sector, he went on to say that competition law can apply to this sector 'in so far as solidarity does not predominate in it'.[141]

---

136 Case C-205/03, *FENIN v Commission* [2006] ECR I-6295. Para. 35.
137 *Ibid.*, para. 36.
138 *Ibid.*, paras 37, 39 and 40.
139 As distinct to what was decided by the Court, AG Maduro proposed that the Court should uphold the second part of FENIN's appeal and refer the case back to the CFI in order to it make the findings necessary to determine whether or not the activities of the SNS were economic in nature. Opinion of Advocate General Maduro in Case C-205/03, *FENIN v Commission* [2006] ECR I-6295, para 57.
140 *Ibid.*, para. 15.
141 *Ibid.*, para. 16.

Accordingly, when the state provides health services pursuing redistributive objectives it is governed by the solidarity principle, which means that this activity does not involve the objective of capitalisation, and therefore competition rules will not apply because the state is not acting as an undertaking. This is even more true when health services are provided free of charge and based on the principle of equity of access, since in this situation there are no market forces involved and the service is guided only by the principle of solidarity.[142] As Cygan points out, '[t]he reasoning of Advocate General Maduro is interesting because it focuses on the role and objectives of the State as a provider of healthcare services and not as a participant in competitive markets'.[143]

Second, he admits, differently from the CFI, that it is essential to dissociate the two activities performed by the SNS, i.e. that of purchasing goods (upstream market activity) from that of providing free health services (downstream activity).[144] This dissociation makes it possible to subject only the economic part of the activity to competition law.[145]

The third point of his reasoning that deserves attention is the parallel he draws with the case law on freedom to provide services when assessing the nature of the provision of free health care services by the SNS. Indeed, he differentiates between the application and the purpose of competition rules from those of free movement rules when determining the nature of health services. He thus explains that the state can prevent the application of competition rules to certain activities, such as the provision of health care services, by organising them predominantly according to the principle of solidarity. In contrast, the organisation of these activities based on the principle of solidarity at the national level makes no difference to the application of free movement rules. Accordingly, he concluded that 'although there is no doubt that the provision of health care free of charge is an economic activity for the purpose of Article 49 EC, it does not necessarily follow that the organisations which carry on that activity are subject to competition law'.[146] In other words, health care can simultaneously be subject to free movement rules but remain outside the reach of competition rules. In relation to free movement rules, the requirement of remuneration is important for the classification of the activity as economic or not, whereas in competition law the focus is on the purpose of the activity.[147]

However, as argued above, the requirement of remuneration is one of the shortcomings of the case law on cross-border health care, because the Court only

---

142 *Ibid.*, paras 27 and 31.
143 CYGAN, A. 2008. Public healthcare in the European Union: still a Service of General Interest? *International and Comparative Law Quarterly*, 57: 529–60.
144 In his view, 'it is essential to consider each activity separately, in order to determine whether it should be classified as an economic activity'. Opinion of Advocate General Maduro in Case C-205/03, *FENIN v Commission* [2006] ECR I-6295, para. 43.
145 *Ibid.*, para. 68.
146 Opinion of Advocate General Maduro in Case C-205/03, *FENIN v Commission* [2006] ECR I-6295, para. 51.
147 CYGAN, A. 2008. *Op. cit.*

takes account of the relationship between the patient and the foreign health care provider, disregarding the fact that from the moment when the patient is reimbursed by his or her health system of affiliation, the element of remuneration disappears and the service becomes free of charge.

Therefore, it is possible to conclude that, according to the AG's reasoning, under competition law the principle of solidarity and the social objectives pursued by the health system do play a role and thus protect health services from the full force of the Treaty rules. However, when free movement rules are at stake, solidarity has no importance, since what matters in this case is the requirement of remuneration rather than the purpose of the activity.

AOK Bundesverband and Others   This competition case concerns references made to the ECJ by German courts raised in actions between German sickness funds and pharmaceutical companies producing medicinal products. The Court had to answer whether the German sickness funds were acting as undertakings for the purpose of ex Article 81 EC (now Article 101 TFEU) when fixing the maximum amounts payable to pharmaceutical companies regarding the cost of medicinal products. The determination of fixed maximum amounts was introduced by the German law on health reform aimed at reducing costs in the health sector. According to this system, an independent body composed of doctors' representatives and representatives of the sickness funds in the German statutory health scheme established the groups of medicinal products for which fixed maximum amounts must be determined.[148] This list of products was then submitted for approval by the Ministry of Health. In a second stage, the sickness fund associations determined the uniform fixed maximum amounts applicable to the medicinal products defined in the list.

In answering the questions referred by the German courts, the ECJ first admitted that the German sickness funds involved in the management of the social security scheme fulfilled an exclusive and non-profit-making social function based on the principle of solidarity.[149] Therefore, according to the Court, the activity of the funds must be regarded as non-economic.

When analysing the specific activity of determining fixed amounts to medicinal products, the Court, even if considering that this could be regarded as an economic activity, also concluded that it did not fall outside the social objectives pursued by the sickness funds and thus in doing that they were not acting as undertakings.[150]

As with *FENIN*, here again the social objectives pursued by the health services provider – grounded on the principle of solidarity – played an important role in determining whether the funds were acting as undertakings or not. Thus, even if the activity could, in principle, be regarded as economic, once part of the social objectives of the health system, it fell outside the application of competition rules.

---

148 Joined Cases C-264/01, C-306/01, C-354/01 and C-355/01 *AOK Bundesverband and Others* [2004] ECR I-2493, para. 13.
149 *Ibid.*, para 51.
150 *Ibid.*, paras 55 and 63.

These two decisions of the ECJ show that the Court is very cautious when applying the Treaty rules on competition to providers of health services. It adopted the concept of solidarity to protect a range of state welfare schemes by finding that the activity is non-economic or social in character. In contrast to the competition case law, the Court adopts a different position when dealing with health services in the context of free movement rules.[151] In the case law regarding patient mobility, i.e. recipients of services, the Court assumes that the provision of health care is economic in character, as seen in previous sections of this book.

Even in competition law cases where the Court determined that the first test was passed, by concluding that the bodies/organisations in question were undertakings in abuse of a dominant position in the respective markets, it was cautious in then applying the proportionality test. This is the situation of two other cases, namely *Ambulanz Glöckner* and *AG2R Prévoyance*. In the former, the issue at stake at national level was the refusal by public authorities to authorise the provision of patient transport services in a certain geographical area of Germany to *Ambulanz Glöckner*, a private firm operating ambulance services. This refusal was based on the fact that the other two aid organisations entrusted with the task of providing public ambulance services were already operating at a loss and the entry of another provider into this market would entail an increase in user charges. The question referred to the ECJ was whether the creation of a monopoly, through the granting of exclusive rights to some medical aid organisations for the provision of public ambulance services over a defined geographical area, was compatible with EU competition law, specifically with what is now Article 106(1) and Articles 101 and 102. In other words, was it an abuse of a dominant position or were the organisations in question undertakings operating a service of general economic interest whose performance would be negatively affected if EU competition law were to apply?[152] The Court concluded that (1) patient transport services constituted an economic activity and, therefore, that the organisations entrusted with the task of providing these services were undertakings;[153] (2) the reservation of patient transport services to certain medical aid organisations entrusted with a public ambulance service was a measure that conferred a special or exclusive right to these organisations;[154] and (3) there was an abuse of a dominant position, because reserving to certain medical aid organisations an ancillary transport activity that could be carried out by independent operators had the effect of limiting markets. Then, the Court applied the proportionality test in order to determine 'whether this restriction of competition was necessary to enable the holder of an exclusive right to perform its task of general interest in economically acceptable conditions'.[155] The conclusion of the ECJ was that the entry into the market of private

151 SZYSZCZAK, E. 2009. *Op. cit.*
152 HERVEY, T.K. 2011a. *Op. cit.*, p. 200.
153 Case C-475/99, *Ambulanz Glöckner* [2001] ECR I-8089, paras 20 and 22.
154 *Ibid.*, para 25.
155 *Ibid.*, para. 57.

operators of patient transport services 'could affect the degree of economic viability of the service provided by the medical aid organisations and, consequently jeopardise the quality and reliability of that service'.[156] Therefore, the measure of barring an authorisation to private operators was justified if the medical aid organisations that occupy a dominant position on the markets in question were in fact able to satisfy demand in the area of emergency ambulance and patient transport services.

In *AG2R Prévoyance* the ECJ reached a similar conclusion. In this case the facts of the dispute concerned the refusal of Beadout Père et Fils SARL – a company in the bakery sector in France – to join the scheme of supplementary health insurance managed by AG2R – the insurance company appointed under a collective agreement by the traditional bakery sector in France to provide supplementary health insurance to this sector's employees. The question the Court was asked to answer was:

> whether a decision by the public authorities to make compulsory, at the request of the organisations representing employers and employees within a given sector of activities, an agreement resulting from collective bargaining which provides for compulsory affiliation to a scheme for supplementary reimbursement of healthcare costs managed by a designated body, without possibility of exemption is compatible with European Union law.[157]

In terms of Treaty provisions, the question submitted to the Court required the interpretation of Articles 101 and 102 TFEU, read together, respectively, with Articles 4(3) EU and 106 TFEU.[158] In this regard, in order to answer the questions posed to it, the ECJ started by deciding whether AG2R Prévoyance was engaged in economic activities when providing the scheme of supplementary health insurance. The Court concluded that, although being non-profit making, pursuing a social objective and, hence, acting on the basis of the principle of solidarity, AG2R was an undertaking and so the Treaty rules were applicable. Then it continued by deciding that AG2R could be regarded as occupying a dominant position in the market since it had a statutory monopoly in a substantial part of the common market.[159] However, the Court then found that the provision of such a scheme of supplementary health insurance could be regarded as an operation of services of general interest and that the exclusive right of that body to manage such a scheme, without there being any possibility of exemption from affiliation, was justified because otherwise it would render the service provided by AG2R less competitive than a comparable service provided by insurance companies not subject to those constraints.[160]

---

156   *Ibid.*, para. 61.
157   Case C-437/09, *AG2R Prévoyance* [2011] ECR I-00973, para. 23.
158   *Ibid.*, para. 27.
159   *Ibid.*, para. 67.
160   *Ibid.*, paras 79 and 80.

ECJ: Free movement v. competition case law   Comparing the approach applied in free movement disputes to that in competition law, it is possible to say that they differ considerably. The provision of a health service free of charge, pursuing redistributive objectives and governed by the solidarity principle, which was decisive with *FENIN* in order to protect health services from the application of the Treaty rules, was disregarded in cross-border health care cases, even if the activity performed by national health systems in this situation was that of the downstream market and, thus, non-economic in nature. The 'generous' view of solidarity adopted in competition cases does not extend to free movement disputes. In fact, as Cygan argues, '[t]he Court's resolution of this dispute can be viewed as unhelpful to Member States because by promoting individual economic rights and citizenship the judgement undermines arguments of social solidarity'.[161] Accordingly, although it has been argued that competition and free movement rules show convergence and are complementary, the case law of the ECJ demonstrates a different reality.[162] For example, the proportionality tests applied by the ECJ in free movement and competition law cases regarding health care services present different versions. That applied to free movement cases is the strong or strict version of the proportionality test; according to this version, 'the Member State must show that the measure constitutes the least restrictive means of protecting the objective of public interest, and that no other imaginable measure could achieve that objective with a lesser detrimental effect on free movement'.[163] Instead, the version of the test applied in competition cases is the milder one, according to which the measure is permissible if it is suitable to achieving the objective in question and is not manifestly disproportionate.[164]

The problem with the application of the strict version of proportionality in cross-border health care cases is that it is almost impossible to meet because it is very difficult for Member States to show that the specific measure or policy, which is just one part of the public health system, can jeopardise the financial viability of the whole system. In fact, in none of the cases on cross-border health care decided by the ECJ were Member States able to meet the test. As Alexander Somek put it:

> the Member States are systematically in a weak position to prove that either an expected mass exodus of clients or the satisfaction of numerous reimbursement requests would affect the viability of established systems in the long run. Consequently, in isolated instances of service provision, it is next to impossible for them to establish that a burden is 'unreasonable', in particular, where the matter is not one of empirical forecast alone but involves an evaluation of the priorities that a system ought to attend to.[165]

161 CYGAN, A. 2008. *Op. cit.*
162 MORTELMANS, K. 2001. Towards convergence in the application of the rules on free movement and on competition? *Common Market Law Review*, 38: 613–49.
163 HERVEY, T.K. 2011a. *Op. cit.*, p. 230.
164 *Ibid.*, p. 201.
165 SOMEK, A. 2007. *Op. cit.*, p. 26.

It seems that the ECJ has considered that the application of EU competition law provisions to the health care sector at the national level can be potentially problematic due to the political sensitivities involved. In fact, competition rules have the potential to weaken, if not destroy, the solidaristic foundations of EU health systems.[166] Apparently, there is no clear explanation for the differing approaches taken by the Court, which clearly demonstrates a lower threshold for the application of EU free movement rules to the health care sector at the national level in comparison to the application of EU competition law rules to this same sector.[167] A possible explanation, as suggested by Krajewski, is that '[c]ompetition law concerns a general principle, which, by its nature as a "general" principle, can accommodate structured exceptions to its application, without its effectiveness being undermined. The free movement of services, on the other hand, is a fundamental individual right, a basic freedom, which would be affected to a greater degree by such exceptions'.[168]

Another explanation is suggested by Neergaard, who argues that:

> The protection through the principle of solidarity may as mentioned be observed to be stronger in the competition law regime, than what may be observed on residing regimes. This may to a certain degree be explained by the circumstance that the competition law regime if coming into force might be considered to be more dominated by market economics and with fewer possibilities of exemptions.[169]

In a similar vein is the argument of Van de Gronden and Sauter, who analyse the issue of how EU institutions deal with competition law and health care, concluding that health care-specific concerns play an important role in cases regarding competition law, especially those which deal with the concept of under-taking, such as AOK and FENIN. Consequently, solidarity plays an important role in the undertaking test developed by the Court, which 'pays due consideration to health-care specific-concerns, as solidarity is one of the constituting elements of health-care policy'.[170]

In my opinion this is the more convincing explanation for the different approaches taken by the ECJ regarding cross-border (free movement) and competition law cases in health care: in the former cases, health care-specific concerns are not taken into consideration, but only Internal Market arguments, whereas in the latter they are crucial for the decisions taken. It seems, therefore, that in free movement cases the economic 'side' of health care, which is seen purely

166 HANCHER, L. & SAUTER, W. 2012. *EU Competition and Internal Market Law in the Healthcare Sector*. Oxford: Oxford University Press, p. 224.

167 *Ibid.*, p. 314.

168 KRAJEWSKI, M. 2007. Non-economic activities in upstream and downstream markets and the scope of competition law after FENIN. *European Law Review*, 32(1): 111–24.

169 NEERGAARD, U. 2011. *Op. cit.*, p. 49.

170 GRONDEN, J.V.D. & SAUTER, W. 2011. Taking the temperature: EU Competition Law and Health Care. *Legal Issues of Economic Integration*, 38(3): 213–41, p. 222.

as an economic activity, is decisive while in competition law this side is neutralised by virtue of solidarity.

In any case, although these theoretical explanations are useful in establishing the differences between the free movement and competition law approaches taken by EU institutions, they do not help in solving the contradictions already present in the reality of health services. Instead, they seem to reflect the same uncertainty and controversy seen since the beginning of the EU regulation of health services in the Commission's documents concerning these services.

Secondary legislation

Legislation on the coordination of social security systems: Regulation 883/2004[171] *(former Regulation 1408/71)*[172]

Patient mobility in the EU can manifest in different ways. First, patients can pay for their care privately, either paying for treatment out of their own pocket or using private health insurance. Second, it can be covered by agreements between insurers and providers in another Member State. Third, care can be covered by Member States' health systems through the use of the EU legal framework that ensures that socially insured patients obtain public cover for care abroad under certain circumstances.[173] This book is concerned with this last form of patient mobility.

For almost 30 years patient mobility was regulated solely by the rules established by the legislation on the coordination of social security schemes: by the framework provided by Regulation 1408/71, which continued its existence as Regulation 883/2004. This scenario, however, has changed over the last two decades as a result of the ECJ case law on patient mobility.

The first piece of legislation enacted on the coordination of social security schemes was Council Regulation n. 3,[174] which came into force just one year after the enforcement of the Treaty of Rome. This Regulation was then replaced by Regulation 1408/71, and since by Regulation 883/2004. Measures in this specific area were not aimed at harmonising the social security systems of Member States but at securing and promoting the freedom of movement of migrant workers by coordinating the relevant provisions at the national level.[175]

---

171 EUROPEAN PARLIAMENT AND THE COUNCIL OF THE EUROPEAN UNION 2004. Regulation (EC) No 883/2004 of the European Parliament and of the Council of 29 April 2004 on the coordination of social security systems. *L 166.*

172 COUNCIL OF THE EUROPEAN COMMUNITIES 1971. Regulation (EEC) No 1408/71 on the application of social security schemes to employed persons and their families moving within the Community *OJ L 149.*

173 FOOTMAN, K., *et al.* 2014. *Op. cit.*

174 COUNCIL OF THE EUROPEAN COMMUNITIES 1958. Regulation (EEC) No 3 on social security for migrant workers. *OJ N. 30.*

175 MEYER, H. 2011. Current legislation on cross-border healthcare in the European Union. Petrie-Flom Annual Conference: The Globalization of Health Care: Legal and Ethical Challenges. Harvard Law School, Petrie-Flom Center for Health Law Policy, Biotechnology, and Bioethics, p. 4.

In general terms, the rules on the coordination of social security systems have from the outset concerned the basic principles of aggregation of periods, equal treatment and the export of benefits. These principles have remained unchanged since Regulation n. 3. However, 'technical details, the procedures and especially the scope of application of the rules have evolved significantly'.[176]

In regard to planned cross-border health care, as seen in a previous section of this chapter, the decisions of the ECJ, based on the Treaty provisions on freedom of goods and services, overruled the procedure established under the legislation on the coordination of social security systems. As a consequence, 'a dual system came into existence: health care for which authorisation was given according to the rules of the Regulation and health care for which no authorisation was given but which had to be reimbursed on the basis of the Treaty'.[177]

Consiering the differences between the procedure established under Regulation 883/2004 and the rules established by the ECJ and incorporated by the Directive on patients' rights, in this section I will describe the main aspects of Regulation 883/2004 in relation to planned cross-border health care in order to identify the aforementioned differences.

Broadly, the system established under Regulation 883/2004 is based on four overarching principles: non-discrimination on grounds of nationality, the principle of apportionment of benefit rights, the exportability of benefits, and the 'single state' rule in terms of affiliation, liability to contribute and benefit entitlement.[178] In terms of its personal scope, the Regulation 'applies to all nationals of a Member State, stateless persons and refugees who are, or have been, subject to the legislation of one or more Member States and to the members of their families and to their survivors'.[179] Moreover, the Regulation also applies to third-country nationals according to the specific circumstances provided by Regulation 859/2003. In terms of its material scope, 'the Regulation concerns all sickness benefits in kind which are covered by statutory benefit schemes'.[180]

With regard to cross-border health care, the Regulation provides for two different situations: that provided for by Article 19, in which care becomes necessary, on medical grounds, during the stay of a person in the territory of another Member State, and that provided for by Article 20, concerning planned care, in which the patient travels to another Member State in order to receive care. In the first case, the patient does not need authorisation from the Member State of affiliation in order to receive care because it is provided for by taking into account the notion of emergency. This mechanism is put in practice through the use of the European health insurance card, which ensures that the person will get the same

---

176 *Ibid.*, p. 5.
177 PENNINGS, F. 2011. The Draft Patient Mobility Directive and the Coordination Regulations of Social Security. *In:* GRONDEN, J.W.V.D., SZYSZCZAK, E., NEERGAARD, U. & KRAJEWSKI, M. (eds) *Health care and EU law.* The Hague: T.M.C. Asser, p. 134.
178 HERVEY, T.K. & MCHALE, J.V. 2004. *Op. cit.,* p. 113.
179 PENNINGS, F. 2011. *Op. cit.,* p. 135.
180 *Ibid.*

access to public sector health care (e.g. a doctor, a pharmacy, a hospital or a health care centre) as a national of the country he or she is visiting.[181]

In the case of planned health care abroad, patients must obtain prior authorisation from their social security scheme. In this regard, it is important to note that the Regulation does not provide for the conditions governing the granting of prior authorisation, but it states only the situations in which the authorisation cannot be refused, namely when the treatment required is provided by the benefits package of the health care system of the patient's Member State of residence, and when the treatment cannot be provided to the patient in his or her Member State of residence within the time normally necessary for obtaining the treatment in question. Therefore, if a person obtains prior authorisation from his or her Member State of affiliation, he or she will normally receive the benefits in kind provided, on behalf of the competent institution, by the institution of the place of stay, i.e. the cost of the treatment is to be borne by the Member State of affiliation, which refunds the institution of the Member State of treatment directly and not the patient.[182]

It is in fact this mechanism of authorisation that has always been used by Union patients to make use of cross-border health care. However, with the case law of the ECJ and now with the entry into force of Directive 2011/24/EU on the application of patients' rights in cross-border healthcare, the mechanism established by Regulation 883/2004 is no longer the only way to obtain cross-border health care, as will be explained in the next section. Table 4.2 shows the differences between the mechanisms used to obtain cross-border health care provided for by Regulation 883/2004 and that established by the case law of the ECJ (and further by Directive 2011/24). The main differences regard the questions of authorisation and reimbursement.

As Erika Szyszczak puts it:

> The conceptual legal right at the EU level of an individual to travel between the Member States of the EU to receive medical care has altered over time. It appeared from an employment-based social security route under Regulation 1408/71/EC to a dual system of access to care under Regulation 1408/71 and an individual economic right (or freedom) to receive services in another Member State using Article 56 TFEU.[183]

Now this right is codified by the Directive on patients' rights, which is the subject of the next section.

---

181 'The European Health Insurance Card makes it easier for people from the European Union's 27 Member States plus Iceland, Liechtenstein, Norway and Switzerland to access healthcare services during temporary visits abroad. So, if you are going on holiday, a business trip or a short break or are heading off to study abroad, remember to make sure that you have obtained a card. It will help save you time, hassle and money if you fall ill or suffer an injury while abroad'. Available at http://ec.europa.eu/social/main.jsp?catId=559&langId=en [Accessed 6 January 2016].
182 PENNINGS, F. 2011. *Op. cit.*, p. 138.
183 SZYSZCZAK, E. 2011. *Op. cit.*, p. 109.

Table 4.2 Patient mobility according to Regulation 883/2004 and according to ECJ case law

	Regulation 1408/71 (and later 883/04)	PLANNED CARE		EMERGENCY CARE
		ECJ case law, applying Article 49		*Regulation 1408/71 (and later 883/04) only*
Prior authorisation for 'hospital care'	Obligatory	May be required by the Member States (MS)		No prior authorisation
Prior authorisation for 'non-hospital care'	Obligatory	Not needed		No prior authorisation
Means of payment	Benefits in kind provided according to the legislation of the MS of treatment (i.e. in some countries free of charge, in some countries out-of-pocket payment may be required). Settlement of costs between the social security institutions of the two countries concerned.	Out-of-pocket payment with subsequent reimbursement from the social security institution of the patient's home MS.		Benefits in kind provided according to the legislation of the MS of treatment. Settlement of costs between the social security institutions of the two countries concerned.
Level of reimbursement	Always the most beneficial level: the MS of treatment or MS of affiliation.	According to the rules of the patient's MS of affiliation. In any event, only actual costs of the treatment are reimbursed (i.e. a patient cannot make a profit)		According to the rules of the MS of treatment.

Source: adapted from the Commission Staff Working Document – Accompanying Document to the Proposal for a Directive of the European Parliament and of the Council on the application of patients' rights in cross-border healthcare – Impact Assessment {COM(2008) 414 final} {SEC(2008) 2164}

Directive 2011/24/EU

The objective of this section is to discuss the most important issues of the Directive on patients' rights (hereinafter 'the Directive'), which, after almost three years of debates in both Parliament and Council, was finally adopted in March 2011. Before analysing the Directive itself, I will give an overview of the background conditions for the adoption of this piece of legislation. Following that, and in order to systematise the work of this section, the issues from the Directive that will be analysed are: (1) the aims and objectives; (2) the legal basis; (3) the question of reimbursement and prior authorisation; (4) the responsibility of the Member State of affiliation and of treatment; and (5) the administrative procedures provided for in the Directive.

BACKGROUND CONDITIONS FOR THE ADOPTION OF THE DIRECTIVE

At first glance, the case law of the ECJ on patient mobility seems to be the main motivation of the Commission for the adoption of the Directive. However, since the 1990s, following the introduction of the first EU legal powers in the field of public health, the EU has been taking a more central role in this field, using different methods of governance such as the Open Method of Coordination.[184] The choice of soft methods of coordination was due to the fact that the EU had (and still has) limited legal competence in the area of health. Accordingly, many EU documents started to be produced, following the introduction of Article 129 EC by the Treaty of Maastricht, as already explained at the beginning of the chapter. Then, following the first judgements of the ECJ on patient mobility, the High Level Committee on Health[185] produced a report to the Commission entitled 'The Internal Market and Health Services' concerning the impact of the *Kholl*, *Decker* and *Smits* and *Peerbooms* cases.[186] This report led to a 'high level reflection process' whose outcome was a document with 19 recommendations, presented by the Commission in December 2003.[187] In February 2004, the Commission

---

184 In this regard, see, for example, HERVEY, T.K. 2002a. *Op. cit.*; HERVEY, T.K. 2008. The European Union's Governance of Health Care and the Welfare Modernization Agenda. *Regulation and Governance*, 2: 103–20; HERVEY, T.K. 2011a. *Op. cit.*

185 The High Level Committee on Health provides advice to the Commission services on matters related to the development of the Community's health strategy. This includes input on initiatives and activities in the public health field as well as on links between public health policy and other health-related policy areas. Moreover, it is a forum for the exchange of information between the Commission services and Member States' authorities. The Committee members are designated by the respective Departments of Health, and candidate country representatives are taking part as observers. EUROPEAN COMMISSION 2001. Report of the High Level Committee on Health 'The Internal Market and Health Services'. Available at http://ec.europa.eu/health/ph_overview/Documents/key06_en.pdf [Accessed 3 December 2015].

186 *Ibid.*

187 EUROPEAN COMMISSION 2003. High level process of reflection on patient mobility and healthcare developments in the European Union. Available at http://ec.europa.eu/health/ph_overview/Documents/key01_mobility_en.pdf [Accessed 3 December 2015].

presented another communication regarding health care as a 'Follow-up to the high level reflection process on patient mobility and healthcare developments in the EU'.[188] At the same time, in the area of SGI other documents referring to health services, such as the Green and White papers, were produced, as explained in the previous section on SGI. In addition, in November 2002, the Citizenship Network also produced the European Charter of Patients' Rights.[189] This increasing production of documents and interest regarding health care culminated in the inclusion of health services in Article 23 of the draft of the Services Directive put forward in March 2004. However, this provision was dropped by the Council and the European Parliament. Following that, other documents regarding health services were prepared by EU institutions. In 2006, the Council adopted a statement of Common Values and Principles in European Union Health Systems,[190] analysed in the previous chapter. At the same time, the Commission prepared a consultation on health services, put forward in the form of a communication.[191] In 2007, the European Parliament adopted a Resolution on Community action on health services.[192] In that same year the Parliament also adopted a report on the impact and consequences of the exclusion of health services from the Services Directive.[193] Finally, in July 2008, the Proposal for a Directive on patients' rights was put forward.[194] As Erika Szyszczak argues, '[t]he fierce resistance to framing health services within an economic liberal agenda did not deter the Commission from proposing a new Directive in patient mobility in 2008'.

In April 2009 the European Parliament voted in favour of the proposal, but made 122 amendments to the text. Following this, a compromise text was discussed but the Council reached political agreement for the adoption of a new text only in May 2010. Following that, the text was remitted to the Parliament for a second reading and finally adopted in March 2011. The Directive contains 23 articles divided over five sections.

188 COMMISSION OF THE EUROPEAN COMMUNITIES 2004a. Communication from the Commission – Follow-up to the high level reflection process on patient mobility and healthcare developments in the European Union. Available at http://eur-lex.europa.eu/LexUriServ/LexUriServ.do?uri=COM:2004:0301:FIN:EN:PDF [Accessed 6 January 2016].
189 Available at www.activecitizenship.net/files/patients_rights/civic_assessment/european_patients_rights_day_report_light.pdf [Accessed 14 December 2015].
190 COUNCIL OF THE EUROPEAN UNION 2006. Council Conclusions on Common values and principles in European Union Health Systems. 2006/C 146/01.
191 COMMISSION OF THE EUROPEAN COMMUNITIES 2006a. Communication from the Commission. Consultation regarding community action on health services. SEC (2006) 1195/4.
192 EUROPEAN PARLIAMENT 2007a. European Parliament resolution of 15 March 2007 on Community action on the provision of cross-border healthcare. B6–0098/2007.
193 EUROPEAN PARLIAMENT 2007c. Report on the impact and consequences of the exclusion of health services from the Directive on services in the internal market, 10 May 2007. A6–0173/2007.
194 COMMISSION OF THE EUROPEAN COMMUNITIES 2008a. Proposal for a directive of the European parliament and of the Council on the application of patients' rights in cross-border healthcare. 2008/0142 (COD).

OBJECTIVES

As established in recitals 8 and 10 and Article 1, the Directive has three main objectives: first, it aims to establish rules for facilitating access to safe and high-quality cross-border health care; second, to ensure patient mobility according to the principles established by the ECJ, by codifying these principles; and third, to promote cooperation on health care among Member States. Moreover, the Directive also intends to clarify the relationship with the existing framework on the coordination of social security systems, especially with Regulation (EC) No 883/2004.[195] As Elisabetta Zanon contends, the underpinning rationale of the Directive 'is that it should be easy as possible for patients to have access to health care abroad, subject to the same conditions that apply to accessing health care at home'.[196]

Regarding the relationship between the TFEU and the Directive, i.e. whether the Directive covers a field or imposes only minimum harmonisation requirements, it is possible to conclude from the wording of Recital 10 and Article 1 that the Directive is a minimum harmonisation measure. The referred recital and provision make clear that the rules established by the Directive aim at facilitating access to health care and fully respect national competencies in organising and delivering health care. This means that it sets 'only a floor of harmonisation, then stricter different national rules, which protect a legitimate public interest, are not pre-empted by it'.[197] As a consequence, there is still the opportunity for Member States to claim that restrictions on cross-border health care are justified. This can be especially important in relation to non-hospital care, which seems to be fully exempted from any systems of prior authorisation, as will be seen below.

THE DIRECTIVE'S LEGAL BASIS

As provided in its recital, Directive 2011/24/EU has two legal bases: Articles 114 and 168 TFEU. Despite these two legal bases, one in the Internal Market and the other in public health, the former is in fact the main basis of the Directive. In fact, this focus on the Internal Market is clearly stated in recital 2, which provides that 'Article 114 TFEU is the appropriate legal basis since the majority of the provisions of this Directive aim to improve the functioning of the internal market and the free movement of goods, persons and services'.

The focus on the Internal Market is demonstrated further in this same recital, when it is stated that 'Union legislation has to rely on this legal basis even when public health protection is a decisive factor in the choices made'. Indeed, the use of the public health provision (Article 168) was justified mostly for the fact that a 'high level of human health protection is to be ensured also when the Union adopts

---

195 See recitals 8 and 10.
196 ZANON, E. 2011. Health care across borders: Implications of the EU Directive on cross-border health care for the English NHS. *Eurohealth*, 17: 34–6.
197 HERVEY, T.K. 2011a. *Op. cit.*, p. 237.

acts under other Treaty provisions' (recital 1), in this case the Internal Market provision. Moreover, Article 114 (3) also requires that a high level of protection is to be taken into account when the adoption of measures concerning health, 'in particular of any new development based on scientific facts'. Accordingly, this book takes the view that it was not the fact that the Directive regulates several issues in the field of health that determined the choice of the public health provision as one of its legal bases, but the general requirement of protecting public health. This was the solution for the Directive encompassing health concerns. Otherwise, this Directive would merely be one concerning the Internal Market.

The fact that the majority of the provisions are aimed at improving the functioning of the Internal Market already signals the rationale of the Directive, i.e. that health care is addressed as an economic service and that all health services are economic in nature. In effect, this is what is mentioned in recital 6, which, recalling the ECJ's judgements on cross-border health care, states that '[. . .] all types of medical care fall within the scope of the TFEU'.

It is important to point out, however, that the Internal Market legal basis was controversial because of 'its explicit linkage to the free movement right of health care services as an economic right but also by subsuming the progress made through soft law and soft governance processes as part of the functioning of the Internal Market'.[198] During the procedure for the adoption of the Directive, the legal basis was severely criticised by interest groups. For this reason, the Committee of Regions supported the use of a joint legal basis, combining Article 114 and Article 168 TFEU, which was, in the end, adopted. Nevertheless, as will be seen, many objectives of the Directive are incompatible with the prohibition of harmonisation provided by Article 168. Even though in theory the Directive states that it fully respects 'the responsibilities of Member States for the definition of social security benefits relating to health and for the organisation and delivery of healthcare' (recital 10), it seems almost impossible to establish rules for facilitating access to cross-border health care (recital 10) without interfering with Member States' policies regarding the delivery of health services. In any case, this conflict can always be resolved through the powers of the Union to regulate the Internal Market. Furthermore, once it is established by law that health services are economic services, there will be always the possibility of recourse to the Internal Market 'solution'.

In effect, it is possible to say that the Directive will have deregulatory effects at the national level, since Member States will have to adapt or change their legislation concerning the delivery of health care services in order to cope with the rules established by Union legislation. For some Member States, these deregulatory effects have already occurred since some countries have amended their legislation to comply with the ECJ's rulings on patient mobility. In this regard, Germany, for example, codified in 2004 the provisions of the ECJ's rulings in its SGB V. Therefore citizens insured by a German sickness fund can consume healthcare

198 SZYSZCZAK, E. 2011. *Op. cit.*, p. 119.

services in other Member States without referring specifically to the Court's rulings, and sickness funds have been allowed to conclude contracts with health care providers in other EU Member States.[199]

The deregulatory effects at the national level were then followed by a re-regulation of health services at the EU level, with the codification – or harmonisation – brought about by the Directive. This process of re-regulation is only possible through the use of the provisions regulating the Internal Market because, as demonstrated, there are limited Union competences to regulate health services from the point of view of welfare services.

REIMBURSEMENT AND PRIOR AUTHORISATION: SUBSTANTIVE OBLIGATIONS UPON THE MEMBER STATE OF AFFILIATION

The general rule regarding reimbursement provided for in Article 7, paragraph 1, of the Directive is that the Member State of affiliation has an obligation to ensure that the costs incurred by individuals with health care provided in another Member State are reimbursed if the type of care provided is among the benefits to which the patient is entitled in the Member State of affiliation. Therefore, according to this rule, prior authorisation is not required in order for a patient to have the costs of treatment in another Member State reimbursed.

Regarding the costs to be reimbursed, paragraph 4 of Article 7 establishes that the Member State of affiliation has the obligation to reimburse up to the level of costs that it would have assumed if the treatment had been provided in its own territory. Furthermore, the cost of treatment should not exceed the actual costs of the treatment. However, the Member State 'has the option, if it so desires to assume further costs, including higher costs of treatment and also travel and accommodation expenses'.[200]

The general rule is that prior authorisation is no longer required in order for a patient to be reimbursed for cross-border healthcare (Article 8 (6)). However, there are exceptions to this rule, contained in Article 8 of the Directive. Therefore, in some situations the Member State of affiliation may require prior authorisation in order to reimburse the health care provided abroad (Article 8, paragraph 2). The first situation in which prior authorisation is justified is when planning requirements are at stake, i.e. when prior authorisation relates to the need for the maintenance of sufficient and permanent access to the health system or when there is a need to contain costs and avoid the waste of financial, technical and human resources. In this regard, Quinn and De Hert recall that:

> As stated in Smits and Peerbooms such prior authorisation may be required as the number of hospitals, their geographic distribution, the way in which

---

199   KOSTERA, T. 2008. *Op. cit.*, p. 22.
200   QUINN, P. & HERT, P.D. 2011. The Patients' Rights Directive (2011/24/EU) – Providing (some) rights to EU residents seeking healthcare in other Member States. *Computer Law & Security Review*, 27: 497–502, p. 500.

they are organised and the facilities they are able to offer are all matters for which a high level planning will be required.[201]

This rule, however, must be combined with one of the two criteria contained in paragraph 2 of Article 8. Accordingly, even when planning requirements are at stake, the treatment subject to prior authorisation must fall into one of these two cases: (1) when the treatment involves overnight hospital accommodation (at least one night) or (2) when it requires the use of highly specialised and cost-intensive medical infrastructure or equipment. The second situation in which prior authorisation is justified is when the treatment presents a risk to the patient or the population (Article 8 (2), b) and, finally, the third situation relates to cases where the treatment gives rise to serious and specific concerns relating to safety and quality, the exception to this rule being those treatments subject to Union legislation ensuring minimum levels of safety and quality (Article 8 (2), c).

Acceptable grounds for refusal of prior authorisation   The Directive not only restricts the situations in which prior authorisation may be required, but it also restricts the situations in which prior authorisation may be refused (Article 8 (6)). Therefore, according to the Directive, the Member State may refuse prior authorisation when the treatment in question: (1) will expose the patient to risk that is not considered acceptable, this risk being attested previously after a clinical evaluation of the patient; (2) will expose the general public with reasonable certainty to a substantial safety hazard; (3) will be provided by a health care provider that raises serious and specific concerns regarding the respect of safety and quality standards and guidelines; and (4) can be provided in the territory of the Member State of affiliation within a time limit that is medically justifiable, taking into account the state of health of the patient and the course of the illness.

RESPONSIBILITIES UPON THE MEMBER STATE OF AFFILIATION: INFORMATIONAL AND PROCEDURAL OBLIGATIONS

Article 5 contains most of the obligations incumbent upon the Member State of affiliation. However, there are other obligations that are contained in other Articles of the Directive, such as Articles 8 and 9. With regard to Article 5, the first obligation regards the compliance with the rules of reimbursement established in the Directive. The second is to provide mechanisms which make available information on rights and entitlements regarding cross-border health care for those patients that wish to receive care abroad. This obligation includes not only the provision of information on the terms and conditions for reimbursement, but also the assurance of available procedures for accessing cross-border health care, including rights of appeal and redress should patients consider that their rights have not been respected. Moreover, a clear distinction must be made between the

201   *Ibid.*, p. 498.

rights arising under the Directive and those arising under Regulation 883/2004.[202] The third obligation concerns the provision of a medical follow-up, when judged necessary, in the same conditions under which a medical follow-up would have been provided had the treatment had been carried out in the territory of the Member State of affiliation. The last obligation provided for in Article 5 is to guarantee that patients who seek or do receive treatment abroad have remote access to, or at least a copy of, the medical records. This obligation should comply with Union rules regarding personal data.

Article 8 (7) also provides for an obligation incumbent upon the Member State of affiliation concerning prior authorisation. According to this Article, the Member State shall make publicly available the types of care that are subject to prior authorisation and relevant information on the system of prior authorisation.

Furthermore, Article 9, which concerns the administrative procedures regarding cross-border health care, establishes the criteria that the Member State shall ensure in regarding these procedures. According to the Article, the procedure must be: (1) based on objective, non-discriminatory criteria that are necessary and proportionate to the objective to be achieved; (2) easily accessible, and information relating to such a procedure must be made publicly available at the appropriate level; and (3) capable of ensuring that requests are dealt with objectively and impartially. Moreover, regarding the administrative procedures, the Member State must set out and make public the reasonable periods of time within which the requests for cross-border health care should be dealt with. For this purpose, the Member State must take into account the specific medical condition, the urgency and individual circumstances (Article 9 (3)).

Article 9 (4) also establishes the criteria that must be followed by decisions on the administrative procedures. These decisions, including those of reimbursement, must be: (1) reasoned; (2) subject, on a case-by-case basis, to review; and (3) capable of being judicially challenged.

RESPONSIBILITIES UPON THE MEMBER STATE OF TREATMENT: INFORMATIONAL AND PROCEDURAL OBLIGATIONS

Article 4 provides not only for the principles governing the treatment received abroad and the rules regarding such treatment, but also for the responsibilities of the Member State of treatment. The general principles regarding health care received abroad are in fact those already stated by the Council Conclusions on Common values and principles in European Union Health Systems and analysed in the previous chapter. These are: universality, good-quality care, equity and solidarity. Concerning the rules governing health care abroad, the first is that the legislation applicable is that of the Member State of treatment; the same applies to the standards and guidelines on quality and safety. Second, with regard to the legislation on safety standards, the Union legislation is applicable (Article 4 (1)).

---

202 *Ibid.*, p. 500.

In relation to the responsibilities, the first is the setting up of National Contact Points for cross-border health care. These bodies must be able to provide information on the standards and guidelines on quality and safety of care, as well as information on the accessibility of hospitals for persons with disabilities (Article 4 (2) 'a'). Article 6 (3) also establishes obligations upon the Member State of treatment regarding national contact points, which include the provision of information on patients' rights, complaints procedures and mechanisms for seeking remedies, according to the legislation of that Member State, as well as the legal and administrative options available to settle disputes, including in the event of harm arising from the treatment received abroad. The second obligation is to ensure that health care providers provide the necessary information: (1) on treatment options, their availability, quality and level of safety in order to help patients to make an informed choice; (2) on prices; (3) on their authorisation or registration status; and (4) on their professional liability, such as insurance cover or other means of personal or collective protection (Article 4 (2) 'b'). The third obligation upon the Member State of treatment is to make available, according to its legislation, transparent complaints procedures and mechanisms that allow patients to seek remedies in the case of harm arising from the treatment received (Article 4 (2) 'c'). The fourth is to ensure that there are systems of professional liability insurance or similar arrangements with regard to the treatment provided on its territory (Article 4 (2) 'd'). The fifth is to ensure that patients have access to their medical records in order to allow the continuity of care. This obligation must be in conformity with the Union rules on the protection of personal data, since the Member State must also ensure the protection of the fundamental right to privacy (Article 4 (2) 'e' and 'f'). In relation to this obligation, Quinn and De Hert highlight that '[a]n important factor in this area will be whether the exception allowed in Article 8 (3) of the Data Protection Directive for the processing of medical data for medical purposes applies'.[203]

Finally, the Member State must also guarantee the application of the principle of non-discrimination in relation to patients coming from other Member States, which also includes the application of the same scale of fees as those charged from national patients in similar health situations. In relation to the non-discrimination principle, the Directive also provides exceptions. Therefore, in the case of overriding reasons of general interest, such as planning requirements necessary for the maintenance of sufficient and permanent access to care within the health system of that Member State, this Member State may adopt necessary and proportionate measures that may somehow violate the principle of non-discrimination (Article 4 (3) and (4)).

Apart from the issues analysed in this section, the Commission was able to include in the Directive novel elements that were neither part of the case law of the ECJ on cross-border health care nor related to patients' rights, though could be linked to patient mobility.[204] This is the case of the system of mutual recognition

203 *Ibid.*
204 *Ibid.*, p. 501.

of prescriptions, European reference networks, cooperation on rare diseases, e-health and cooperation on health technology assessment. Considering that these novelties are not directly related to patient mobility, I will only give an overview of the provisions of the Directive regarding these issues.

In relation to prescriptions, the general rule provided for in Article 11 is that medicinal products authorised to be marketed in the territory of a Member State must have their prescriptions recognised and dispensed in the territory of another Member State in compliance with the national legislation in force in that Member State. The exceptions to this rule are provided by this same article and include (1) restrictions that are non-discriminatory, and necessary and proportional to safeguard human health; and (2) situations in which there are legitimate and justified doubts about the authenticity, content or comprehensibility of an individual prescription.

With regard to European reference networks, according to Article 12, the Commission will support Member States in the development of these networks between health care providers and centres of expertise, especially in the area of rare diseases. As Quinn and De Hert explain, '[t]he idea for European Reference Network is based upon a pilot study aiming to share expertise among clinicians in the treatment of rare diseases'.[205]

Concerning rare diseases, Article 13 also provides for the Commission's support in cooperation among Member States in relation to the development of diagnosis and treatment of these diseases. The idea is to make health professionals, patients and the bodies responsible for the funding of health care aware of the tools and options of diagnosis and treatment of rare diseases.

Finally, Article 14 provides for cooperation on e-health. This cooperation is to be supported by the Union, and aims at exchanging information among Member States and should work in the form of a voluntary network connecting national authorities responsible for e-health.

As already mentioned, the Directive is a codification of the ECJ's case law on patient mobility. It is supposed to facilitate 'access to safe and high-quality cross-border health care in the European Union and to ensure patient mobility throughout Europe'.[206] It can also be viewed as a form of Europeanisation of other health care issues,[207] considering that it gave the European Commission the potential to interfere in the organisation of national health systems.[208]

The deadline for transposition of the Directive by Member States was 25 October 2013. Since then, 26 infringement proceedings have been launched against 26 Member States based on late or incomplete notification of such measures. Although as of 1 July only four of these proceedings have remained

---

205 QUINN, P. & HERT, P.D. 2011. *Op. cit.*, p. 501.
206 MEYER, H. *Op. cit.*, p. 19.
207 SZYSZCZAK, E. 2011.*Op. cit.*, p. 128.
208 HOUDRY, V. 2015. *Op. cit.*, p. 80.

open,[209] the Directive is still in an early stage of implementation and many of its fields of application are not sufficiently mature to be evaluated.

Moreover, the monitoring practices of inbound and outbound patients differ significantly and not all Member States are able to supply reliable data on numbers of cross-border health care referrals.[210] In addition, there are different frameworks within which patient mobility occurs, such as waiver agreements between countries, treatment reimbursed under the social security rules regulations, treatments obtained abroad that are not covered by the home national health system,[211] and most Member States are able to supply only aggregate figures on all types of cross-border health care, which makes it impossible to know the number of referrals specifically under the Directive.

Therefore, this makes problematic any deep analysis of the actual impact of the Directive. For example, in the report under Article 20(3) of Directive 2011/24/EU,[212] adopted by the European Commission in 2014, it was noted that the coming into operation of the Directive could affect the use of social security regulations. In this regard, this report set out in detail the data needed in order to assess this issue. However, until September 2015 these data were unavailable, rendering impossible this analysis by the European Commission.[213]

It was nevertheless possible to evaluate some aspects of the Directive in the study prepared for the Commission in 2015, carried out by a group of experts from KPMG, Technopolis and Empirica GmbH.[214] This group analysed the functioning of the Directive by means of a number of evaluative questions that concentrated on certain issues of the Directive, namely: reimbursement, quality and safety of cross-border health care, and undue delay. I will comment on some of the conclusions of this study in the final chapter of this book, when analysing the impact of the Directive on the principles governing EU health systems.

Therefore, although it is somewhat premature to discuss the impact of the Directive in practice, it is possible to do so from a theoretical point of view. Many works have been produced in this regard, pointing out the opportunity to create an effective framework for cross-border health care issues at EU level and an iterative framework for the modernisation of a social service of general interest.[215] In relation to patients, authors usually highlight the increase in individual

209 EUROPEAN COMMISSION 2015. Report from the Commission to the European Parliament and the Council. Commission report on the operation of Directive 2011/24/EU on the application of patients' rights in cross-border healthcare. COM (2015) 421 final.
210 ZUCCA, G. *et al.* 2015. *Op. cit.*, pp. 14 and 39.
211 FOOTMAN, K. *et al.* 2014. *Op. cit.*, p. 11.
212 EUROPEAN COMISSION 2014. Report from the Commission to the Council and the European Parliament compliant with the obligations foreseen under Article 20(3) of Directive 2011/24/EU of the European Parliament and of the Council of 9 March 2011 on the application of patients' rights in cross-border healthcare. COM/2014/044 final.
213 See n. 563 supra.
214 ZUCCA, G. *et al.* 2015. *Op. cit.*
215 SZYSZCZAK, E. 2011. *Op. cit.*, p. 127.

rights,[216] including safeguards on quality, safety, reliability, redress, continuity and information on healthcare matters.[217] These rights also include the reimbursement of treatment abroad for the larger part of outpatient care without prior authorisation of patients' Member State of affiliation. Another advantage of the Directive that is constantly stressed is patient choice.[218]

However, compared to the older framework for reimbursement of planned cross-border health care provided for by Regulation 883/2004, the Directive offers poorer opportunities for patients. First, it is least beneficial in terms of reimbursement tariffs because under the Directive reimbursement is made according to the tariffs of the patient's home Member State whereas under the Regulation the most beneficial tariff was always guaranteed, i.e. either that of the Member State of treatment or that of the patient's home Member State. Second, under the Directive the patient must in principle pay for treatment abroad upfront whereas under the Regulation, providers abroad were paid through the same mechanism of domestic providers. Moreover, patients have the burden to prove that the treatment undergone abroad complies with the criteria and conditions of reimbursement that apply for care at home, which includes the presentation of invoices and their translations.[219]

Furthermore, other aspects of the Directive are also subject to criticism. For example, it is argued that it affects Member States' autonomy in relation to their health systems and creates an over-reaching EU competence in this area because it makes greater inroads into national regulatory autonomy and moves the ownership of health care away from the state and from a service of general interest within closed boundaries into the EU regulatory field.[220] In addition, the impact of this codification and Europeanisation of health care may in fact violate the principles governing health care throughout the Union, namely universality, equity, solidarity and quality of care. Indeed, some aspects that are seen as an advantage, such as the increase in individual rights, also present the other side of the coin – the reinforcement of patients' rights also has the potential to erode important values behind the provision of health care. This will be analysed in detail in the final chapter.

This book, although supporting the view that the individualist approach taken by the Directive may erode important values of health care and poses risks to national health systems, recognises that the legislature was more coherent with the solidaristic feature of EU health systems than the ECJ. In many ways the Directive represents a step back to the revolutionary and activist approach of the ECJ: it reinstated prior authorisation for most major operations by expanding the concept

216   MEYER, H. 2011. *Op. cit.*
217   SZYSZCZAK, E. 2011.*Op. cit.*, p. 127.
218   BAETEN, R. 2014. Cross-border patient mobility in the European Union: in search of benefits from the new legal framework. *Journal of Health Services Research & Policy*, 19(4): 195–7.
219   *Ibid.*
220   SZYSZCZAK, E. 2011. *Op. cit.*, p. 129.

of 'hospital treatment' to treatments requiring the use of highly specialised and cost-intensive infrastructure, and by creating new situations where authorisation is allowed; it allowed Member States to limit the list of treatments covered; and it excluded top-up payments. The traditional patients' rights, which are connected to a more individualist view of health care rights, were traded off against new types of rights, such as information and quality. [221]

Conclusion

The objective of this chapter was to explain the framework that governs the provision of health services within the EU. This included the analysis of specific rules regarding health services, such as Article 168 TFEU, Regulation 883/2004 and Directive 2011/24/EU, as well as other Treaty provisions pertaining to policy areas intersecting with those of health services, such as the provisions on the Internal Market and those regarding competition law. This analysis was complemented by the use of the ECJ's case law concerning cross-border health care and competition law in order to illustrate the Court's interpretation of the referred Treaty provisions. Moreover, the chapter also provided an explanation of the relationship between health services and SGI, which aimed at showing how the European Commission addresses health services in this context.

221 HATZOPOULOS, V. & HERVEY, T. 2013. *Op. cit.*

5 Insights from Human Rights law and practice[1]

The core elements of the right to access health care services as a human right

Having analysed the situation of health services in the context of EU law, the book moves now to another field of law, namely that of human rights. The objective of this chapter is to provide an overview of how health services are situated within this field of law. This will be done through the analysis of the most important human rights documents concerning health services. Then, I will outline the relationship between the content of these documents and theories of distributive justice, especially the communitarian and individualist views of health care. The idea is to show that a human rights approach to health care is inspired by egalitarian and communitarian theories, supporting, thus, the view taken by this book, i.e. that these theories are the most appropriate to be used as basis for the development of health systems and policies based on the principle of solidarity, as is the case of EU health systems.

Key legal texts at the international level

The notion of a right to health is related to the public health movement that began in the 19th century and to the recognition of a third generation of rights in the 20th century, the so-called social rights. The Constitution of the World Health Organization (WHO) of 1946 was the first international human rights document to formulate the concept of a right to health, stating in its recital that 'the enjoyment of the highest attainable standard of health is one of the fundamental rights of every human being'.[2] The subsequent documents of the United Nations containing a right to health provision were inspired by the WHO definition. Thus, two years later, the Universal Declaration of Human Rights addressed the right to health in its Article 25(I).

---

1 Part of this Chapter was included in a previous work published by the author. BORGES, D.D.C.L. 2011b. Making sense of human rights in the context of European Union health-care policy: individualist and communitarian views. *International Journal of Law in Context*, 7(3): 335–56.
2 WORLD HEALTH ORGANIZATION. Constitution of the World Health Organization. Available at www.who.int/about/mission/en/ [Date accessed 06 January 2016].

However, the first specific clause in an international human rights document with regard to the right to health only appeared in 1966, in Article 12 of the International Covenant on Economic, Social and Cultural Rights (ICESCR).[3] Along the same lines as the ICESCR, the International Convention on the Elimination of All Forms of Discrimination Against Women (CEDAW),[4] in its Article 12, and the Convention on the Rights of the Child (CRC),[5] in its Article 24, also specifically address the right to health in relation to the respective groups protected by the Conventions.

It is, however, the ICESCR that provides the fullest and most definitive conception of the right to health. The provision has a broad scope and is concerned not only with a right to health care services but also with background conditions that affect health. Regarding the right to health care, with which this book is concerned, the provision does not say much. Thus, to understand the content of this provision better, it is necessary to consider the General Comments of the UN Committee on Economic Social and Cultural Rights in order to infuse concrete substance to this right, identifying its elements and related principles.

In 2000, the Committee put forward the General Comment 14,[6] which can be considered the official interpretation of Article 12 of the Covenant. This document addresses several issues concerning the right to health, but especially the content of the right, state obligations, violations and implementation at national level. The text starts by stating that the 'realization of the right to health may be pursued by through numerous, complementary approaches, such as the formulation of health policies, or the implementation of health programmes developed by the WHO, or the adoption of specific legal instruments'. From this introduction it can already be seen that the document is much more concerned with states' duties in terms of the realisation of the right to health, which includes the provision of a range of facilities, services and conditions, than with individuals' entitlements.

Content, principles, entitlements and obligations related to the right to health

In terms of the content of the right to health (Article 12.1), the Comment refers to the right to health as containing both freedoms and entitlements. The issue of

3 UNITED NATIONS (UN). International Covenant on Economic, Social and Cultural Rights 1966. Available at www.ohchr.org/EN/ProfessionalInterest/Pages/CESCR.aspx [Accessed 6 January 2016].
4 UNITED NATIONS (UN). Convention on the Elimination of All Forms of Discrimination against Women (CEDAW) 1979. Available at www.un.org/womenwatch/daw/cedaw/ [Accessed 6 January 2016].
5 UNITED NATIONS (UN). Convention on the Rights of the Child (CRC) 1989. Available at www.ohchr.org/en/professionalinterest/pages/crc.aspx [Accessed 6 January 2016].
6 UNITED NATIONS (UN) COMMITTEE ON ECONOMIC SOCIAL AND CULTURAL RIGHTS – CESCR 2000. Substantive issues arising in the implementation of the International Covenant on Economic, Social and Cultural Rights – General Comment No. 14 (E/C. 12/ 2000/4). Available at http://data.unaids.org/publications/external-documents/ecosoc_cescr-gc 14_en.pdf [Accessed 8 December 2015].

freedoms is related to negative rights pursued by individuals that must be respected by states, such as the right to control one's health and body, including sexual and reproductive freedom, and the right to be free from torture, non-consensual medical treatment and experimentation. Entitlements, by contrast, are related to positive rights, which have an individual as well as a collective dimension. Hence, according to the Comment, Article 12 includes both these dimensions. Collective rights are critical in the field of health because modern public health policy relies heavily on prevention and promotion – which are approaches directed primarily at groups – rather than on curative care, which is directed at the individual. In this regard, the Comment does not address the question of entitlements from the point of view of an individual right, but rather refers to 'the right to a system of health protection which provides equality of opportunity for people to enjoy the highest attainable level of health',[7] which seems to be consonant with the forms of the realisation of this right described at the beginning of the document.

Furthermore, the right to health is interpreted by the Committee as an inclusive right extending not only to timely and appropriate care, but also to the underlying determinants of health, such as access to safe and potable water and adequate sanitation, sufficient supply of safe food, nutrition and housing, healthy occupational and environmental conditions, and access to health-related education and information, including on sexual and reproductive health. The Committee also considers the participation of the population in all health-related decision-making at community, national and international levels as an aspect of the right to health.

Yet in relation to the content of the right to health, this document is very helpful because it states the four fundamental principles related to this right, namely, availability, accessibility, acceptability and quality. The principle of availability means that functioning public health and health care facilities, goods, services and programmes have to be available in sufficient quantity within the state, including safe and potable water and adequate sanitation facilities, hospitals, clinics, trained medical and professional personnel, and essential drugs. According to the document, however, other factors have to be considered when addressing states' obligations regarding this principle, such as the country's condition of development.

The principle of accessibility is divided into four categories or dimensions: non-discrimination, physical accessibility, economic accessibility or affordability, and information accessibility.

The principle of acceptability means that health services must be respectful of medical ethics and culturally appropriate, respecting minorities and sensitive to gender and life cycle requirements.

Finally, the principle of quality means that health facilities, goods and services must be scientifically and medically appropriate and of good quality. According to the Comment, this requires 'skilled medical personnel, scientifically approved

---

7   *Ibid.*, para. 8.

and unexpired drugs and hospital equipment, safe and potable water, and adequate sanitation'.[8]

It is important to note that Article 12.2 provides for some examples regarding the action to be taken by states in the realisation of the right to health care services. In this regard, the General Comment emphasises that equality and non-discrimination are the principles that must guide the provision of health care facilities. Moreover, the document points out that appropriate resource allocation is an important tool to prevent discrimination.[9]

In regard to obligations, the General Comment, although acknowledging the limits of available resources, considers that two main obligations are of immediate direct effect: to guarantee that the right to health will be exercised without discrimination and to take steps towards the full realisation of the right. Furthermore, as with other human rights, the right to health imposes three types or levels of obligation on states parties: the obligation to respect, protect and fulfil. The first is directly related to individuals' freedoms and requires states to refrain from interfering directly or indirectly with the enjoyment of the right to health. The obligation to protect requires states to take measures to prevent third parties from interfering with the guarantees provided for in Article 12. Finally, the obligation to fulfil requires states to adopt, for example, appropriate legislative, administrative, budgetary, judicial and promotional measures towards the realisation of the right to health.

In terms of provision and access to health care services, with which this book is concerned, the obligation to fulfil is the most important. According to the General Comment, the obligation to adopt a national health policy with a detailed plan to realising the right to health falls within the scope of the obligation to fulfil. This includes the provision of a health system which is affordable for all and that provides health care facilities, goods and services on a non-discriminatory and equitable basis.

With regard to violations, and especially violations related to the obligation to fulfil, which is the most important for the provision and access to health care services, some of the examples given by the General Comment are 'the failure to adopt or implement a national health policy designed to ensure the right to health for everyone; insufficient expenditure or misallocation of public resources which results in the non-enjoyment of the right to health by individuals or groups, particularly the vulnerable or marginalized [. . .]'.[10]

Finally, in relation to the implementation of the right to health, the basic tool referred to by the Comment is the adoption of a framework legislation containing national policies and strategies to ensure to all the enjoyment of the right to health, as well as identifying the available resources to attain its objectives. Other tools mentioned by the document are the adoption of health indicators and benchmarks,

8   *Ibid.*, para. 12(d).
9   *Ibid.*, para. 19.
10   *Ibid.*, para. 52.

and remedies and accountability. With regards to remedies, the Comment states that '[a]ny person or victim of a violation of the right to health should have access to effective judicial or other appropriate remedies at both national and international levels'. The incorporation into the domestic legal order of international instruments recognising the right to health is also referred to as a way of enhancing the scope and effectiveness of the right to health.

From the analysis of General Comment 14, especially concerning the right to provision and access to health care facilities, it is possible to say that the principles of equality and non-discrimination play an important role in relation to this right and both of them are akin to the principle of equity. In terms of the human right to health, these principles mean that 'outreach (and other) programmes must be in place to ensure that disadvantaged individuals and communities enjoy, in practice, the same access as those who are more advantaged'.[11] According to the Comment, they are embedded in the content of the right to health, thus influencing all the approaches taken in relation to this right, be it in terms of obligations, violations or its implementation.

Key human rights documents at the European level

The most important human rights documents at European level were adopted by the Council of Europe. The best known of these is the European Convention on Human Rights.[12] However, in this Convention there is no specific provision concerning the right to health, which is regarded as part of the right to life or as part of the right to a private life, provided for, respectively, in Articles 2 and 8 of the Convention. Thus, it is difficult to initiate a discussion about the content and principles of the right to health in relation to this legal text.

Nonetheless, two other European legal texts provide specifically for the right to health and the right to access health care: the European Social Charter (ESC)[13] and the Convention on Human Rights and Biomedicine (CHRB).[14] The ESC is considered a complement to the European Convention on Human Rights,[15] since

11 HUNT, P. & BACKMAN, G. 2013. Health Systems and the Right to the Highest Attainable Standard of Health. *In*: GRONDIN, M. *et al.* (eds) *Health and human rights in a changing world*. New York: Routledge, pp. 62–76, p. 64.

12 COUNCIL OF EUROPE 1950. Convention for the Protection of Human Rights and Fundamental Freedoms as amended by Protocols No. 11 and 14.

13 COUNCIL OF EUROPE 1961. European Social Charter.

14 COUNCIL OF EUROPE 1997. Convention for the protection of human rights and dignity of the human being with regard to the application of biology and medicine: Convention on human rights and biomedicine.

15 'The Committee notes that the right to protection of health guaranteed in Article 11 of the Charter complements Articles 2 and 3 of the European Convention on Human Rights – as interpreted by the European Court of Human Rights – by imposing a range of positive obligations designed to secure its effective exercise. This normative partnership between the two instruments is underscored by the Committee's emphasis on human dignity'. Conclusions XVII – 2, Vol. 1, from 30 June 2005. Statement of interpretation of Article 11; 11–1; 2 of the European Social Charter.

it guarantees economic and social human rights while the Convention protects civil and political human rights. However, there is a considerable difference between these two legal texts, since the Charter is not binding on states and violations are not subject to the European Court of Human Rights.

In spite of the non-binding effects of the Social Charter, this legal document is part of a different mechanism of governance within Europe, which includes a collective complaints procedure and a monitoring procedure based on national reports. This mechanism was introduced by the Additional Protocol adopted in 1995 which came into force in 1998. According to this mechanism, the European Committee of Social Rights (ECSR) examines the reports and decides whether or not the situations in the countries concerned are in conformity with the Charter. As Hendriks explains:

> In the case the ECSR finds the complaint admissible, it will submit a report with its findings and its conclusions on the merits of the case. These mostly well reasoned reports, followed by a resolution adopted by the Committee of Ministers deciding on whether the complaint is upheld, are very authoritative even though they do not have the same status as legally binding decisions.[16]

With regard to the right to health, the Social Charter provides for it in its Article 11. This provision has already been interpreted by the European Committee of Social Rights,[17] and its interpretation clearly points out the principles and elements embedded in the provision and access to health care services. In this regard, according to the Committee's interpretation, the system of health care must be accessible for the entire population and states should take as their main criterion for judging the success of health system reforms, effective access to health care for all, without discrimination, as a basic human right. Furthermore, the Committee considers that the right to access to health care implies that: (1) the cost of health care should be borne, at least in part, by the community as a whole; (b) health costs should not place an excessive financial burden on individuals – steps must therefore be taken to reduce the financial burden on patients from the most disadvantaged sections of the population; (c) arrangements for such access must not lead to unnecessary delays in its provision; and (4) the number of health care professionals and equipment must be adequate (the criterion is three beds per thousand population).

There are some examples of collective complaints based on Article 11. In 2006, the ECSR reported that Greece had failed to comply with Article 11 because of health hazards caused by lignite mined in certain parts of the country. In 2008, a

---

16 HENDRIKS, A. 2012. Health and Human Rights: The European Institutions. *In:* TOEBES, B., HARTLEV, M., HENDRIKS, A. & HERRMANN, J.R. (eds) *Health and Human Rights in Europe.* Cambridge; Antwerp; Portland, OR: Intersentia Publishing, p. 45.

17 COUNCIL OF EUROPE 2008. Digest of the Case Law of the European Committee of Social Rights. Available at www.coe.int/t/dghl/monitoring/socialcharter/Digest/DigestSept2008_en.pdf [Accessed 3 December 2015].

complaint was addressed against Bulgaria because of discriminatory provisions against some groups, such as Roma, found in the Bulgarian health insurance legislation.[18]

These examples show that the ECSR addresses the right to health in a collective manner, that is, the measures found to be in violation of Article 11 are measures which affect the health of populations or which discriminate against specific social groups. No examples of complaints based on individual rights have been found.

Therefore, it is possible to argue that the principles stated by the Committee's interpretation are very similar to those found in Article 12 of the ICESCR. Accessibility, non-discrimination and quality are expressly referred to in the interpretation of Article 11. Moreover, although not clearly mentioned, equality is an embedded principle contained in this Article, insofar as there is a special concern for reducing the financial burden on patients from the most disadvantaged sections of the population.

The Convention on Human Rights and Biomedicine, in turn, refers specifically to access to health care in its Article 3. The principles of equity and quality are clearly stated by this provision. The explanatory report on this Convention clarifies the meaning of these principles and provides for definitions of some terms used in Article 3.[19] The report gives a definition of the term 'health care', stating that it means the services that offer diagnostic, preventive, therapeutic and rehabilitative interventions, designed to maintain or improve a person's state of health or alleviate a person's suffering. This care must be of a fitting standard in the light of scientific progress and be subject to a continuous quality assessment. Regarding the expression 'equitable access', the report considers that 'equitable' means first and foremost the absence of unjustified discrimination. Although not synonymous with absolute equality, equitable access implies effectively obtaining a satisfactory degree of care.

Moreover, the report also provides an important clarification for the general aim of the provision, explaining that the purpose of Article 3 is not to create an individual right on which each person may rely in legal proceedings against the state, but rather to prompt the state to adopt the requisite measures as part of its social policy in order to ensure equitable access to health care. This option for a more collective approach to the right to access health care is aligned with the position adopted by the Committee on Economic Social and Cultural Rights over the interpretation of Article 12 ICESCR.

Therefore, considering the text of Article 3 and the clarifications provided in the explanatory report, it is possible to conclude that the principles of equity, quality and non-discrimination are the focus of the Convention on Human Rights and Biomedicine in relation to access and provision of health care services.

---

18 HENDRIKS, A. 2012. *Op. cit.*, p. 46.
19 COUNCIL OF EUROPE 1996. Explanatory Report to the Convention on human rights and biomedicine. Available at https://rm.coe.int/CoERMPublicCommonSearchServices/Display DCTMContent?documentId=09000016800ccde5 [Accessed 3 December 2015].

Finally, it is also important to mention the Charter of Fundamental Rights of the European Union.[20] Although not a human rights document, the Charter proclaims in its Article 35 that:

> Everyone has the right of access to preventive health care and the right to benefit from medical treatment under the conditions established by national laws and practices. A high level of human health protection shall be ensured in the definition and implementation of all Union policies and activities.

Compared to the documents of the Council of Europe, the Charter has its application restricted to the EU level. At the Union level, the Charter now plays a very important role with the entry into force of the Treaty of Lisbon, since, according to Article 6 of the Treaty on European Union, it is considered to have the same legal value as the Treaties. Before being considered part of EU law, Article 35 of the Charter was rarely mentioned by the ECJ in cases concerning the provision of health care services. One example of the use of the Charter by the Court is the opinion of Advocate General Colomer in Stalatemaki.[21] The Advocate states that:

> However, although the case-law takes as the main point of reference the fundamental freedoms established in the Treaty, there is another aspect which is becoming more and more important in the Community sphere, namely the right of citizens to health care, proclaimed in Article 35 of the Charter of Fundamental Rights of the European Union, since, 'being a fundamental asset, health cannot be considered solely in terms of social expenditure and latent economic difficulties'. This right is perceived as a personal entitlement, unconnected to a person's relationship with social security, and the Court of Justice cannot overlook that aspect.[22]

In this case the Charter is used to support free movement rights. Nevertheless, in my opinion, and as maintained in this book, the right to health care is not construed based on individual claims because this is not the appropriate way to advocate this right, which has in fact a much broader perspective. As Herrmann and Toebes put it, '[t]he question then arises, whether such claims actually construe a right to healthcare, or whether they are essentially free movement claims. Furthermore, they may lead to concerns about resource allocation at national level'.[23] Yet with the new binding effects of the Charter it is likely that the ECJ

---

20 EUROPEAN PARLIAMENT AND COUNCIL OF THE EUROPEAN UNION 2000. Charter of Fundamental Rights of the European Union (2000/C 364/01).

21 Case C-444/05, *Stamatelaki* [2007] ECR I-3185.

22 Opinion of Advocate General Colomer in Case C-444/05, *Stamatelaki* [2007] ECR I-3185, para 40.

23 HERRMANN, J.R. & TOEBES, B. 2012. The European Union and Health and Human Rights. *In:* TOEBES, B., HARTLEV, M., HENDRIKS, A. & HERRMANN, J.R. (eds) *Health and human rights in Europe.* Cambridge; Antwerp; Portland, OR: Intersentia, p. 56.

will use it more often in order to support its decisions, and we will see the dimension that the Court truly wants to attribute to this right.

According to Article 35 of the Charter, health care is a fundamental right, be it at the level of preventive care or at the level of curative care (medical treatment). The reference to 'everyone' can be understood as a reference to the principle of accessibility to health care, as well as to the principle of equality and non-discrimination. Indeed, due to the importance of these two last principles as fundamental rights, they are addressed separately in Articles 20 and 21 of the Charter. The second part of Article 35 addresses the issue of public health in relation to other policies. It is important to note, however, that the Charter does not provide for a personal entitlement in relation to the right to health care. Instead, this right is subject to the conditions established by national laws and practices, which is aligned with Article 168 (7) of the TFEU.

The analysis of the international and European documents regarding the right to health enables us to identify the common and core principles related to the provision and access to health care services in human rights law. Although not necessarily written explicitly, the principles of non-discrimination and equality can be drawn on from all the provisions regarding the right to health care. Moreover, they are expressly mentioned in the documents and reports that interpret and discuss the content of some provisions. The principle of equality means not only equality under the law. Equality in terms of access to health care services, goods and facilities is an aspect of equity in health care, and this encompasses the horizontal and the vertical aspects of equity.

The principle of accessibility (meaning both economic and geographical) is also present in all of those documents. It is closely related to the principle of equal access, but in the case of accessibility, access must be provided to all without the precondition of measuring needs, as required in the principle of equal access.

The principle of quality can also be considered as a common element present in all of those human rights texts. This principle shows concern not only for the quality of health care services, goods and facilities, including health professionals, but also for the safety of patients.

Two final points deserve to be addressed. First, it is important to note that all of those documents acknowledge the constraints imposed by the limits of available resources. This leads to the conclusion that access to health care is to be guaranteed by a specific set of benefits that varies from country to country, and not to every service that people may need or want. In the specific context of health systems, finite budgets require a balance between competing human rights and tough police choices. In guiding this process, human rights require that questions be decided in a fair, transparent and participatory way, taking into account explicit criteria, such as the well-being of disadvantaged groups, assuring thus the construction of an effective health system that ensures access to all.[24] The second point is that those documents also show concern over the participation of the population in all

---

24 HUNT, P. & BACKMAN, G. 2013. *Op. cit.*, p. 69.

health-related decision-making processes. Hence, the definition of health policies and actions will vary according to states' wealth, and the decisions over these policies, including those about the allocation of resources, must have the participation of the community.

Individualist and communitarian views on the right to access health care services and their relationship with human rights documents

After identifying the core elements and principles associated with the right to access health care services, as defined in the most important international and European human rights law texts, as well as the individual entitlements and state obligations formed on the basis of this right, I will now analyse those elements and principles in light of the theories of distributive justice discussed in Chapter 1 regarding the distribution of health care, namely egalitarianism and libertarianism, in order to determine whether human rights documents in the field of health propose an individualist or communitarian view of health rights, especially the right of access to health care.

As already explained in Chapter 1, the discourse over an individualist view of health care relies on libertarianism and on the basic principle of self-ownership, according to which personal liberty and freedom of choice are basic values.[25] In this case, health care is viewed as a commodity to be purchased in a market like other commodities.[26] Accordingly, this view promotes choice and individual patient rights as dominant values, and patients are referred to as consumers in health care markets.[27] The principle of equity and the concern for the community as a whole have a secondary role for the individualist rhetoric. By contrast, a communitarian view of health care relates to the egalitarian ideology and to the idea of being a citizen belonging to some community. Communitarianism is a critical philosophical movement that gained expression during the 1980s, especially in the Anglo-American world.[28] By defending the idea that communitarianism is the politics of the common good as opposed to the individualism diffused by liberalism, which is the politics of rights, communitarian philosophers have sought to move ethics away from individual rights and universal rules toward theories that give moral importance to culture, community and specific relationships.

In relation to health care, a communitarian view suggests that, by virtue of that membership, individuals must have a concern for the health of others. Hence, by acknowledging values and bonds that unify and identify societies, this view

---

25   WISEMAN, V. 1998. From Selfish Individualism to Citizenship: Avoiding Health Economics' Reputed 'Dead End'. *Health Care Analysis*, 6: 113–22.

26   DANIELS, N. 2008b. *Op. cit.*

27   NEWDICK, C. & DERRETT, S. 2006. Access, Equity and the Role of Rights in Health Care. *Health Care Analysis*, 14: 157–68.

28   Notable political philosophers of communitarianism include Michael Sandel, David Miller, Michael Walzer and Charles Taylor.

promotes equity as an important value and attaches a special moral importance to health care: it distinguishes health care from other market goods in such a way that it becomes a community or social good.[29] Therefore, competing interests and health needs have to be weighted and balanced with community interests in order to accomplish the protection of health needs in an equitable way.

Furthermore, a second distinction that can be made between these two views of health care is that an individualist view will lead to the application of the rules of commutative or retributive justice whereas a communitarian view of health care claims that distributive justice rules apply, which call for the equal distribution of goods among social groups according to their needs.

Based on these differences between the individualist and the communitarian views of health care, it may now be suggested that a human rights approach to the right to access health care services promotes a communitarian view of this right.

Why a human rights approach to the right to health care promotes a communitarian view of this right

Considering the definition used to characterise a communitarian view of health care and the importance of the principle of equal access, as well as the balance between individual and societal interests contained in this approach to health care, it is possible to argue that the international and regional human rights documents analysed in the previous section suggest a communitarian view of health care.

Starting with Article 12 of the ICESCR and its interpretation by General Comment n. 14, it can be seen that this document starts its analysis about the normative content of Article 12, stating that the entitlements provided for therein include 'the right to a system of health protection which provides equality of opportunity for people to enjoy the highest attainable level of health'.[30] Therefore, although referring to an entitlement in relation to the right to health, this entitlement expresses not only an individual right since it is combined with the principle of equality. The reference of 'equality of opportunity for people' is a clear demonstration of the balance between the individual right and the public interest.

When referring to the interrelated and essential elements of the right to health (availability, accessibility, acceptability and quality), the document refers several times to the question of non-discrimination, especially on social grounds, and equity. The document states, for example, that 'health facilities must be accessible to all, especially the most vulnerable or marginalized sections of the population, in law and in fact, without discrimination in any prohibited grounds'.[31] It also provides, with regard to economic accessibility (or affordability), that '[e]quity demands that poorer households should not be disproportionately burdened with

---

29 MOONEY, G. & HOUSTON, S. 2008. Equity in health care and institutional trust. *Cadernos de Saúde Pública*, 24(5): 1162–7.
30 General Comment n. 14 (E/C. 12/2000/4), para. 8.
31 *Ibid.*, para. 12 (b).

health expenses as compared to richer households'.[32] This is a reference to the vertical aspect of equity – which requires that persons with greater needs should be treated more favourably – and shows that human rights law is very much concerned with the health of individuals in less favourable social conditions. Since a communitarian view of health care suggests that by virtue of our membership of a certain society we must have a concern for the health of others, these references are also a reflection of a communitarian view of health care.

Furthermore, it is important to point out that the General Comment addresses the question of equality also from the point of view of the allocation of resources within the health system. It thus states that:

> investments must be mostly directed towards primary and preventive health care, which can benefit a far larger part of the population, rather than to expensive curative health services, which are often accessible only to a small, privileged fraction of the population rather than primary and preventive health care benefiting a far larger part of the population.[33]

In respect to the questions of the fulfilment and implementation of the right to health at national level, the document is also devoted to measures that favour the whole community, such as the provision of a health system affordable for all, the promotion of medical research and health education as well as the adoption of a legal framework in order to implement health policies.

Finally, it is important to note that the Comment recognises the collective as well as the individual dimensions of the right to health. However, it highlights the importance of the collective dimension due to the fact that modern public health policies rely heavily on strategies devoted to groups, such as prevention and promotion.

Like the ICESCR, the European documents can be interpreted as promoting a communitarian view of the right to health and health care. The provisions contained in the ESC and CHRB consider the principle of equity as the core principle in the field of health care. In the case of Article 11 of the ESC, although the principle is not provided clearly in the wording of the Article, the interpretation put forward by ECSR considers the importance of equality in the provision of health care, regarding health care as a social good. By establishing that the cost of health care should be borne, at least in part, by the community, the ECSR shows that health care is an important good for the whole society and, thus, that the notions of reciprocity, mutuality and community must be present in the provision of this good. Furthermore, the concern about the most disadvantaged sections of the population demonstrates that equality is an essential principle governing the access to health care.

---

32 *Ibid.*, para. 12 (b).
33 *Ibid.*, para. 19.

Article 3 of the Convention on Human Rights and Biomedicine is even clearer about the role of equality in health care, since the Article itself establishes as a state obligation the provision of 'equitable access to health care'. Moreover, the report on the interpretation of this legal norm expressly mentions that the scope of Article 3 is not to create an individual right on which each person may rely in legal proceedings against the state, but rather to prompt the state to adopt the requisite measures as part of its social policy in order to ensure equitable access to health care protection.

As can be seen, the European human rights documents are even clearer in adopting a communitarian view in relation to the right to health. The report on Article 3 of the Convention on Human Rights and Biomedicine leaves no doubt that any interpretation of this right has to be focused on equality and the question of equal access rather than on the issue of entitlements. In fact, the European Court of Human Rights (ECtHR) had the opportunity to give its opinion about rights and entitlements in the field of health care when analysing the admissibility of a case involving the provision of health care services/goods. The case referred to the provision of a robotic arm designed to be mounted on a wheelchair in order to give more autonomy to a person suffering from Duchene Muscular Dystrophy (DMD).[34] The device costs about €36,000 and its provision was refused in the national proceedings. The applicant appealed to the ECtHR, submitting that the right to respect for his private life, guaranteed by Article 8 of the European Convention on Human Rights, 'entailed a positive obligation for the State to provide him with, or pay for, this medical device'.[35]

Although the application was declared inadmissible, the Court went through the question of individual entitlements in the field of health care and the balance between the individual and community interests, arguing that 'regard must be made to the fair balance that has to be struck between the competing interests of the individual and the community as whole [. . .]'.[36]

The same approach was taken by the Court in the case of *N. v. the United Kingdom*.[37] The case concerned an allegation of a violation of Article 3 of the Convention related to the expulsion of a Uganda citizen who had her claim for asylum in the UK territory denied. The applicant was HIV positive and had been treated with antiretroviral drugs in the UK territory, and basically contended that in her home country she could not continue with the AIDS treatment insofar the hospital in her home town was very small and unable to cope with AIDS. The Court held by 14 votes to 3 that there would be no violation of Article 3 of the Convention in the event of the applicant being removed to Uganda. To reach this conclusion the ECtHR analysed several issues, including the balance between community demands and the protection of an individual's fundamental rights, stating that:

34 Nikky Sentges v. the Netherlands (Admissibility) [2003] ECtHR Application n. 27677/02.
35 *Ibid.*, p. 5.
36 *Ibid.*, p. 7.
37 N. v. The United Kingdom [2008] ECtHR Application n. 26565/05.

inherent in the whole of the Convention is a search for a fair balance between the demands of the general interest of the community and the requirements of the protection of the individual's fundamental rights (. . .) Advances in medical science, together with social and economic differences between countries, entail that the level of treatment available in the Contracting State and the country of origin may vary considerably. While it is necessary, given the fundamental importance of Article 3 in the Convention system, for the Court to retain a degree of flexibility to prevent expulsion in very exceptional cases, Article 3 does not place an obligation on the Contracting State to alleviate such disparities through the provision of free and unlimited health care to all aliens without a right to stay within its jurisdiction. A finding to the contrary would place too great a burden on the Contracting States.[38]

The analysis of the ECtHR in these two cases shows that a human rights approach to the right to health care regards the individual as part of the community and requires a balance between both interests. The concern about the principle of equality in access is also present in the human rights approach, insofar as the first judgement shows that equal services must be provided for people with the same health needs. This does not mean, however, that a human rights approach trivialises the language of rights and sets aside individual rights and entitlements in relation to the provision of health care. The rights discourse may shape health policy and enable insistence on the choices and decisions, including those relating to the structure of the health system, based on the fundamental principles provided for in human rights law, such as equality and non-discrimination, and accessibility.[39] Moreover, a human rights approach also leaves space for the introduction of individual rights and entitlements provided that these rights are weighed against community interests and prove to be adequate in a certain social context. In other words, a human rights approach to health care recognises individual rights in this field but subjects them to a strict proportionality control as against the general interest, balancing, therefore, the interests of the individual against those of the community.

Why the type of policy developed at the EU level may be said to promote an individualist view of the right to access health care services

The view of health care suggested by human rights law is considerably different from what EU law has attributed to it. The following chapter will deal specifically with the impact of EU law on principles governing the provision of health care at the national level. In this section, however, I will put forward some elements that

---

38 *Ibid.*, para. 44.
39 MARKS, S. & CLAPHAM, A. 2005. *International human rights lexicon*. Oxford: Oxford University Press.

will help in the analysis to be carried out in the following chapter; I will argue that the EU approach to health care rights suggests an individualist view of this right.

First, it is clear from the judgements regarding cross-border health care and from the new directive on patients' rights discussed in the previous chapter that, according to the EU approach, all types of health care services, including hospital or non-hospital services, have an economic character and, thus, are similar to other services provided in the market (in this case, in the Internal Market context).[40] The assumption that all types of health services are economic services and thus fall within the scope of the rules on the freedom to provide services is the first point that can be said to be promoting an individualist view of the provision of health services. As discussed in this book, one of the differences between the egalitarian and libertarian theories of distributive justice applied to health care, and which reflects respectively communitarian and individualist views of health care, is that the first attributes a moral importance to health care, which is seen as a social good, whereas the latter does not acknowledge this special moral importance, viewing it only as a commodity to be purchased in the market place just like any other. Accordingly, from the moment that health care services become an issue pertaining to the Internal Market rather than to social security matters, they lose their special nature as a social good, becoming a commodity subject to the rules applied to any other kind of service. Furthermore, in this way the patient is considered in isolation rather than part of the community as a whole, which contrasts with the redistributive nature of health care as a social service.[41]

The case law of the ECJ and the new Directive on patients' rights show that the process of European economic integration has spilled over into some areas which were not thought to be affected by the Internal Market rules or the fundamental freedoms. Accordingly, when this process reaches the provision of health services it implicates a more prominent role of the market in the provision of these services.

Second, the approach taken at the EU level promotes freedom of choice for patients. As Kaczorowska argues, 'the ECJ created a right to effective and speedy medical treatment for patients'.[42] Although choice may be a mechanism of delivering health services in public health systems, as in the case of the quasi-market model explained in Chapter 1, this mechanism requires a specific policy design in order to avoid inequalities that can arise in a normal market due to the differences in people's purchasing power. Therefore, promoting choice within the national health system and using a specific policy design is different from promoting it at the EU level. At the national level, the choice mechanism is planned and developed as part of the health policies whereas at the EU level the promotion of choice in

40   See, for example, Preamble of Directive 2011/24/EU, para. 6.
41   BORGES, D.D.C.L. 2011a. EU health systems and the Internal Market: Reshaping Ideology? *Health Care Analysis*, 19(4): 365–87.
42   KACZOROWSKA, A. 2006. A Review of the Creation by the European Court of Justice of the Right to Effective and Speedy Medical Treatment and its Outcomes. *European Law Journal*, 12: 345–70.

relation to health services is part of the Internal Market, which is a normal market where inequalities are likely to arise.

Third, it may be contended that the approach taken at the Union level in relation to health care does not show concern about equity, which is an essential principle within the egalitarian ideology and the communitarian view. As argued in the previous chapter, equal access to health care means meeting population needs of health services in an equal way. However, the new rules put forward by the Directive on patients' rights – which reflects the ECJ's decisions in cases of cross-border health care – may seriously affect the principle of equal access to care. Assuming that equity of access is also measured according to the nature and extent of barriers imposed on patients, the costs of receiving treatment abroad – which are initially paid by patients and then reimbursed by the Member State of affiliation – can be regarded as a financial barrier to access. Moreover, it should be taken into account that income-related inequalities in the use of health care already exist in many EU countries and this type of financial barrier is likely to increase these inequalities.[43] In fact, it is possible to argue that this mechanism of cross-border health care is based on the ability to pay, which is a value common in libertarian systems.

The main objective of Directive 2011/24/EU is ensuring the freedom of patients and providers to receive and provide health care. To achieve this objective, the directive uses more flexible mechanisms than those stated in Regulation 883/2004. This rule also provides for the case of planned health care abroad (Article 20). However, in this situation patients must obtain prior authorisation from their social security scheme. By contrast, the mechanisms provided for in Directive 2011/24/EU are based on reimbursement, i.e. patients travel abroad to receive medical care through out-of-pocket payments which are then reimbursed by their own health systems. The concerns about the impact of this mechanism in the principle of equal access to care refer mainly to the case of non-hospital care, since the case of hospital and specialised care is still subject to authorisation, which is a mechanism already used by Regulation 883/2004.

A good way to understand this argument is by trying to answer the question: What kind of patients will benefit from this new EU market for health care? If people who travel abroad to receive non-hospital care have to pay for it up-front, it is only those with enough resources to bear the expenses of travelling and of paying the costs of the treatment who will be able to exercise their patients' free movement rights. In this regard, it is important to bear in mind that many health systems within the EU operate on a benefits-in-kind basis. Thus, in these countries, people are not used to paying for receiving health services. Therefore, in theory, the Directive ensures patients' rights for all, but, in practice, it will benefit a vocal minority, composed of the wealthier members of society, who can really make use

---

43 DOORSLAER, E.V., KOOLMAN, X. & JONES, A.M. 2004. Explaining income-related inequalities in doctor utilisation in Europe. *Health Economics*, 13: 629–47.

of these new rights. This ensures only equality under the law, but not equality in terms of equal access to care and needs.

Therefore, although conferred upon all EU citizens, cross-border health care is likely to be exercised by a minority of Europeans who can afford the price of mobility. It seems thus that the kind of policy that is being developed at the EU level in relation to access to health services, although in theory supposed to respect equity, is much more concerned with providing freedom of choice to patients and health providers, without caring about the impact that this may have on access to care. Individual rights may be won at the expense of the principle of equal access for equal needs and the objective of reducing inequalities in health care between social groups. This policy is actually creating a mechanism based on the ability to pay, common in health systems such as that of the United States, which provokes unequal access to care.

Accordingly, the Union policy in terms of health care is promoting an individualist view of health care, setting aside principles that inform a commu-nitarian view of health care, especially the principle of equal access to services, based on actual needs. As Greer claims, '[e]quity concerns are not very important – it takes a creative mind to argue that patient mobility is anything other than a boon to the wealthy and articulate'.[44]

It is true that it is very easy to sympathise with the individual rights discourse and with the idea of providing freedom to patients to receive treatment. However, a better analysis of the subject shows us that there is a serious risk of promoting these rights just for the wealthier and well-represented members of society, causing huge inequality in the health system in terms of access to care. In fact, a first look at the situation of an individual seeking to receive health care abroad may lead to the conclusion that this individual is realising his or her right to health care, as guaranteed by international human rights law. But a better look at this situation can show a different reality, because this is only

> a small component of the right to health, as most people will continue to make use of healthcare services nationally. The primary responsibility for realising a right to health (care) lies with national governments, and such free movement claims can never replace this responsibility. Being able to travel abroad to make use of healthcare services is one thing, but the main essential part of the right to health implies that individuals can enjoy good quality and accessible health services in their own country.[45]

Nevertheless, it is important to note that enforceable individual rights and entitlements play an important role in contexts where people are socially excluded and marginalised. In this case, the balance between the individual right and the

---

44 GREER, S.L. 2008b. Power: struggle: the politics and policy consequences of patient mobility in Europe. *Observatoire social européen*. Policy Paper 2, July 2008.
45 HERRMANN, J.R. & TOEBES, B. 2012. *Op. cit.*, p. 69.

community interests shows that enforcing individual rights is the only way to achieve equity.[46] This is the case of some courts' decisions in developing countries concerning the access to health services.[47]

However, this is not the case of cross-border health care in the EU. The level of prosperity of EU health systems is higher than those of South Africa or other developing countries. In the case of the EU, shifting focus towards individual rights threatens to undermine equity in the health systems, because in such a context the rights and entitlements created will benefit mostly the socially advantaged, that is, those patients who can afford the costs involved in going abroad for a health treatment, which sometimes can also involve litigation before administrative and judicial bodies.

It is then possible to conclude that EU health care policy has been developed as an Internal Market issue. This shows that health policies can be shaped by trade rather than by health departments.[48] However, even if shaped by the market environment, the development of health policies requires a clear view and a statement of aims, priorities, limitations, responsibilities, methods and resource implications. Moreover, there is a need to preserve basic principles that are central to EU health systems, such as the principle of equal access to health care services. Otherwise, the notions of reciprocity, mutuality and public interest are at risk of disappearing from the provision of health services within the EU. Other aspects of this individualistic view, especially the impact of EU health policies on equity, will be addressed in the following chapter.

Conclusion

The objective of this chapter was to present the main human rights documents in the field of health and show how they relate to theories of distributive justice in the field of health care, especially the individualist and communitarian views. The chapter also demonstrates why a human rights approach to health services promotes a communitarian view of these services while the EU approach has been promoting an individualist view of health services. By doing that, the chapter provides a critical analysis of the way EU institutions have been dealing with health services, presenting some elements that will be used in the following chapter, which deals specifically with the impact of EU law on common principles governing the provision of health care.

---

46 Yamin, A.E. 2014. Promoting Equity in Health: What Role for the Courts? *Health and Human Rights Journal*, 16(2): 183–6.

47 See, for example, a case involving AIDS policy, submitted to the Constitutional Court of South Africa – *Minister of Health and Others v Treatment Action Campaign and Others (right to health care and access to HIV/Aids treatment)* [2002] ZACC CCT8/02.

48 GREER, S.L. 2008a. Choosing paths in European Union health services policy: a political analysis of a critical juncture. *Journal of European Social Policy*, 18: 219–31.

6 The EU approach to health care and the development of new values in the provision of health services

The objective of this final chapter is threefold. The first is to show that the present EU approach to health policy introduced market mechanisms into the field of health services, inserting these services in a more liberal context that contrasts with the traditional solidaristic origin of health policy in Europe. In this analysis I will also consider some possible explanations for the development of this type of health policy at the EU level. The second is to show how this change of approach affects principles and values of national health systems. Last, I will present some possible solutions in order for this policy to be in conformity with communitarian and solidaristic national values.

The EU and the development of market values in the field of health services: motivation and consequences

As shown in the previous chapters, health services became a policy area of increased interest from the EU. Since the signature of the Treaty of Rome, the approach to health services at the EU level has changed significantly, moving from a public service and social security issue to an economic matter subject to the rules of the Internal Market. This change, in my opinion, was not due to the several health system reforms adopted at national level in the last decades aiming at reducing costs, which introduced some market mechanisms into the health systems.[1] As discussed in the first chapter, it is possible to introduce market values into the system without interfering with the principles governing EU health systems, such as universality, equity and solidarity. This book supports the view that this change of approach was due to an intentional spill-over from the process of economic integration that embraced issues initially excluded from this process of Europeanisation, moving them from a social logic to an economic logic, making therefore the regulation of such issues possible at the EU level, as in the case of health services. Yet it is not only the possibility of regulating health care at Union

---

1 Szyszczak is of the opinion that '[e]conomic factors in the shape of rising health care costs and deeper public sector deficits create a greater demand for the liberalisation and privatisation of welfare provision from governments'. SZYSZCZAK, E. 2011. *Op. cit.*, p. 128.

level that was responsible for this change of approach; other factors also worked as a motivation. The increased interest of private providers pushed the process of liberalisation of health care. In this respect, Szyszczak argues that:

> The liberalisation of health care markets has been facilitated by a new breed of medical tourist facilitators, ranging from the cheap flights offered by 'nofrills' airlines, to clinics which can arrange medical package holidays, to insurance companies providing medical tourism insurance schemes.[2]

The case of Hungarian dental clinics illustrates this situation very well. As Földes documented in her thesis, the city of Sopron in Hungary has one of the highest concentrations of dentists per residents between 150 and 400 dentists for 50,000 inhabitants whereas normally the concentration for a population of this size would be of 20 dentists.[3] Hungarian clinics use multilingual internet advertisements, press advertisements and agents located in targeted countries in order to reach out to patients. Some of them even provide accommodation and other travel related arrangements for patients.[4] In Poland, for example, medical tourism is seen as an export specialty. This led to the inclusion of medical tourism in the project 'Promotion of Poland as an attractive and business-friendly country with a huge investment potential', and stimulates companies to build medical facilities in order to receive foreign patients.[5]

Therefore, in an era of globalisation, Europeanisation of health care emerges as a possibility to create new markets for this service. In this regard, the provision of health care across borders creates the possibility of a new range of health professionals and providers. Patients will have new options and can shop around for the best provider and price. In this context, a new relationship arises and patients are no longer seen as users of a welfare service but as consumers in health care markets. In this regard, it is important to note that the view of patients as consumers is an important feature of health systems governed by liberal values. For instance, there is a movement in the United States called consumer-driven health care that advocates, *inter alia*, that one of the most effective ways to introduce market competition into health care is by letting people make health care purchasing decisions just as they make purchasing decisions for any other good.[6] However, this type of movement is in stark contrast to solidarity, which is, in fact, severely criticised by those who advocate consumer-driven health care.

---

2   *Ibid.*, p. 128.
3   FÖLDES, M.É. 2009. *Op. cit.*, p. 255.
4   This is the case of Rosengarten clinic mentioned by Földes in her thesis. Available at www.rosengarten.hu/dental-treatments.html [Accessed 8 December 2015]; *Ibid.*, p. 257.
5   Project *Promotion of Poland as an attractive and business-friendly country with a huge investment potential*. Available at www.forum-ekonomiczne.pl/public/upload/ibrowser/InwestujMedycyna.pdf [Accessed 8 December 2015].
6   For a deeper analysis of the consumer-driven movement see JOST, T.S. 2007. *Health care at risk: a critique of the consumer-driven movement*. Durham, NC: Duke University Press.

Indeed, authors who have analysed the actual impact of the ECJ's jurisprudence on cross-border health care in national health systems have concluded that it makes these systems more business-like. In some countries it has encouraged more competitive behaviour from insurers and more commercial behaviour and price increases from providers.[7]

This rise in new market opportunities for health care within the EU has been influenced not only by private providers but also by EU institutions, which have successfully included health care within their political agenda by redefining this service as an economic activity. Moreover, the cross-border aspect of health care also facilitated the governance of these services from EU institutions. It must be noted, however, that, although cross-border health care has been advocated as an issue of patients' rights, it goes beyond this aspect.[8] In this respect, European institutions have already envisaged the market opportunities offered by cross-border health care. The explanatory statement of the report from the European Parliament's Committee on the Environment, Public Health and Food Safety about the proposal for a Directive on the application of patients' rights in cross-border health care states, for example, that:

> It is likely that we will see an increase in the number of 'health brokers' setting up to give patients independent advice on packages of treatment and care, in the same way as an insurance broker shops around on behalf of his client to find the best options to meet his or her needs. Clearly it is for each Member State to decide its policy in this area and each Member State will in due course also have to decide whether the role or training of the health broker needs to be regulated or self-regulated in some way.[9]

This statement clearly shows how EU institutions have taken a market approach to health services and that EU health policy is more about markets than about individual or aggregate health outcomes.[10] The idea of a health broker is only

7   BAETEN, R., VANHERCKE, B. & COUCHEIR, M. 2010. The Europeanisation of National Health Care Systems: Creative Adaptation in the Shadow of Patient Mobility Case Law. *OSE Paper Series*. Research paper n. 3. Brussels: Observatoire social européen.

8   In this respect, when comparing the proposal for the Directive on patients' rights in relation to the draft of the Services Directive, Baeten argued that 'a general "clean-up", had been carried out in order to eliminate any notion of "health services" from the text. Instead, the provisions were presented under the heading of "patients' rights". This general tidying up did however not concern the legal basis of the proposal, which remained Art. 95 of the EC Treaty, concerning the internal market'. BAETEN, R. 2009. The proposal for a directive on patients' rights in cross-border healthcare. *In:* DEGRYSE, C. (ed.) *Social developments in the European Union 2008*. Brussels: Trade Union Institute (ETUI), Observatoire social européen (OSE), p. 157.

9   EUROPEAN PARLIAMENT. 2009. Committee on the Environment, Public Health and Food Safety. Report on the proposal for a directive on the application of patients' rights in cross-border healthcare (Explanatory Statement). A6–0233/2009. Available at www.europarl.europa.eu/sides/getDoc.do?type=REPORT&reference=A6–2009–0233&language=EN#title2 [Accessed 3 December 2015].

10   GREER, S. & JARMAN, H. 2012. *Op. Cit.*

possible when health care is completely inserted in a market context governed by liberal values. This view poses a risk for EU health systems that were built based in egalitarian values, opening the door for a different market phenomenon. One of these is health tourism, which is often called medical tourism.[11]

It is possible to conclude, therefore, that this economic view towards health care brought these services into a market perspective, moving away from the social logic that permeates them at the national level. This move can be said to be promoting a libertarian ideology in the provision of health services, contrasting with important values of EU health systems. As already noted in this book, one of the main differences between egalitarian and libertarian ideologies is that the former attributes a moral importance to health care, which is seen as a social good, whereas the latter does not acknowledge this special moral importance, viewing it only as a commodity to be purchased in a market just like any other. Furthermore, in this way the patient is considered in isolation rather than part of the community as a whole, which contrasts with the redistributive nature of health care as welfare services.

The decoupling of the provision of health care from its social nature seems to be part of a trend of liberalisation and commodification of health services within the EU. This trend can be observed in various dimensions of different policies developed by EU institutions. It can be argued, thus, that health policies, and especially health care, are becoming a means of serving the priorities of the process of economic integration.[12]

As will be shown in the following sections of this chapter, this liberal trend not only creates the potential for the presence of other market phenomena, but can also have a negative effect on national values governing the provision of health services.

Health tourism as a market phenomenon

Health or medical tourism is very common in countries such as the United States, where, as explained in the first chapter, health care is not universal and is inserted in a market context. According to Lee and Balaban:

> 'Medical tourism' is the term commonly used to describe people traveling outside their home country for medical treatment. Traditionally, international medical travel involved patients from less-developed countries traveling to a medical center in a developed country for treatment that was not available in their home country. In the United States, the term 'medical tourism' generally refers to people traveling to less-developed countries for medical care. Medical

11 REISMAN, D. 2010. *Health tourism: social welfare through international trade*. Cheltenham, UK: Edward Elgar.
12 KOIVUSALO, M.T. 2005. The future of European health policies. *Journal of Health Services*, 35(2): 325–42.

tourism is a worldwide, multibillion-dollar phenomenon that is expected to grow substantially in the next 5–10 years. However, little reliable epidemiologic data on medical tourism exist. Studies using different definitions and methods have estimated anywhere from 60,000 to 750,000 medical tourists annually.[13]

Although within the EU context health tourism has different features, it can become a phenomenon similar to that described above. In this regard, it is important to highlight that mobility within the EU is often underestimated.[14] It is true that the overall number of patients receiving cross-border care remains low compared with total populations, but indications are clear that it is moving at a fast pace and has an immense potential to grow in the future.[15] Moreover, 49% of European citizens showed a willingness to travel abroad to receive medical treatment, according to a special Eurobarometer survey on cross-border healthcare conducted in 2014.[16]

This change in approach towards a more liberal view of health care is thus something that may change EU health systems and the way health services are delivered. As argued above, EU institutions, at least the Commission and the Parliament, are aware of these changes and the consequences they can bring. Indeed, it is possible to say that a more liberalised health care market is one of the aims of this change in approach.

Nevertheless, in relation to the ECJ, which is also responsible for this change of view, I am not so sure that its position when deciding cases on patient mobility was also inspired by liberal values and the idea of a potential market for health services within the EU. The position of the ECJ was guided by another motivation which is not so clear. Newdick, in a speculative analysis about the ECJ's motivation, proposes that one of the explanations for the Court's position is that it misunderstood the distinction between civil and political rights and social and economic rights. The former can be enforced as substantive rights because they are generally negative in character, whereas the latter are enforceable as procedural rather than substantive rights, especially when they arise from finite, public funds. The ECJ, however, enforced health care rights as if they were civil or political rights. Another explanation suggested by Newdick is the 'intuitive mistrust of

13 LEE, C.V. & BALABAN, V. 2011. The Pre-Travel Consultation Counseling & Advice for Travelers. *Travelers' Health 2011 Yellow Book*. Centers for Disease Control and Prevention. Available at www.nc.cdc.gov/travel/yellowbook/2012/chapter-2-the-pre-travel-consultation/medical-tourism.htm [Accessed 10 December 2015].

14 GINNEKEN, E.V. & BUSSE, R. 2011. Cross-border health care data. *In:* WISMAR, M., PALM, W., FIGUERAS, J., ERNST, K. & GINNEKEN, E.V. (eds) *Cross-border health care in the European Union: mapping and analysing practices and policies*. Copenhagen: World Health Organization, on behalf of the European Observatory on Health Systems and Policies.

15 ZUCCA, G. *et al.* 2015. *Op. cit.*, p. 11.

16 Special Eurobarometer 425. Available at http://ec.europa.eu/public_opinion/archives/ebs/ebs_425_en.pdf [Accessed 10 December 2015].

national governments and anxiety about their willingness to ignore individual rights'.[17]

One of the problems with cross-border health care becoming medical tourism within the EU, as seems to be the intention of EU institutions, is that it will benefit nationals from countries where the cost of care is more expensive since according to the Directive the costs of reimbursement are determined by the Member State of affiliation. Therefore, nationals from these Member States can seek cheaper care but the contrary is not likely to happen, once individuals from Member States with cheaper tariffs for health care will have to bear the difference between the tariffs of reimbursement and the actual cost of care in the Member State of treatment in order to receive health care across borders. Giving as an example the situation of Hungary, Földes contends that Hungarian patients are in a clearly disadvantaged situation when compared to their Western counterparts. According to her:

> The disadvantage becomes particularly obvious when comparing the situation of a Hungarian patient seeking treatment in a Western state to a Western patient seeking treatment in Hungary. Although it is a common argument that certain population categories always benefit more from the EU market freedoms than others, in this case the disadvantage of Hungarian patients is systemic due to the cost-assumption rules applied under the Kohll and Decker mechanism combined with the significantly lower cost of health care in Hungary.[18]

Another problem arising from medical tourism is the 'race to the bottom'. In this regard, Member States that provide a higher standard of services, better value for money or a greater choice for medical 'consumers' are likely to attract more patients to receive these services. The same applies to Member States whose medical profession enjoys a high reputation. The worst scenario, if such pressures reach extreme levels, is the temptation on the part of the national authorities of those states to reduce the quality of service provided, in order to discourage such 'medical tourism', resulting in a classic race to the bottom.[19]

Considering that health systems within the EU are guided by the principle of solidarity and that, by virtue of the concept of Union citizenship, the principle of equality is also fundamental for the Union, the possibility of nationals from one Member State having more advantages with regard to cross-border health care than nationals from other Member States is something that clearly goes against these principles and consequently should be avoided by both EU institutions and Member States when developing and putting into practice cross-border health care policies and legislation.

---

17 NEWDICK, C. 2011. Disrupting the Community – Saving Public Health Ethics from the EU Internal Market. *In:* GRONDEN, J.V.D., SZYSZCZAK, E., NEERGAARD, U. & KRAJEWSKI, M. (eds) *Health care and EU law.* The Hague: T.M.C. Asser, p. 223.

18 FÖLDES, M.É. 2009. *Op. cit.*, p. 240.

19 HERVEY, T.K. 2002a. *Op. cit.*, p. 85.

Health care, judicialisation of politics and multilateral conflicts

A third explanation, in my opinion, is the misconceiving of technical issues related to health care, such as health planning. In this regard, it is important to remind ourselves that the ECJ played an important role in the development of the principles governing the provision of health services across borders. However, as a judicial body, the Court is not the most appropriate institution to develop policies regarding the provision of welfare. In theory, these policies should be decided by technical and administrative bodies and not by a judicial one. This is in fact a consequence of the judicialisation of politics,[20] which in Europe has been described well by Alec Stone Sweet.[21] This phenomenon can be explained by the expansion of judicial power provoked by the inevitable relationship between law and politics.[22]

However, judicialisation can be very harmful to collectivity when social welfare is involved because in these disputes judges are dealing with communitarian demands that result in multilateral conflicts.[23] These conflicts differ from bilateral ones, in which the referral of a conflict to a judge for adjudication may be effected by either one of the parties, without the other's consent. In these cases the decision has the effect of law, binding on the parties to the dispute, but also may have precedential value to the extent that the decision serves to clarify the rules relevant to particular behaviours or relations.[24]

In multilateral conflicts it is not only one of the parties that will be affected by a judicial decision: it is the whole community, a macro-universe compared with that affected by bilateral conflicts. Multilateral conflicts deal with distributive justice and are usually present when public goods are at stake, such as in the case of health care provided by national governments. When deciding these cases, judges are not only applying the law, but also exercising their normative power, which is not so different from that of the legislature.[25]Accordingly, the decisions taken by courts in this type of conflict cannot follow the same criteria used in bilateral conflicts.

Courts are not so familiar as executive bodies in dealing with multilateral conflicts regarding social welfare demands, because most of the time they determine solutions in bilateral conflicts. Moreover, multilateral conflicts usually require knowledge of technical issues, such as planning and management of systems and resources. In this respect, Cappelletti maintains that:

---

20 In this regard, see TATE, C.N. & VALLINDER, T. (eds) 1995. *The global expansion of judicial power.* New York: New York University Press.
21 SWEET, A.S. 2000. *Governing with judges.* Oxford: Oxford University Press.
22 TATE, C.N. 1995. When courts go marching in. *In:* TATE, C.N. & VALLINDER, T. (eds) *The global expansion of judicial power.* New York: New York University Press, p. 13.
23 In this regard, see LOPES, J.R.D.L. 2006. *Direitos sociais: teoria e prática.* São Paulo: Editora Método.
24 SWEET, A.S. 2000. *Op. cit.* p. 19.
25 In this regard, see FARIA, J.E. (ed.) 2005. *Direitos humanos, direitos sociais e justiça,* São Paulo: Malheiros.

Indeed, for the creation of law are necessary instruments that are not available to the courts and 'go far beyond the mere knowledge of the existing law and how it performs.' Judges, according to this understanding, are unable to personally develop the type of research required for a creative work that cannot be limited to the laws and precedents, but involve complex issues and social, economic and political data, they do not even have the resources, including financial, whereby parliaments, legislative committees and ministries are able to instruct others to carry out research that often, neither legislators nor administrators would develop themselves.[26]

The case law of the ECJ on patient mobility can be regarded as a type of multilateral conflict where social welfare is at stake. Therefore, the ECJ should be aware of the consequences and impacts of its decisions in such a type of conflict. The Court has never explained the logic of its thinking, or the role it perceives for national health care planning.[27] Although the decisions on these disputes have elements of policy making, since they had an actual impact on administrative issues of national health systems, including the allocation of resources, they did not take into account principles used to make policy in the field of social welfare and health services. Even so, the ECJ felt 'so strongly motivated to develop policy in this area with, it seems, so little understanding of the consequences of its actions in terms of fairness and equality'.[28]

Furthermore, the transference of welfare decision-making to a judicial body presents the problem of legitimacy. Indeed, the competent body to deal with decisions on the allocation of resources is the legislature and not the judiciary. Considering that judicial decisions are not only mere acts of law enforcement – even more so in the case of the ECJ, which is empowered to apply and interpret EU law – but rather, constitute the law itself, there is an overlapping of competences when courts make this type of decision. In the case of the EU, the question of legitimacy takes on a greater dimension by virtue of its multi-level structure. Hence, it is not only the problem of a judicial body acting as a legislature, but the fact that this judicial body acts at supranational level. Therefore, the 'politically unconstrained powers of the ECJ reach much further than the powers of judicial review under any national constitution'.[29]

A good example of how far EU law can reach, and indeed be different from national (constitutional) law, is given by Hervey. She explains, using the *Watts* case as an example, that although it is uncontroversial under EU law that British patients are entitled to look for treatment abroad, under UK law, including Human Rights law, there is no basis from which patients could claim a 'right to treatment'.[30]

---

26 CAPPELLETTI, M. 1993. *Juízes legisladores?* Porto Alegre: Sérgio Fabris Editor., p. 87. Author's free translation.
27 NEWDICK, C. 2011. *Op. cit.*
28 *Ibid.*, p. 225.
29 SCHARPF, F.W. 2009. Legitimacy in the Multilevel European Polity. *MPIfG Working Papers*, 09/1, p. 18.
30 HERVEY, T.K. 2011a. *Op. cit.*, p. 243.

Moreover, a further reason justifies the definition of policies and priorities by the national legislature: health needs and priorities should be decided according to specific social contexts, because the rights and entitlements they create are aimed at meeting populations' health needs fairly.[31] Considering that there is still discussion about the lack of democracy regarding EU institutions,[32] establishing priorities at the EU level may interfere with this fair deliberative process and lead to undesirable outcomes in terms of health needs. In this regard, Somek contends that:

> Determining who is to get treatment for what type of ailment and after how much of a waiting period are political questions. Granting individuals, on the basis of Article 49 EC Treaty, the right to bypass national queues and to have services that were obtained abroad reimbursed at home gives rise to problems of opportunity cost. The ECJ's opens the door for a vocal minority. Lending them the hand of EC law may indirectly divert resources from clients who are more poorly represented on a transnational scale. The choices made by the national political process become undercut by the ECJ which loves to posture as the sentinel of consumer interests. The Union appears to be 'brought closer to its citizens', but at the expense of democratic control.[33]

It is true that now the principles established by the jurisprudence on cross-border health care are codified by a Directive and, as a consequence, the issue of competence is somehow solved, since Member States agreed on that piece of legislation.[34] However, even with the entry into force of the Directive, it is likely that the ECJ will have to decide on cases concerning cross-border health care because Member States still have a margin of discretion to decide on prior authorisation concerning certain types of treatment. In addition, there is the issue of the implementation of the rule at the national level, which also might be subject to disputes before the Court. In this context, it is difficult to avoid the fact that issues regarding national health policies pass before the jurisdiction of the Court. Therefore, it is for the Court to take a more cautious approach when interpreting and applying EU law in fields in which the impact on national policies and priorities is inevitable, as is the case with health policies. Furthermore, the Court has recently shown that this more cautious approach is needed, as it demonstrated in *Commission v. France*, analysed in Chapter 4 of this book.

---

31 DANIELS, N. 2008a.*Op. cit.*, p. 28. In this regard, see also DWORKIN, R. 1993. *Op. cit.*
32 HERVEY, T.K. 2002a.*Op. cit.*
33 SOMEK, A. 2007. *Op. cit.*, p. 55.
34 Even if agreed by Member States, the Directive might have a liberalising and deregulatory impact on national health care policies because it arose as a consequence of the principles developed by the ECJ. In this regard, Scharpf argues that 'the overall pattern is now shaped by an institutional constellation in which political legislation must be negotiated in the shadow of judicial decisions which, for structural reasons, have a liberalizing and deregulatory impact'. SCHARPF, F. W. 2009. *Op. cit.*, p. 17.

Other consequences of the application of liberal values to EU health care services: how these new values affect the principles of equity, solidarity, universality and quality

After analysing the new values involved in the provision of health services in the EU, as well as the motivation and some of the consequences of this new approach, this book will now examine how it affects the principles governing the provision of health services in the EU. Although the impact on these principles are analysed separately, the analysis is interrelated since all the principles are grounded in the more general egalitarian ideology and most of them fall under the umbrella of solidarity.

Solidarity

The option to start the discussion with the principle of solidarity is due to the fact that this principle works as a kind of umbrella, embedding in its core ideas, for example, equity and universality, which will be discussed in the following sections. Therefore, discussing the impact on solidarity also means discussing the impact on these other principles.

As already discussed in Chapter 2, solidarity and the welfare state are highly interrelated since it is the sense of belonging to nation states (welfare states) that permits citizens to develop the sentiments of solidarity and trust. Moreover, in Chapter 3 the operational meaning of solidarity within health systems was explained, i.e. what types of cross-subsidisation solidarity entails. In this regard, it was shown that solidarity implies cross-subsidisation between different social groups, between the healthy and unhealthy, and between different age groups. Yet, more than that, '[s]olidarity also implies that, as coverage is based on the medical needs of the patient, all patients are treated equally, regardless of their contributions to the system'.[35]Having this in mind, the impact of EU law and the Internal Market on national health systems, especially with regard to their solidaristic feature, is not difficult to demonstrate. Indeed, this is one of the aspects continuously discussed by authors in this field. For this reason, and considering also the fact that analysing the impact on equity and universality presupposes indirectly analysing the impact on solidarity, I will not take long to develop my ideas in this respect.

As Szyszczak argues, 'the demands of individuals have proved difficult to reconcile with the respect for the solidaristic and the social welfare nature of health care systems in the EU (. . .)'.[36] This is because solidarity is grounded in social values that stem from the common good and sense of community whereas the demands of individuals, as in the case of cross-border health care, are grounded in the logic of the Internal Market, which is based on the individualist premises of the economic

35　HERVEY, T.K. 2011a. *Op. cit.*, p. 186.
36　SZYSZCZAK, E. 2011.*Op. cit.*, p. 128.

fundamental freedoms guaranteed by the Treaty. This includes access to a wider market and consequent efficiencies and economies of scale, values which stand in stark contrast to the closure required by the organisation of health systems at the national level.[37]

The importance of the principle of solidarity to welfare systems is immense. In fact, it works as a kind of 'shield' to protect national welfare systems against market values. Indeed, in the case of health care, this principle could have been used more than in fact it was to 'protect' national health systems from the application of the fundamental freedoms of the Treaty. As demonstrated in Chapter 4, solidarity was used much more in cases regarding competition law than in those about freedom to receive health services across borders.

However, at the national level, solidarity still plays an important role. Regardless of the fact that Member States have been experimenting with market mechanisms within their health systems, this has not changed the solidaristic nature of these systems. At the national level, the provision of health services is still seen as a social matter. This contrasts starkly with the economic view of these services at the EU level. This already creates a complex relationship in this field. Moreover, the fact that the EU does not have redistributional competences does not create supranational obligations of solidarity in the health field, making this issue even more complex – the openness required by market integration contrasts with the closure needed to organise a health system. If we consider that Western societies are constantly exposed to and influenced by market and consumerist ideas, the closure required by national solidarity may turn out to be something 'bad' or 'ugly', as Somek predicts.[38] In this context, the benefits of mutual assistance and closure required to construct welfare systems seem to be of less relevance. As this author explains:

> [. . .] the public perception of national health care systems changes. Earlier, their existence nurtured a sense of national belonging. Each citizen's life was experienced as being tied up with the life of all others. Now these systems come to be perceived as outdated and overly defensive. Repeatedly, they are forced to express their reluctance to assist those who obtained a service abroad (hence, they seem to be *not caring*) and constantly sounding the alarm about their financial viability (hence, they seem to be *potentially crumbling*). The perception of systems, which rest on enormous historical achievements, as uncaring, stingy and prone to financial crisis 'erodes their credibility'. It begins to seem more promising to shift to privatisation and to allow for more flexible arrangements. Why not dismantle existing health care monopolies and preserve their 'cross-subsidy element' (the good risks pay for the bad risks, the higher earners for the lower earners) by using the tax and transfer system to attain the

---

37   HERVEY, T.K. 2011a. *Op. cit.*, p. 216.
38   SOMEK, A. 2007. *Op. cit.*

redistributive effect in a privatised system supplemented by subsidies? Does not a competitive system hold out the promise of better and more flexible services owing to its superior efficiency?[39]

If the example of the case of cross-border health care is taken, it is possible to say that the market forces won the dispute. The option at EU level was to regard health services as an economic issue and to privilege choice and ability to pay instead of solidarity and equity. Nevertheless, as will be shown, choice and ability to pay as envisaged by EU health policies seriously affect the egalitarian premises of EU health systems.

Ultimately, solidarity comprises the promotion of social welfare. Thus, one could argue that choice and competition are elements that improve general welfare and, even if they may have negative effects for some aspects of solidarity, this is a trade-off resulting from the application of the market in relation to national health systems. However, not even in relation to this aspect can the impact be said to be positive. It is true that freedom of choice and competition have the effect of improving general welfare, since the effect on life satisfaction can be said to be positive, as proved by a recent study on this subject.[40] Nevertheless, when it comes to social welfare the impact is not positive. The same study asserts that the positive effects only apply to what are defined as 'middle class' individuals with a good income and high education.[41] In the same vein, another recent study in the field of economics, which analysed the welfare effects of patient mobility in the EU, concluded that in the long run the use of high reimbursement for mobility may lead to a decrease in total welfare.[42] Moreover, cross-border shopping may not be compatible with local welfare maximization.[43]

Therefore, the lower classes do not benefit in the same way as wealthier classes from the application of market values. Accordingly, if we consider that social welfare has equity concerns and that these values are positive only for the middle classes, the impact for social welfare is not positive at all. In this regard, another study that investigated, from an economic point of view, the relationships among patient mobility, health care quality and welfare, concluded that 'if the EU is enforcing the rights for patients to obtain health care in another country without establishing a proper transfer payment system, the impact on health care quality

39 SOMEK, A. 2007.*Op. cit.*, pp. 56–7.
40 ZIGANTE, V. 2011. Assessing Welfare Effects of the European Choice Agenda: The case of health care in the United Kingdom. *LSE 'Europe in Question' Discussion Paper Series*, LEQS Paper No. 35/2011, p. 26.
41 *Ibid.*, p. 26.
42 LEVAGGI, L. & LEVAGGI, R. 2014. Patients' mobility across borders: a welfare analysis. *In:* LEVAGGI, R. & MONTEFIORI (eds), *Health care provision and patient mobility: health integration in the European Union.* Italy: Springer, pp. 179–200.
43 LEVAGGI, R. & MENONCIN, F. 2014. Cross-border health care provision: who gains, who loses. *In:* LEVAGGI, R. & MONTEFIORI, M. (eds) *Health care provision and patient mobility: health integration in the European Union.* Italy: Springer, pp. 223–44.

and financing might be detrimental not just to regional welfare but also to global (interregional) welfare'.[44]

Accordingly, the principle of solidarity can be said to be severely affected by the EU approach in relation to national health systems. The 'vertical' application of market values to EU health systems has the effect not only of diminishing the sense of social solidarity built nationally, but also of dismantling the egalitarian premises on which social welfare is grounded. The following analysis about equity will explore this in more depth.

Equity

In the previous chapter, when explaining the reasons why EU policies in the field of health care are based on individualist premises, I analysed some of these policies' impacts on equity. Aside from what was said about equity there, here it is important to address other ways in which equity may be affected. In practice, this principle is the one likely to be most affected by market values. A good way to start this discussion is by giving the following example: patient A and patient B are affiliated to the same national health system, which operates on a benefits-in-kind basis. They have the same health problem, the same need for care and, thus, the same prescription for a non-hospital treatment, for which there is a waiting list under the national health system. Patient A has sufficient resources to travel and to pay up-front for this treatment and decides to have the treatment abroad, where he will not have to wait. By contrast, patient B, who is not as wealthy as patient A, will go on the waiting list of the system in order to have the same treatment provided within the national borders.

This example clearly shows how equity can be affected by a policy governed by values based mainly on market freedoms. Not only will the wealthier patient receive health care more quickly, but this possibility may also represent a way of bypassing policy choices made for the allocation of resources by national health systems.[45] Therefore, the impact on equity has two aspects: one is illustrated by the example above that refers to one individual in relation to another having the same need for care; and the second is the individual in relation to collectivity.

These two aspects of liberal values affecting the principles of equity are also shown by a situation experienced in Canada, where some cases challenging the Canadian public health system were submitted to the Canadian Constitutional Court. The Chaoulli case[46] is probably the best known and has had greatest

44 BREKKE, K.R., LEVAGGI, R., SICILIANI, L. & STRAUME, O.R. 2011. Patient Mobility, Health Care Quality and Welfare. *Discussion Paper, Norwegian School of Economics.* Available at www.nhh.no/Files/Filer/institutter/sam/Discussion%20papers/2011/13.pdf [Accessed 14 December 2015], p. 29.

45 HERVEY, T.K. 2011a. *Op. cit.,* p. 245.

46 Decision of the Supreme Court of Canada, *Chaoulli v. Quebec (Attorney General)*, [2005] 1 S.C.R. 791, 2005 SCC 35.

repercussions. Basically, it refers to the right of an individual to obtain private health care at his/her own expense – which is prohibited under Canadian law – by reason of the long waiting lists within the public system. The Constitutional Court decided in favour of the right of the individual and struck down the local legislation as infringing the constitutional rights to life and security. This decision has been described as portending the fall of Medicare, Canada's most cherished social programme, because of its abandonment of the principle that need should determine access.[47] It has been claimed that it allows for access to be determined by wealth, which could result in the creation of a two-tier system structure.[48]

As demonstrated by the example of Canada, cross-border health care within the EU also has the potential to create a two-tier system: first, because lower-income groups are less likely to access health care abroad because it represents a financial barrier to them. As explained in Chapter 3, access to care is also measured according to the nature and extent of barriers imposed on patients, and hence the payment of treatments up-front and travel expenses impose a financial barrier to access. In this context, cross-border health care will be accessed mostly by wealthier individuals, who, incidentally, are not usually those in the greatest need of care.[49] Likewise, lower-income groups may also be discouraged to travel due to cultural and linguistic aspects. This can be said to work as a personal barrier to access care. Furthermore, the wealthier have a stronger voice and are more articulate. Indeed, it was wealthier patients who brought the cases on cross-border health care before the ECJ. Therefore, if national health services start to be abandoned by those patients, they will not use their voice to 'fight' for a system that they do not use. In this context, the worst scenario could be that of closure of domestic infrastructure led by a large net outflow of patients, 'which might decrease local access to care for the patients who do not go abroad'.[50]

In this regard, a recent study assessing the welfare effects of the European Choice Agenda concluded that choice policies in health care are not equitable because choice is indeed 'a middle class policy, mainly benefiting well educated, high income individuals who are able to make optimal use of the available choice'.[51] Furthermore, this is not likely to change with the Directive on patients because it facilitates access to cross-border health care without paying attention to social status or ability to pay. Although emphasising the significance of important values in the

47 GROSS, A.M. 2007. The right to health in an era of privatisation and globalisation: national and international perspectives. *In:* BARAK-EREZ, D. & GROSS, A.M. (eds) *Exploring social rights: between theory and practice.* Oxford; Portland, OR: Hart. *Op. cit,* p. 311.

48 MARCHILDON, G.P. 2005. The Chaoulli Case: A Two-Tier Magna Carta? *Healthcare Quarterly,* 8(4): 49–52.

49 HERVEY, T.K. 2011a. *Op. cit.,* p. 245.

50 BAETEN, R. 2011. Past impacts of cross-border health care. *In:* WISMAR, M., PALM, W., FIGUERAS, J., ERNST, K. & GINNEKEN, E.V. (eds) *Cross-border health care in the European Union.* Copenhagen: World Health Organization, on Behalf of the European Observatory on Health Systems and Policies, p. 282.

51 ZIGANTE, V. 2011.*Op. cit.,* p. 26.

health field, of which equity is included, the Directive does not manage to convert these values into rights and does not provide any mechanisms to counterbalance the effects of choice. As De La Rosa contends:

> Yet, facilitating equal access to care, regardless of one's social status or ability to pay, is an essential aspect of equity. Curiously, or perhaps deliberately, the text is silent on social and territorial inequalities in access to care. It does not really attach great importance to disadvantaged individuals or groups, often cut off from public policy on care. Nor does it promote access to cross-border healthcare for patients in a state of necessity. Notwithstanding its display of values, the Directive is aimed primarily at individuals or groups of individuals who have the cognitive and social resources required to engage in a process of mobility. This is one of the challenges of concretely transforming mobility issues into EU law: it is intended for a public that is sufficiently informed to be able to engage in this kind of process.[52]

In this same vein, a study on cross-border health care found that it has a negative impact on equity because it widens the gaps in access to care between different social groups, insofar as '[s]ocially advantaged groups are likely to make more use of the possibilities to receive care abroad. Also it is easier for patients who are fit to travel to access cross-border care, as they have no co-morbidity and their treatment is relatively easier'.[53]

Moreover, another way in which the EU approach to health care can affect the principle of equity of access is the use of free movement rights by those wealthier patients as a way of by-passing waiting lists and gatekeeping systems. The creation of a two-tier system not only has an impact on equity but also on the principle of non-discrimination. In this respect, Szyszczak suggests that cross-border health care based on free movement is discriminatory because:

> The free movement perspective has been driven by patients who are knowledgeable of their EU right and have the economic means to travel abroad for treatment and stay abroad for fairly short periods to receive treatment, often returning back to the home State system for after care and support.[54]

Furthermore, cross-border health care can also be said to be discriminatory in relation to people with complex health problems or chronic diseases: first, because patients need to be fit to travel; and second, because these patients need longer and more complex forms of long-term care, which can be problematic in

---

52 ROSA, S.D.L. 2012. The Directive on Cross-Border Healthcare or the Art of Codifying Complex Case Law. *Common Market Law Review*, 49: 15–46, pp. 38–9.

53 BAETEN, R. 2011. *Op. cit.*, p. 282.

54 SZYSZCZAK, E. 2011. *Op. cit.*, p. 111.

a cross-border setting.[55] Indeed, long-term care is excluded from the scope of the Directive, as asserted by Article 1.3 (a), and the preamble (recital 14) is very vague in explaining the reasons for this exclusion.[56]

The Directive also raises discrimination concerns in relation to funding levels, which vary considerably between countries. Treatments are reimbursed at different levels depending on the Member State, and such variation could impede access to cross-border care to nationals from countries where the tariffs and reimbursement of treatment are lower than the tariffs in the country of treatment.[57] In this regard, data on patient flows covering the calendar year 2014 suggest that this is actually what has been happening, since wealthier Member States, such as Finland, Luxembourg, France and Denmark, reported a much higher volume of patient mobility than other EU Member States.[58]

Cross-border health care may also affect expenditure control mechanisms of national health systems. While cross-border care is reimbursed on a fee-for-service basis, remuneration in some Member States is subject to expenditure control mechanisms. Hence, official rates used for cross-border care can be too high because they do not take into account reduction fees due to targeted budgets, creating thereby a tension between resource allocation and policies aiming for cost control within Member States and the fee-for-service reimbursement of cross-border care.[59]

In addition, the discriminatory aspect of cross-border health care and its impact on equity can also give rise to reverse discrimination, which will be analysed in the next section of this chapter.

Therefore, it is possible to argue that introducing values such as freedom of choice and ability to pay – which have a libertarian nature – into the provision of health care across borders in the EU has a serious impact on the principle of equity. This is, more than ever, an issue of concern in the EU because the progress made by EU Member States between 2005 and 2009 in improving access to health care changed drastically with the financial crisis. In this regard, the number of people reporting unmet need fell steadily from 24 million in 2005 to 15 million in 2009. Since 2009, however, this positive trend has been reversed – a visible sign of the damage caused by the financial and economic crisis. By 2013, the number

55 BAETEN, R. 2012. *Op. cit.*, p. 27.
56 NYS, H. 2014. The Transposition of the Directive on Patients' Rights in Cross-Care Healthcare in National Law by the Member States: Still a Lot of Effort to Be Made and Questions to Be Answered. *European Journal of Health Law*, 21: 1–14.
57 FOOTMAN, K. *et al.* 2014. *Op. cit.*, p. 11.
58 EUROPEAN COMMISSION 2015. Report from the Commission to the European Parliament and the Council. Commission report on the operation of Directive 2011/24/EU on the application of patients' rights in cross-border healthcare. COM (2015) 421 final.
59 KIFMANN, M. & WAGNER, C. 2014. Implications of the EU Patients' Rights Directive in Cross-Border Healthcare on the German Sickness Fund System. *In*: LEVAGGI, R. & MONTEFIORI, M. *Health care provision and patient mobility: health integration in the European Union*. Italy: Springer, pp. 49–66.

of people reporting unmet need for health care had risen to 18 million (3.6% of the population).[60] Therefore, considering what was explained in Chapter 3 about access to health care, choice and ability to pay are values that have the potential to affect access based on need (horizontal equity) since lower-income groups and people with mobility difficulties are less likely to make use of cross-border health care insofar as the costs involved in this form of care represent a financial barrier to access. Moreover, personal barriers, such as cultural and linguistic aspects, may discourage these groups from accessing care abroad.

Reverse discrimination and the provision of health care services

As already explained, the free movement provisions have as their main aim the establishment of the Internal Market. Therefore, in theory, these provisions only apply to situations where the application of a national measure deters a Member State national from exercising an economic activity in an inter-state context. As a way of filtering situations unconnected to the aim of creating the Internal Market, the ECJ has established in its case law that situations regarding individuals who remain confined within the territory of their own Member State do not entail the application of EU law (free movement provisions), since they are purely internal to the respective Member State and escape the ambit of Internal Market creation. This is called the purely internal rule, which was applied for the first time in *Saunders*,[61] a case relating to workers and then extended to other fundamental freedoms.[62]

Reverse discrimination arises as a consequence of the purely internal rule, and can be explained as a 'disadvantage' imposed on those individuals who do not exercise an economic activity in an inter-state context and for this reason do not benefit from the more flexible rules or grants established by EU law to individuals who exercise free movement rights. As Alina Tryfonidou explains:

> [. . .] reverse discrimination is a difference in treatment based on the fact that a person has not contributed to the construction of the internal market. In other words, reverse discrimination is a difference in treatment between the following two categories of persons: a) Union citizens who can point to a contribution to the aim of establishing and maintaining an internal market (the 'favoured' ones) and b) Union citizens who are unable to illustrate any link with the internal market aims of the Community (the 'reversely discriminated' ones).[63]

60 Expert Panel on effective ways of investing in Health 175 (EXPH). Preliminary Report on Access to Health Services in the European Union. Available at http://ec.europa.eu/health/expert_panel/opinions/docs/010_access_healthcare_en.pdf [Accessed 14 December 2015].
61 Case 175/78 *R. v Saunders* [1979] ECR 1129, para. 11.
62 TRYFONIDOU, A. 2008. Reverse Discrimination in Purely Internal Situations: An Incongruity in a Citizens' Europe. *Legal Issues of Economic Integration*, 35(1): 43–67.
63 *Ibid.*, p. 54.

Therefore, those who can establish a link with the Internal Market are somehow favoured because usually EU law imposes more flexible or generous rules on situations that fall within its scope. By contrast, persons who remain confined within their Member State of origin have to comply with the more restrictive laws of the respective Member State once the presence of EU citizens in their own Member States *per se* generates no EU obligations at all.[64] This difference in treatment may arise even in cases involving the same factual situation where the only distinguishing factor is the connection or not with the completion of the Internal Market, i.e. the connection with the free movement (inter-state) element.

Traditionally, the problem of reverse discrimination has been considered by the ECJ as a permissible difference in treatment that is not prohibited by EU law and falls outside its scope. In the view of the Court, this was a type of necessary evil of the EU's system of governance that should be dealt with at the national level.[65] Therefore, in the case of provision of services, for example as in the case of health care, if the provision is within one and the same Member State, Article 56 TFEU cannot be used as the basis of a claim. In this situation, claims can only be based on national law.[66]

However, more recently the Court has tried to extend the scope of the fundamental freedoms to situations that presented a tenuous link with the aims of these provisions in order to address the problem of reverse discrimination. As a consequence, situations that did not comprise inter-state movement entailed the application of EU law as a way of preventing the emergence of reverse discrimination. In the words of Tryfonidou, 'there is no longer a need for a link to be established between a deterrent effect on the exercise of one of the fundamental freedoms and the national measure that is contested for being in violation of the relevant Treaty provision'. [67] This new approach of the Court arose in part as a reply to the fact that in some Member States reverse discrimination is prohibited by national constitutions by virtue of the principle of equality,[68] but it is also a concern with the emergence of a difference in treatment between Union citizens based on the criterion of the Internal Market, which appears to be outdated in face of the status of European citizenship.[69]

In the view of Spaventa, for example, the introduction of the status of Union citizenship changes the migrant paradigm in relation to the personal scope of the Treaty. As a consequence, it is no longer necessary to exercise movement within the Union in order to be a potential right-holder (personal scope). The wording of Article 20(1) TFEU – ex Article 17(1) EC, in fact, supports this view, by making

---

64 SHUIBHNE, N.N. 2002. Free Movement of Persons and the Wholly Internal Rule: Time to Move On? *Common Market Law Review*, 39: 731–71, p. 750.

65 TRYFONIDOU, A. 2008. *Op. cit.*, p. 54.

66 TRYFONIDOU, A. 2009. *Reverse discrimination in EC law*. The Netherlands: Kluwer Law International, p. 51.

67 TRYFONIDOU, A. 2008. *Op. cit.*, p. 50.

68 TRYFONIDOU, A. 2009. *Op. cit.*, p.121.

69 TRYFONIDOU, A. 2008. *Op. cit.*, p. 51.

European citizenship conditional only upon the possession of nationality of one of the Member States.[70] Therefore, this leads to a result that any EU citizen falls within the personal scope of the Treaty, even those static ones who have not exercised migration within the Union. However, of course, there are limits or boundaries to this interpretation and they are somehow defined by the material scope of the Treaty, that is, by the potential rights that static citizens are able to claim using the Treaty.

This new approach first appeared in custom duties cases,[71] as *Lancry*,[72] *Simitzi*[73] and *Carbonati Apuani*,[74] and was then transplanted to cases concerning family reunification, such as *Carpenter*[75] and *Jia*.[76] More recently, in cases concerning citizenship, the ECJ has put in the same position Union citizens who have contributed to the Internal Market and those who have not, by making basic rights granted by EU law available to the latter group. Examples of this are cases such as *Ruiz Zambrano, Morgan and Grzelczyk*, analysed in Chapter 2 of this book. Especially in those cases involving citizenship of the Union, the Court abandoned the traditional economic migrant approach, moving beyond the labels of work, goods, establishment and services.[77]

The purpose of looking at this new approach of the Court in relation to movement and the problem of reverse discrimination is because it is a problem that can arise too in the provision of health care in the EU. This can arise because the rules for the provision of health care across borders, now codified by Directive 2011/24/EU, confer rights – such as choice of provider – to individuals who opt to be treated outside their country of origin/residence, which are most of the time not conferred to individuals who are treated inside the country. These 'static' individuals, instead, are subject to national rules, which, in general, are stricter since they do not confer the possibility of mobility and choice, as in the case of cross-border health care. Therefore, citizens who opt for cross-border health care are in an advantageous situation insofar as they are free, in relation to many types of health treatment, to seek a provider of their choice wherever in the EU. In this regard, Baeten and Palm sustain that:

> [. . .] we could question whether the Court itself does not introduce some degree of inconsistency when ruling that patients are at liberty to go to the care provider of their choice in another Member State, whereas, domestically they only can receive reimbursement of treatment from contracted providers.

70 SPAVENTA, E. 2008. Seeing the wood despite the trees? On the scope of Union Citizenship and its Constitutional effects. *Common Market Law Review*, 45: 13–45.
71 TRYFONIDOU, A. 2008. *Op. cit.*, p. 48.
72 Joined Cases C-363/93, C-407/93, C-409/93 and C-411/93, *Lancry* [1994] ECR I–3957.
73 Joined Cases C-485/93 and C-486/93, *Simitzi* [1995] ECR I-2655.
74 Case C-72/03, *Carbonati Apuani Srl v. Comune di Carrara* [2004] ECR I-8027.
75 Case C-60/00, *Carpenter* [2002] ECR I-6279.
76 Case C-1/05, *Jia v. Migrationverket* [2007] ECR I-1 583.
77 SHUIBHNE, N.N. 2002. *Op. cit.*, p. 751.

Even if this could seem to create an inconsistency in the policy, the Court does, however, not forbid this so-called reverse discrimination since EU law does not deal with purely internal situations.[78]

It is not difficult to imagine this situation in many countries around the EU. In Italy, for example, where the provision of health care is decentralised to the regional level, it is well-known that provision is better in central and northern regions of the country, such as Tuscany and Lombardy. Accordingly, if the same right granted to cross-border patients were granted to patients within the country, people living in Calabria or Sicily could choose to be treated by a private provider in these other regions. Indeed, this would be much easier for Italian patients than seeking a provider outside their country, because it is usually cheaper travelling within the country where health professionals speak the same language. This is likely to be the case for many other countries in the EU, not only in those having a decentralised system for the provision of health care but also in those with centralised provision. This is in fact what happens in Spain, where a patient may be reimbursed for treatment carried out in a private provider in another EU Member State, but may not be reimbursed for treatment carried out by a domestic private provider.[79]

The solution to this situation would be to extend access to non-contracted providers to domestic patients. This was what happened in Germany and the Netherlands when they implemented the ECJ rulings on patient mobility.[80] However, this is not the case in most Member States.

Domestic patients are also in a worse situation in Member States where reimbursement of domestic private providers is partially covered. In Finland, for example, costs of some private treatments are reimbursed by 20–60% of the total price whereas treatments carried out on a Finnish patient by a private provider in another Member State will be fully reimbursed.[81]

Likewise, this situation also poses the question of discrimination against private providers of the state of affiliation. The fact that patients are free to seek private health care outside their home country, but are circumscribed to those with which the national system has arrangements, is a situation that discriminates against local private providers.

Although Article 8 2 (c) of the Directive establishes that health care may be subject to prior authorisation when the provider gives rise to serious and specific

78 BAETEN, R. & PALM, W. 2011. The Compatibility of Health Care Capacity Planning Policies with EU Internal Market Rules. *In:* GRONDEN, J.W.V.D., SZYSZCZAK, E., NEERGAARD, U. & KRAJEWSKI, M. (eds) *Health care and EU law.* The Hague: T.M.C. Asser, p. 410.

79 REQUEJO, M. 2014. Cross-border care in Spain and the implementation of the Directive 2011/24/EU on the application of patients' rights in cross-border healthcare. *European Journal of Health Law*, 21(1): 79–96.

80 BAETEN, R. 2012. *Op. cit.*, p. 20.

81 KATTELUS, M. 2014. Implementation of the Directive on the application on patient's rights in cross-border healthcare (2011/24/eu) in Finland. *European Journal of Health Law*, 21(1): 23–32.

concerns relating to the quality or safety of the care, in my opinion this quality and safety exception could not be used to require prior authorisation to every private or non-contracted provider only on this basis.[82]

Some commentators are of the opinion that domestic patients too should benefit from the Directive, since the definition of 'patient' in Article 3(h) does not distinguish between mobile and domestic patients.[83] I understand, nevertheless, that this is the case with regard to some rights provided for in the Directive, such as the right of information (Article 4 2(b)), but it does not apply to the specific right of reimbursement without prior authorisation as envisaged by Article 7.

Although the ECJ has moved on to try to give a new approach to situations where reverse discrimination can arise, and has progressed the scope of EU law beyond the Internal Market, as shown by the cases on citizenship, the question of movement is still a decisive factor for the Court. Therefore, in order to invoke the Treaty (or to fall within its material scope) some sort of movement is necessary, even if indirectly. What about a situation that does not present any kind of link with movement? Could the rights conferred by the Treaty be invoked in a situation like this? This is what I would like to explore here in relation to health care, and more specifically to determine whether non-migrant EU citizens are able to claim the right to choose a health care provider within their own Member States, as migrant patients are according to Directive 2011/24/EU. Considering that in order to establish the true scope of EU law it is important to define the class of individuals who are able to claim rights (the personal scope) and the potential rights that they are able to claim (the material scope), it is important to analyse the situation of a potential claim involving health care having regard to the personal and material scopes of EU law.

Even if the Court has already decided on cases involving social security benefits, as I will show below, a situation involving the provision of health care has not yet been studied or subject to the scrutiny of the ECJ. Therefore, having regard to the possibilities offered by the Treaty, the Charter of Fundamental Rights and national legislation, we will now discuss the basis for a claim regarding the situation of a static individual who wishes to choose a health provider within the territory of his or her Member State, in the same way that migrant patients are able to do.

One could argue that a possible solution in a situation like this, in which patients are not allowed by national legislation to seek a provider of their choice inside their own Member State, would be a claim based on the fundamental right to health provided for in either national constitutions or Article 35 of the Charter of Fundamental Rights. However, national constitutions usually do not provide for the right to health as an entitlement to treatment. Likewise, the Charter, although talking of a fundamental right, provides for the respect for national laws.

---

82 BAETEN, R. & PALM, W. 2013. Preserving General Interest in healthcare through secondary and soft EU Law: the case of the Patients' Rights Directive. *In*: NEERGARD, U. *et al.* (eds) *Social services of general interest in the EU*. The Hague: T.M.C. Asser, pp. 385–412.

83 NYS, H. 2014. *Op. cit.*

The Charter by itself would not be sufficient to base a claim like this. However, it could be used in conjunction with other legal provisions. In this regard, an alternative solution would be a claim based on citizenship of the Union (Article 20(1) TFEU), which would support the idea that static citizens also fall within the scope of EU law (personal scope). Besides that, the claim could be based on two other different rights: first, the right of equal treatment before the law, which is one of the founding principles of the EU (Article 2 TEU). Practically applied to the envisaged situation, this would entail that a static citizen should have the same right to choice of health care provider within national borders as a cross-border patient. It is important to note that in relation to the principle of non-discrimination on the grounds of nationality, established by Article 18 TFEU, it could not be used in this situation since the comparison would be between individuals from the same nationality. Second, the right to move freely within the territory of the Member States as established by Article 21(1) TFEU. However, with regard to this right, the first problem that I see is whether it could constitute the claim of a right to move anywhere within the territory of one's own Member State. Despite the broad and teleological interpretation that has been given to this provision, the Court indicated in *Garcia Avello*,[84] for example, that it does not apply to situations with no cross-border element.[85] Moreover, the Charter of Fundamental Rights could be used to reinforce the principles of equality and non-discrimination (Articles 20 and 21) and to raise the question of health care as a fundamental right (Article 35). Finally, national legislation, especially constitutional provisions on the principles of equality and non-discrimination, could also be invoked.

A claim like this would probably be subject to the scrutiny of the ECJ, which would have to decide whether the purely internal rule would be applicable or not in this case. As demonstrated in other situations, the Court has put in the same position Union citizens who have contributed to the Internal Market and those who have not, by making available to the latter the basic rights granted by EU law. However, I think that in the case of the provision of health care it would be more difficult for this argument to stand: first, because there are interpretative limits to the development of EU citizenship[86] and the Court has already signalled that citizenship of the Union is not intended to extend the material scope of the Treaty;[87] and second, because within national borders health care is still dealt with as a social issue over which Member States retain competence (Article 168(7)). Therefore, it would be difficult not only to show the link with EU law, but also to apply it to this sensitive field over which Member States retain discretion. In this regard, it is important to note again that national constitutions usually do not provide for the right to health as an entitlement to treatment.

84 Case C-148/02, *Garcia Avello* [2003] ECR I-11613.
85 SPAVENTA, E. 2008. *Op. cit.*, p. 25.
86 SHUIBHNE, N.N. 2009. The Outer Limits of EU Citizenship: Displacing Economic Free Movement Rights? *In:* BARNARD, C. & ODUDU, O. (eds) *The outer limits of European law.* Oxford; Portland, OR: Hart, p. 169.
87 See, for example, judgement of the Court in the joined Cases C-64/96 and C-65/96, *Ueker and Jacquet* [1997] ECR I-3171. Para 23.

The ECJ has not yet dealt with a claim like this. However, in *Government of the French Community and Walloon Government v Flemish Government*,[88] Advocate General Sharpston raised a similar argument. The situation at issue concerned the possibility of an autonomous region of a Member State – *in casu* the Flemish region – of granting a social security benefit conditional on residence in the territory of this autonomous region or in the territory of another Member State. Although the Court limited its decision to the analysis of the conformity of the Flemish legislation in relation to free movement law, especially ex-Articles 39 and 43 EC (now Articles 45 and 49 TFEU), since the social security benefit in question affected mainly migrant workers, the Advocate General also analysed the issue from the point of view of EU citizenship, examining the situation of Belgian citizens who have not made use of their freedom of movement rights. Therefore, this involved the broader issue of the impact of EU law on purely internal situations, i.e. 'an occasion for the Court to reflect on the nature and rationale behind its doctrine in respect of purely internal situations'.[89] Recalling the cases on citizenship and the theory regarding the 'purely internal rule', Advocate General Sharpston started by sustaining that not 'all so-called "internal situations" are automatically deprived of any link to Community law'.[90] In other words, the link with EU law can exist even in internal situations. This was exactly what the Advocate General argued in this case. She constructed her argument in this regard by first explaining that EU citizenship not only grants citizens the right to move but also the right to reside anywhere within the Union territory, and it is possible to exercise this right without first exercising the right to move between Member States.[91] She went on by showing that by virtue of the combination of the application of national law and the application of EC law, the only category of persons residing in the French-speaking or German-speaking region who would not be able to access the Flemish care benefit are Belgians who had not exercised their right of freedom of movement but who had exercised (and still exercise) their right to reside in a particular part of Belgium. In this regard, as she further explains:

> the difference in treatment between such persons on the one hand, and nationals of other Member States and Belgians who have exercised classic economic rights of freedom of movement, on the other hand, arises precisely because EC law intervenes to prevent adverse treatment of the latter group.[92]

Considering this reasoning and the fact that the principle of non-discrimination may also prevent reverse discrimination in the field of social security law, the Advocate General reached the conclusion that the group of Belgian nationals who

---

88 Case C-212/06, *Government of the French Community and Walloon Government v Flemish Government* [2008] ECR I-1683.

89 Opinion of Advocate General in Case C-212/0, para. 121.

90 *Ibid.*, para. 136.

91 *Ibid.*, para. 143–4.

92 *Ibid.*, para. 151.

shave not exercised the classic economic right of movement are nevertheless able to invoke EU law once they are sufficiently affected by its application.[93]

This same reasoning could be transposed to the case of the provision of health care, even though health care differs in some aspects from the situation of this Belgian case: first, because it does not constitute an additional social security benefit; and second, because within borders there are no differences in treatment between persons and health care benefits are conferred the same way on citizens. The fact that one part or region of a Member State has a better provision of health care is generally due to economic reasons rather than to legislation; and third, because the difference in treatment in the case of health care, i.e. the possibility of choice across borders, is established by EU law (Directive 2011/24/EU). Indeed, what happened in the field of health care is that the EU, through the jurisprudence of the ECJ, that is, through negative integration, deregulated some aspects of the provision of health care at the national level, by establishing, for example, that some administrative mechanisms used by Member States were against free movement law. Then Directive 2011/24/EU came into force, and as an instrument of positive integration, established a kind of re-regulation of these services at EU level. In effect, the Directive follows the familiar interaction between negative and positive integration and, in the case of health care:

> this is no less than a watershed given the constitutional barriers that had been erected in the Treaty against harmonization in this field and which have now been breached. Could this mean the scope for applying the EU law concept of citizenship has increased?[94]

The result of this re-regulation is that there are two concurring competences on the same subject (provision of health care), thus creating differences in treatment when compared to the national provision of services that are not subject to the principles of the Directive. Therefore, the fact that a Member State does not allow its citizens to have a choice of health care provider within its own territory does not render this prohibition, in principle, against EU law.[95]

In spite of these differences, I do not see them as an impediment to applying Advocate General Sharpston's reasoning to the case of health care. Accordingly, Member State nationals who have not exercised their right of free movement by crossing the border of their Member State of origin would also be able to choose a provider within the national territory by virtue of the status of citizenship of the Union. For obvious reasons, this type of claim would open the possibility for

---

93 *Ibid.*, para. 154.

94 HANCHER, L. & SAUTER, W. 2012. *Op. cit.*, p. 310.

95 In this respect, Canizarro explains that '[r]everse discrimination, thus, may well be considered as a consequence of the existence of two overlapping spheres of competence in the same matter: of the existence of norms belonging to different legal systems, and having to conform to different objectives and values'. CANNIZZARO, E. 1997. Producing 'Reverse Discrimination' through the Exercise of EC Competences. *Yearbook of European Law*, 17: 29–46, p. 1.

Member States to raise, first, arguments concerning their discretion to organise their health systems. Moreover, Member States could also use objective justifications as counterarguments. In the case of health care, there are a number of plausible arguments that could be used in this regard, amongst which the most important is the protection of public health through the maintenance of a balanced medical and hospital service open to all. This, in effect, was already recognised as a justification in the case law of cross-border health care. Such a justification would be even more crucial in the case of Member States that decentralise the provision of health care services.

Despite the lengthy reasoning of Advocate General Sharpston on the problem of 'purely internal situations', the Court did not decide on this point. It only remarked that the national court, also in situations classed as purely internal, might use EU law.[96] Therefore, it is difficult to predict how the Court would react in a similar situation, as in the case of health care. I am certain, however, that there are many counterarguments that the Court will have to deal with if one day it decides on purely internal situations, based upon the continuing competences of Member States, as in the case of health care. In this respect, Advocate General Sharpston pointed out:

> Given that purely internal situations have traditionally been viewed as falling outside the scope of EC law, it is likely that Member States would indeed wish to present such arguments to the Court, and their arguments need to be considered carefully. [. . .] It might be that, on more detailed examination, the prima facie case that I have outlined above is refuted.[97]

Finally, it should be noted that whilst the application of EU law to purely internal situations, such as that envisaged in the case of health care, can be a way of enforcing individuals' rights at the national level, putting them in the same position as migrant patients, it is likely to affect national procedural rules and the hierarchy of norms,[98] subverting national systems of judicial review since national constitutions usually do not provide for the right to health as an entitlement to treatment. Although here I discussed the possibilities to correct reverse discrimination in the provision of health care through the use of legal instruments, I am not so sure whether this is the best way of addressing the subject. The option of using courts, especially the ECJ, to redress a problem that involves national competence may not be the most democratic way, opening the door for improper judicial-law making. There are, however, other ways of addressing the question of reverse discrimination. Shuibhne, for example, discusses the possibilities for reform and correction of reverse discrimination in terms of the level of governance – EU or national – and the type of governance – legislative or judicial.[99] In my

---

96 Judgement of the Court in Case C-212/06. Para 40.
97 Opinion of Advocate General in Case C-212/06, para. 156.
98 SPAVENTA, E. 2008. *Op. cit.*, p. 37.
99 SHUIBHNE, N.N. 2002. *Op. cit.*

opinion, the legislature should be preferred since it allows for a more democratic political discussion. Moreover, this should have as a starting point the national level because it enables a ground-up form of governance rather than top-down.

Universality

Universal coverage of health services can be defined as a situation in which all people have access to needed health services without the risk of severe financial consequences.[100] Based on this definition it is possible to distinguish countries by degree of universality within the health system. Usually, national health services, such as in the UK, offer universal coverage linked to residence requirements. In social insurance systems, the coverage is quasi-universal, as in the case of Germany. On the opposite side lies the case of the United States, where the degree of universality is low due to the voluntary and private nature of the health system. As a consequence, a considerable number of people are left without health care coverage.[101]

The principle of universality is the one that is likely to be least affected by the market values – freedom of choice and ability to pay – developed by the EU in relation to cross-border health care. If we take into account health systems as a whole, this type of care is just one part of the services offered by the system and thus the main range of services will continue to be available to the population covered by such a system. Hence, in this case there will be no impact on the principle of universality. However, if we take the issue of cross-border health care separately it is possible to imagine a potential impact on universality. Considering that universal coverage is directly related to the number of people covered by the services offered/needed by the population and that cross-border health care based on choice, as provided for in the Directive on patients' rights, will only be affordable for wealthier patients due to the implied costs, it can be stated then that it will have a negative effect on universality. Therefore, although offered to all EU citizens covered by EU health systems, cross-border care will actually be accessible only to a privileged group of citizens that is better informed, more mobile and better-off.

Quality

Quality of health care is a concept that can be interpreted in different ways due to the multiple definitions of quality given by the literature, and highlighted in

---

100 CARRIN, G., MATHAUER, I., XUA, K. & EVANSA, D.B. 2008. Universal coverage of health services: tailoring its implementation. *Bulletin of the World Health Organization*, 86: 857–63. See also ORGANISATION FOR ECONOMIC CO-OPERATION AND DEVELOPMENT (OECD) 1987. Financing and Delivering Health Care: A Comparative Analysis of OECD Countries. *OECD Social Policy Studies*, 4.

101 REIBLING, N. 2010. Healthcare systems in Europe: towards an incorporation of patient access. *Journal of European Social Policy*, 20: 5–18.

Chapter 3. These differences are also reflected in the way each country implements measures to assess the quality of care. In the case of the EU, although there are legislation and policies adopted by the Union, the differences that exist at the national level make this issue a complex one. As Legido-Quigley and colleagues suggest:

> There is considerable variation between and within European Union Member States in the approaches each has adopted and the extent to which legislative measures to ensure quality of care have been implemented.[102]

In relation to the adoption of measures regarding quality in health care, these authors have identified three broad categories of country within the EU: the first refers to those Member States that have no legislation or policy on quality; the second relates to Member States that have recently enacted legislation or implemented policies in this area; and the third category refers to those Member States that have a long tradition of legislation and policies on the quality of care.[103]

These differences within the EU pose a problem for the provision of health care across borders, a situation in which the focus of quality is mainly based on patient safety. Although there are different types of cross-border patient,[104] the object of this analysis is individuals who go abroad on their own initiative to seek treatment. These patients are in a very different situation from those who are sent abroad by their health systems. The schemes for sending patients abroad present several advantages to patients, because:

> First, patients are being guided through the entire process as all medical, logistic and travel aspects of cross-border care are organized for them: transport arrangements such as airplane tickets are booked; hospital rooms are reserved; and medical appointments, including pre- and post-treatment consultations, the actual treatment (e.g. an operation) and if necessary rehabilitation, are organized for the patients. Second, public authorities generally go to great lengths to check the medical expertise and quality standards of the foreign providers to which they send their patients and they have strict requirements on quality, safety and hygiene.[105]

Instead, when patients go abroad on their own, also known as individually driven planned cross-border care,[106] the situation is completely different. In this case the patient is more vulnerable, especially when he or she chooses a private provider.

---

102 LEGIDO-QUIGLEY, H., MCKEE, M., NOLTE, E. & GLINOS, I.A. 2008. *Op. cit.*, p. 17.
103 *Ibid.*
104 See, for example, GLINOS, I.A. & BAETEN, R. 2006. *Op. cit.* and GLINOS, I.A., BAETEN, R., HELBLE, M. & MAARSE, H. 2010. A typology of cross-border patient mobility. *Health Place,* 16(6): 1145–55.
105 LEGIDO-QUIGLEY, H., MCKEE, M., NOLTE, E. & GLINOS, I.A. 2008. *Op. cit.*, p. 49.
106 *Ibid.*

Generally, these patients have fewer guarantees because the quality standards are lower than those guaranteed by the public sector. Moreover, due to the question of information asymmetry, a specific characteristic that permeates the provision of health care, 'patients do not have the necessary knowledge to assess the quality and appropriateness of care they receive, which is why the public system has a role in ensuring standards for quality and safety in the health care sector'.[107] This is accentuated still further when the patient does not speak the language of the country of treatment and is unfamiliar with the health system.

The freedom of choice guaranteed by the Directive on patients' rights creates the possibility for this kind of situation where the safety of patients may be at risk, thus undermining the principle of quality. Although there are many provisions in the Directive aimed at ensuring the quality and safety of health care provided abroad, such as Article 4 (2) b and c, and Article 12 (2) c, this is not easy to put into practice and to monitor, especially in the case of private providers, as explained above. Furthermore, there are insufficient data about patients going abroad to seek treatment on their own, which makes monitoring even more complicated. Regarding this specific issue, the Directive points to a paradox because 'where the European Union needs to facilitate access to safe and high-quality cross-border health care, it is withheld to act on the basis of the subsidiarity principle'.[108]

In addition, patients who face a genuine problem, such as harm arising from the treatment received abroad, will face a further impediment: seeking remedies. In the view of Meyer, for example, 'the biggest obstacle for individual patients to seek cross-border treatment remains the fact that they would rely on foreign complaints procedures and jurisdiction if they suffer harm arising from the healthcare they receive abroad and seek remedies'.[109]

Therefore, the freedom of choice offered by cross-border health care may affect the principle of quality insofar as there are serious difficulties in assuring the safety of patients travelling abroad to receive treatment on their own. The Directive fails to ensure quality and safety of cross-border care, and patients will have to rely on national standards of the host Member State.[110] Moreover, they may also have problems in seeking remedies in the case of liability issues.

Another potential negative effect of freedom of choice on quality relates to the continuity of care in cross-border treatment. In this respect, Baeten, citing various studies, mentions the question of weakness in the care chain, lack of information transfer for aftercare and the availability of drugs and medical devices prescribed abroad.[111]

Finally, another way in which cross-border health care, as provided for in the Directive on patients' rights, may affect quality is by opening the door to a race

107　*Ibid.*, p. 50.
108　PALM, W. & BAETEN, R. 2011. The quality and safety paradox in the patients' rights directive. *European Journal of Public Health*, 21(3): 272–4.
109　MEYER, H. 2011. *Op. cit.*, p. 18.
110　BAETEN, R. 2012. *Op. cit.*, p. 28.
111　BAETEN, R. 2011. *Op. cit.*, p. 269.

to the bottom. As already explained, countries that offer better treatment for a given medical speciality may reduce the quality of services in order to discourage the entry of foreign patients.

How to cope with market values and solidaristic (egalitarian) principles of EU health systems?

As demonstrated above, the principles codified by the Directive on patients' rights are firmly grounded in the economic liberties provided for by the Treaty; it is taken for granted that the provision of health services is purely economic in nature and therefore should be dealt with as any other service offered in the Internal Market. This is the approach that the EU took in relation to health services, which contrasts markedly with that taken at the national level, where health care still belongs in the social sphere. A different path, for example, was followed by the ECJ in relation to education. This is illustrated well by the Court's judgement in *Humbel*.[112]

This book takes the view that dealing with health care services from an exclusively economic point of view is not the best way, because these services are grounded in egalitarian premises and a purely market/economic approach opens the door for, *inter alia*, inequalities in the access to care as well as types of discrimination. Indeed, the current situation regarding the provision of health care is extremely polarised: health care provided at the national level is part of social/welfare policies developed nationally whereas health care provided across borders, based on the Directive on patients' rights, is part of the Internal Market policies developed by the EU.

The codification of the principles developed by the ECJ in this Directive shows that a step towards a more liberal approach in relation to health care was taken and that this choice made at EU level is a tendency that seems unlikely to be reversed. It is possible to imagine scenarios and solutions in the event that the Directive had not been adopted: possible solutions could have been the improvement of the legislation on the coordination of social security systems in order to establish, for example, clearer criteria for the granting of prior authorisation, based on objective and non-discriminatory criteria and restricted to what is necessary and proportionate, as provided for in Article 8 of the Directive. In effect, as De La Rosa argues, 'it is likely that patients will continue to favour cross-border healthcare based on the Regulation, inasmuch as it exempts them from paying fees up front – fees that are borne by the institution of the State of affiliation'.[113]

Another mechanism that could have been used in order to encourage or better coordinate cross-border health care between EU Member States is soft law.[114] Even

112   Case C-263/86, *Humbel* [1988] ECR 5365.
113   ROSA, S.D.L. 2012. *Op. cit*, p. 33.
114   HERVEY, T. & TRUBEK, L. 2007. Freedom to Provide Health Care Services within the EU: An Opportunity for a Transformative Directive. *Columbia Journal of European Law*, 13: 623–47, p. 637.

though the Directive on patients' rights presents some mechanisms of new governance, as in the case of the European reference networks (Article 12), the majority of this piece of legislation is about formal, hard law. The substantive rules governing cross-border health care in the Directive can be considered as a classic method of EU regulation and carry much more weight that the new governance methods present in this rule. I am not saying that legislation does not offer advantages in the regulation of the Internal Market; it does offer valuable aims, such as structure, detail, certainty and the possibility of codification of the Court's case law.[115] What I maintain is that in this sensitive area it would be preferable to have more soft law instruments than classic EU legislation.

In this context, different solutions must be used in order to compensate for the more liberal approach taken by the Directive, thus avoiding a polarised situation in relation to the provision of health care and the dismantling of solid principles guiding health care around the EU, which can give rise, for example, to increase in inequalities related to the use/access to cross-border health care services. In this regard, even though some Member States have already amended their national rules in order to implement the relevant ECJ rulings, as already explained, they have recently brought into force the necessary laws, regulations and procedures in order to transpose the Directive (Article 21), a fact that goes well beyond the amendments necessary to implement ECJ jurisprudence. Moreover, Member States still have some margin of discretion in relation to services that need prior authorisation. Therefore, there is still a lot to be done in relation to the inter-state provision of health care. This can be an opportunity for EU institutions, such as the ECJ and the Commission, to rethink the most critical aspects related to this issue, mainly to find a way to cope with solidaristic and egalitarian values in a market environment. This should include acknowledgement of the special features of EU health systems that include not only the egalitarian-based principles analysed above, but also specific characteristics permeating the provision of health care, such as information asymmetry. Rethinking cross-border health care also means rethinking the policies used to regulate this issue at the EU level. Therefore, I will now develop some ideas regarding the policy instruments that could be used at the EU level to address cross-border health care.

The jurisprudence of the ECJ on patient mobility and the Directive on patients' rights show that cross-border health care has been regulated at the EU level mainly as an Internal Market issue. This is due to the question of competence, since the EU has no powers to legislate on health matters, as explained in Chapter 4. However, this type of provision of care needs to be dealt with also as a health issue. Accordingly, it is important to remember that the health sector has special features that require specific policies. Therefore, the first recommendation is to approach cross-border health care also from the point of view of a health policy issue, which, as a consequence, entails specific models for the development of policies. This could

---

115 KILPATRICK, C. 2011. Internal Market Architecture and the Accommodation of Labour Rights: As Good as it Gets? *EUI Working Papers LAW 2011/04.*

include, for example, the creation of a specific Directorate for health within the European Commission structure. The fact that health is part of a Directorate that is also dedicated to consumer affairs may suggest that policies for the health field are not designed by experts in this area. Moreover, issues related to consumer affairs tend to be influenced much more by market requirements. Once the issue is viewed as a matter requiring health policy regulation, the next step is to choose an appropriate policy design capable of regulating crucial elements of cross-border health care.

As described in Chapter 1, one of the models utilised to deliver health care in some EU countries is the quasi-market model. This model uses choice and competition – market mechanisms – in order to increase efficiency within the health system, but at the same time to offer solutions for the delivery of health care services in publicly provided systems based on solidarity. Considering that cross-border health care, as established by the jurisprudence of the ECJ and the Directive on patients' rights, also makes use of these market mechanisms, the quasi-market model could be applied to the regulation of cross-border health care. However, as explained before, the use of the quasi-market model entails the adoption of a specific policy design in order to avoid undesirable consequences, such as the rising of inequalities, which derives from the differences in peoples' purchasing power, or specific problems within the health care market, such as information asymmetry. Therefore, health care policies in a quasi-market environment must be designed, first of all, to offer the provision of services free at the point of use, which avoids the inequalities that can arise in a normal market due to the differences in people's purchasing power. Second, patients must be informed in order to make appropriate judgements. In this regard, the system must provide arrangements to advise patients on various aspects related to the provision of health care, including not only the choice of provider, but also special needs regarding travel and disability, communication problems in terms of language and transport, navigation in the health system, and help with transport and travel costs, which promotes equity and helps to make competition real.[116]

Indeed, some of the elements described above seem to have been taken into account in the regulation of cross-border health care at EU level: the Directive on patients' rights pays great attention, for example, to the question of patients being informed, as its Article 6 demonstrates, which provides for national contact points and the content of information that they must be able to provide to patients. This provision is concerned not only with the information regarding health care providers, but also that which is necessary in the event of harm arising from the care provided abroad, such as complaints and remedies available in national legislation.

For the moment, however, it is not possible to ensure that the National Contact Points referred to by the Directive will actually be able to provide the information

116 LE GRAND, J. 2007. *Op. cit.*

required by Article 6: first, because the awareness of patients of the existence of ***National Contact Points is considered to be low in most Member States;[117] second, because patients believe that the information currently provided on cross-border health care is too complex for them to understand; and third, patients also believe that they do not have access to all the information required to make an informed decision about whether to travel to another Member State for a medical treatment.[118] Furthermore, the pseudo-patient investigation exercise included in the evaluative study on the Directive prepared for the European Commission indicated that National Contact Points do not directly disclose information on quality and safety relating to health care providers outside of their country or region.[119] With regard to information on reimbursement, stakeholders interviewed in that study stated that citizens are not adequately informed about the opportunities available under the Directive, nor are they aware of the existence of National Contact Points.[120]

Therefore, although in theory the question of information is adequately laid down in the Directive, it is not possible to assert whether it will be sufficient and appropriate to compensate for information asymmetry and certain personal barriers to access. It is especially the question of information asymmetry that needs to be well regulated when the market is opened to private providers, because 'patients are heavily dependent on the decisions of health professionals and care providers, and this distinguishes them from other service consumers'.[121]

Nevertheless, the Directive does not regulate other measures required by the quasi-market model. The more problematic issues are the provision of services free at the point of use and help with transport and travel costs. These are measures that avoid the increase of inequalities. In fact, when describing the impact of the Directive on the principle of equity, I highlighted the consequences of offering freedom of choice in cross-border health care.[122] Therefore, in order to make the application of the quasi-market model feasible for the provision of cross-border health care, measures need to be taken at both the EU and national level. The issue of provision being free at the point of delivery seems to be the most problematic because patients, in principle, can go to any private provider within the EU. For this issue, one possible solution would be a system of accreditation of EU health providers, including both public and private. The credentials granted

---

117   ZUCCA, G. *et al.* 2015. *Op. cit.*, p. 31.
118   EUROPEAN COMMISSION. 2014. Impact of information on patients' choice within the context of the Directive 2011/24/EU of the European Parliament and of the Council on the application of patients' rights in cross-border healthcare (Final Report). Available at http://ec.europa.eu/health/cross_border_care/docs/cbhc_information_patientschoice_en.pdf [Accessed 14 December 2015].
119   ZUCCA, G. *et al.* 2015. *Op. cit.*, p. 13.
120   *Ibid.*, p. 12.
121   FÖLDES, M.É. 2009. *Op. cit.*, p. 169–70.
122   This problem does not occur when cross-border health care is provided through the mechanism of coordination of social security systems, i.e. when it is the national health system that sends the patient abroad.

to these providers would ensure that they have a certain level of quality standards. For this reason, this would also help with assuring that the principle of quality is protected. The EU would issue this certificate – through its specialised bodies, including committees and experts dedicated to health – and once the provider received the certification, a scheme could be established where Member States could reimburse the provider directly for treatment carried out on their nationals. Thus, patients would not have to bear the treatment expenses up-front. This system of accreditation should be followed also by incentive measures that encourage health providers to acquire the certification. Apparently this would not entail changes in the Directive.

In regard to the question of help with transport and travel costs, the EU could create a fund that would provide subsidies for Member States to give financial aid to those patients with earnings beneath a given threshold and who wish to undergo health treatment abroad under one of those certified providers. This, in fact, could represent the EU's first step towards redistributive policies in the field of health. One could argue that these measures would be discriminatory in relation to providers not certified by the accreditation system. However, the current situation already entails forms of discrimination as explained above. Moreover, even though these measures would not solve the question of equity of access to cross-border health care, they would neutralise some of the effects of the application of freedom of choice to cross-border health care. In addition, they would assist in assuring the principle of quality in the provision of health services throughout the EU. Therefore, overall these measures would have more positive than negative effects for patients and health providers; they would help in finding a balance between market values and the principles guiding the provision of health care.

It is important to note, however, that the measures suggested above would require financial investment in order to become reality. For this reason, they are unlikely to be part of the EU's health agenda in the next few years, by virtue of the financial crisis that has affected national health policies in almost all EU Member States, which have since adopted measures such as cutting ministry of health budgets, reducing or freezing government budget transfers to health insurance schemes and introducing or tightening controls on growth rates of public spending on health.[123]

Apart from these specific measures, in general terms, EU institutions need to reconceptualise the place occupied by health services within the structure of EU law. The ECJ in particular needs to find a more comprehensive way of solving conflicts that involve the provision of health services in order to accommodate market and solidaristic values of EU health systems. As Hervey argues:

> The underlying structures of EU law need to be reinterpreted, to achieve a different balance between individual entitlements within a market and solidarity, in the context of public healthcare system. The Court (which

123 THOMSON, S. *et al.* 2015. *Op. cit.*

currently decides where, in terms of a binary relationship, a particular fact pattern falls) should now develop a more explicitly value-based approach, which takes account of changes to public health service provision within the Member States.[124]

This author suggests, for example, some provisions of the EU Treaties upon which the Court could base such a new approach. This includes the use of Article 3 TEU, which provides for EU objectives other than just the Internal Market, such as the combating of social exclusion and to work for a 'highly competitive social market economy'. These examples reflect the possibility of interpreting EU law in a more balanced way, according to which market and solidaristic values have equal importance. Another example is Protocol n. 26 on SGI. As already demonstrated, this Protocol gives more flexibility in the interpretation of the role of health care services in the context of EU law, allowing for a more comprehensive categorisation of these services and thus avoiding certain extreme categorisations, such as that already established where all types of health services have an economic nature. The provisions in the Protocol not only offer a sort of counterbalance to the more liberal approach of the Internal Market, but also serve to reassert national competence in the field of health care. Even though this is already established by the jurisprudence of the ECJ and now by the Directive on patients' rights, a more balanced and flexible approach in relation to health services is crucial for including these services in a wider social context: more than simply serving the objective of the functioning of the Internal Market, it serves the objective of the functioning of national health systems, which is one of the most expressive elements of solidaristic welfare states. Ultimately, a more balanced interpretation of EU law in the field of health care is definitely necessary in order to face the major challenge brought about by the extension of the Internal Market, that is, to make use of the opportunities offered by market mechanisms, as freedom of choice and competition, and at the same time to safeguard the social character of health care.

Accordingly, answering the question proposed in the title of this book, it is possible to state that, in fact, there are new paradigms now present in the provision of health services within the EU. These are a consequence of the extension of the Internal Market and EU law into the field of health care, and are clearly illustrated by the case of cross-border health care. However, as demonstrated, there are possibilities for coping with these new values while, at the same time, preserving the solid principles of the EU's health systems. This is important to safeguard not only one of the most important parts of EU welfare states, but also to guarantee that EU citizens will be able to use an important social service when they most need it, i.e. when they become patients.

124 HERVEY, T.K. 2011b. *Op. cit.*, p. 247.

Conclusion

In this final chapter I have pointed out values introduced by the extension of the Internal Market rules to the field of health care and outlined their relationship with a libertarian view of health care. I then demonstrated how these values affect the principles of universality, accessibility, equity and solidarity at the national level. In the last part of the chapter I made my proposals and possible solutions for a more comprehensive and balanced interpretation of the role of the provision of health services in the context of the Internal Market and EU law.

Conclusion

This book sustained the view that the very special nature of health care renders this good different from others offered in a normal market. This view is supported by certain philosophical ideas applied to the field of health, such as the fair equality of opportunity and the capability approach. As a consequence of this difference, the criteria for the distribution of health care are based on egalitarian premises which entail that people with equal health needs should be treated equally by having equal access to health care. The criteria for the distribution of health care offered by the egalitarian theory contrast with those of libertarianism, according to which the distribution of health care is left to the market and no special moral importance is attached to health care.

For matters of ideology and ethics, public health systems providing universal access to health care tend to use the egalitarian theory as the basis for their policies. In the EU, this egalitarian ideology is shared across Member States and is used as a basis for the development of social policies, including health policies. However, no EU health system uses exclusively the egalitarian theory to guide their health policies. Indeed, several EU Member States have chosen to make use of market mechanisms in the delivery of health care without affecting the core of the egalitarian theory. One model that offers this possibility is the quasi-market model already used by some health systems around the EU, such as in Norway, Denmark, France, Germany and the United Kingdom.

The egalitarian theory is especially important for the types of welfare states developed in Europe that promote equity as an important value. This is because EU welfare states have another common feature: their solidaristic base. Solidarity in these welfare states means concern and responsibility for your fellow citizen and implies redistributive obligations. Besides equity and solidarity, other elements are also at the core of EU welfare states. In this regard, citizenship, and especially its social aspect, is a central question in contemporary welfare states insofar as the provision of social rights by the state becames a common strand in welfare states, especially in the EU. Indeed, it is possible to argue that social rights are a product of the welfare states by virtue of the combined ideas relating to citizenship and solidarity. Likewise, the idea of community is also essential in this context because the redistributive obligations originating from solidarity apply to citizens sharing the same territory and most of the time sharing a common history, language and culture. Therefore, equity, solidarity, social rights of citizenship and community are elements that are intrinsically related to the types of welfare state developed in Europe.

However, these elements are perfectly combined only in the context of nation states. This is because welfare states are mainly organised at the national level. Consequently, they have also contributed to the creation of a feeling of national identity.[1] Once they are applied to a wider or supranational dimension, as is the case of the EU, they lose their essential characteristics. Accordingly, social rights work differently at the EU level. This is due to the fact that the project of European integration was guided mainly by economic purposes. As a consequence, there has always been a lack of competence on the EU's part to legislate about social matters and, thereby, a lack of social (redistributive) legislation at EU level. Therefore, the rights originating from the process of economic integration are different from national social rights. Likewise, the traditional notion of social citizenship is different from the notion of a European social citizenship. This latter notion is originally permeated by the idea of a mercantile form of citizenship designed to facilitate economic integration. Hence, EU citizenship was originally conceived to provide rights to mobile citizens who helped the construction and functioning of the Internal Market. More recently, however, the ECJ has shown a different approach to this concept by applying the Treaty provisions on citizenship without the precondition of mobility. Yet, in relation to health care, remains the idea of market citizenship. The situation of cross-border health care illustrates this well because mobile patients can make use of rights and opportunities, such as freedom of choice, not conferred to non-mobile ones. Therefore, it is possible to argue that, in contrast to the national versions of social citizenship and solidarity, the supranational versions of these concepts follow a quite individualist path.

The differences between the national and supranational versions of social citizenship explain why the notions of territory and common culture are crucial to the development of welfare states. In this regard, EU welfare states present different features and ways of evolution that are explained by the history of each individual Member State. In the field of health, this becomes clear when we look at the different models of health systems adopted by Member States. Although there are two basic types – Beveridgean and Bismarkian – each Member State adjusts these types according to its own needs and contexts. Despite the considerable differences in the organisation and financing of EU health systems, they all share common principles and values that are used to shape health policies. At least three of these principles – solidarity, equity and universality – are concerned with the achievement of social justice and social cohesion, as already stated by the Council of the EU in the document 'Council Conclusions on Common values and principles in European Union Health Systems'. This concern about social values can be said to reflect the egalitarian ideology with regard to health care. In spite of the fact that EU health systems have introduced market mechanisms in recent

---

1 BEER, P.D. & KOSTER, F. 2009. *Op. cit.*, p. 50.

decades, the commitment with solidarity, equity and universality is still a reality in the EU. Evidence of that is the fact that the participation of the private sector in EU health systems is still at a reduced level. This situation is very different, for example, from that in the United States, where there is a considerably higher participation of the private sector in the health system. In fact, private health insurance works as the primary source of health coverage in that country.

The introduction of market mechanisms is not the only challenge faced by national health systems. In the last two decades these systems have been also challenged by the direct application of the Treaty rules on situations regarding the provision of health services, especially those provisions related to the Internal Market and competition law. Member States have interpreted this as if the EU were stepping into a field that was not within its competence. After all, Member States managed to include within the Treaty rules on public health a provision that preserved their control over the organisation and provision of health services (now Article 168 (7)).

In fact, the health field may be subject to the interference of supranational governance because it intersects with many areas over which the EU has powers to act and legislate. This is the case of the Internal Market and competition law. Moreover, the nature of health services is sometimes difficult to define or categorise: whereas many services at the national level are clearly publicly provided, others have the participation of private providers – actors that are directly related to the market. Consequently, this influences the nature of health services, which traditionally were regarded as social services. At the national level it still works like this, i.e. health services – even when there are quasi-market or market arrangements – belong to the social sphere. However, at the EU level this works differently. Health services are considered economic services. This economic approach is markedly influenced by the jurisprudence of the ECJ which, through its case law on cross-border health care, asserted more than once that health services are economic in nature. The judicial activism of the Court played, thus, a crucial role in this regard. Likewise, other EU institutions, such as the Commission, also influenced this change of approach. For example, the documents on SGI – as Green and White Papers – gradually changed the discourse in relation to health services, moving from a more social approach to an economic one. Therefore, health services were gradually moulded to become part of EU law and governance. This became a reality with the adoption of the Directive on patients' rights which, although having this very nice and appellative title, is much more about health services in the Internal Market than about patients' rights. In effect, the Directive does not deal with patients' rights in their common usage, not offering protection to such fundamental rights as they are supposed to be.[2] Accordingly, it is possible to conclude that the main driver of EU polices concerning health care and related

---

2 RIAL-SEBBAG, E., CHASSANG, G. & TABOULET, F. 2011. Quelle gouvernance pour les droits des patients en Europe? *Revue des affaires européennes*, 3: 549–61.

fields is the market rather than the interest of the patient. However, as already claimed, health care services cannot be equated to services that are purely subject to conventional market forces and competition.[3]

The exclusion of health services from the Services Directive was the starting point of a process that ended up with the adoption of the Patients' Rights Directive (Directive 2011/24/EU). Indeed, if the ECJ had taken a different approach in cases concerning cross-border health care, for example, by making use of solidarity in some cases as it did very often in competition law cases, the situation could have been different. Instead of the adoption of a Directive concerning cross-border health care, the issue could have been resolved by the amendment of Regulation 1408/71, now Regulation 883/2004, or by the use of soft-law mechanisms in order to make clearer the rules regarding this type of provision of health care.

All these moves regarding health services show a more liberal view in relation to these services, entailing, thereby, the application of values attached to the market, such as freedom of choice, ability to pay and competition. As a consequence, phenomena common to liberal health systems may arise, such as the case of health tourism. The problem is that these liberal values have the potential to affect common principles guiding Member States' health systems, namely equity, solidarity, quality and universality. As demonstrated by the example of cross-border health care, a liberal view has the potential to make access to services less equitable and, ultimately, discriminatory. Moreover, in relation to quality, the assurance of quality in the provision of health care around the EU may be difficult. In relation to universality, it has the potential to make access somehow less universal. Finally, regarding solidarity, market values are grounded in individualist premises that are not compatible with the communitarian basis that supports solidarity. Accordingly, it is important to mention that the interpretation of human rights law regarding health care also supports a communitarian view of health care.

Nevertheless, there is potential for coping with market/liberal values and the common values of EU health systems. In order to do this, a first step would be to rethink health services from the point of view of a health policy issue. This can start with the creation of a specific Directorate dedicated to health within the structure of the European Commission. Furthermore, from the moment that health services are dealt with as a health policy issue, a specific policy model could be applied in order to regulate them at EU level. This book has suggested the application of the quasi-market model, because this allows for the use of freedom of choice and competition without negatively affecting equity and universality. However, to work in this way the use of this model entails the adoption of a specific policy design. At the EU level this would represent the adoption of specific measures. The creation of a system of accreditation was suggested, as well as the creation of an EU fund for cross-border health care, in order to overcome the

3 ROSCAM ABBING, H.D.C. 2015. EU Cross-Border Healthcare and Health Law. *European Journal Health Law*, 22: 1–12, p. 9.

problems posed by cross-border health care. It was recognised, however, that the proposed measures could be unviable by virtue of the financial crises that affected almost all EU Member States.

Finally, considering that Member States have some margin of discretion in relation to services that need prior authorisation, there is still a lot to be done in relation to inter-state provision of health care. Therefore, it was also suggested a reconceptualisation of the place occupied by health services within the structure of EU law. The binary structure – social versus economic – that has often been applied by EU institutions does not fit the singular characteristics of health services provision. In fact, new provisions introduced by the Lisbon Treaty offer the possibility of applying a more flexible approach in relation to health services. This is the case of Article 3 TEU and Protocol n. 26.

These suggested measures aim at overcoming the major challenges brought about by the extension of the Internal Market, allowing the use of the opportunities offered by market mechanisms while at the same time safeguarding the social character of health care.

References

Books, book chapters, articles, working papers, reports and theses

ADAY, L. A. & ANDERSEN, R. 1975. *Development of indices of access to medical care*. Ann Arbor, MI: Health Administration Press.

ALTENSTETTER, C. 1999. From solidarity to market competition? *In:* POWELL, F.D. & WESSEN, A.F. (eds) *Health care systems in transition: an international perspective*. Thousand Oaks, CA: Sage Publications.

AMERICAN COLLEGE OF PHYSICIANS 2008. Achieving a High-Performance Health Care System with Universal Access: What the United States Can Learn from Other Countries. *Annals of Internal Medicine*, 148(1).

ANAND, S., PETER, F. & SEN, A.K. 2004. *Public health, ethics, and equity*. Oxford; New York: Oxford University Press.

ANDRÉ, C. & HERMANN, C. 2008. The privatisation of health care in Europe. *PRESOM Newsletter, n. 5–6 (January/February)* Available at www.raumplanung.tu-dortmund.de/irpud/presom/fileadmin/docs/presom/external/Publications/WP5.pdf [Accessed 25 November 2015].

ANELL, A., GLENNGÅRD, A.H. & MERKUR, S. 2012. Sweden: Health system review. *Health Systems in Transition*, 14(5): 1–159.

ARNESON, R. 1989. Equality and Equal Opportunity for Welfare. *Philosophical Studies*, 56(1): 77.

ARNESON, R. 2002. Egalitarianism. *Stanford Encyclopedia of Philosophy*. Available at http://plato.stanford.edu/entries/egalitarianism/ [Accessed 21 December 2015].

BAETEN, R. 2005. The potential impact of the services directive on health services. *In:* NIHOUL, P. & SIMON, A.-C. (eds) *L'Europe et les soins de santé: marché intérieur, sécurité sociale, concurrence*. Brussels: Larcier.

BAETEN, R. 2009. The proposal for a directive on patients' rights in cross-border healthcare. *In:* DEGRYSE, C. (ed.) *Social developments in the European Union 2008*. Brussels: Trade Union Institute (ETUI), Observatoire social européen (OSE).

BAETEN, R. 2011. Past impacts of cross-border health care. *In:* WISMAR, M., PALM, W., FIGUERAS, J., ERNST, K. & GINNEKEN, E.V. (eds) *Cross-border health care in the European Union*. Copenhagen: World Health Organization, on Behalf of the European Observatory on Health Systems and Policies.

BAETEN, R. 2012. *Europeanization of national health systems: national impact and EU codification of the patient mobility case law*. Report in the context of the EPSU Project. Belgium: European Social Observatory (OSE).

BAETEN, R. 2014. Cross-border patient mobility in the European Union: in search of benefits from the new legal framework. *Journal of Health Services Research & Policy*, 19(4): 195–7.

BAETEN, R. & PALM, W. 2011. The Compatibility of Health Care Capacity Planning Policies with EU Internal Market Rules. *In:* GRONDEN, J.W., SZYSZCZAK, E., NEERGAARD, U. & KRAJEWSKI, M. (eds) *Health care and EU law*. The Hague: T.M.C. Asser.

BAETEN, R. & PALM, W. 2013. Preserving General Interest in healthcare through secondary and soft EU Law: the case of the Patients' Rights Directive. In: NEERGARD, U. *et al.* (eds) *Social services of general interest in the EU*. The Hague: T.M.C. Asser.

BAETEN, R., VANHERCKE, B. & COUCHEIR, M. 2010. The Europeanisation of National Health Care Systems: Creative Adaptation in the Shadow of Patient Mobility Case Law. *OSE Paper Series*. Research paper No. 3. Brussels: Observatoire social européen.

BALDWIN, P. 1990. The politics of social solidarity: class bases of the European welfare state, 1875–1975. Cambridge [UK]; New York: Cambridge University Press.

BARAK-EREZ, D. & GROSS, A.M. 2007. *Exploring social rights: between theory and practice*, Oxford, UK; Portland, OR. Hart.

BARNARD, C. 2005. EU citizenship and the Principle of Solidarity. *In:* SPAVENTA, E. & DOUGAN, M. (eds) *Social Welfare and EU law*. Oxford, UK; Portland, OR: Hart.

BARNARD, C. 2010. Solidarity and the Commission's 'Renewed Social Agenda'. *In:* ROSS, M. & BORGMANN-PREBIL, Y. (eds) *Promoting Solidarity in the European Union*. Oxford: Oxford University Press.

BARROS, P., MACHADO, S. & SIMÕES, J. 2011. Portugal: Health system review. *Health Systems in Transition*, 13(4): 1–156.

BARRY, B. 1974. Review: [untitled]. *British Journal of Political Science*, 4: 79–107.

BAYERTZ, K. 1999. Four uses of 'Solidarity'. *In:* BAYERTZ, K. (ed.) *Solidarity*. Dordrecht, Netherlands; London: Kluwer Academic.

BEAUCHAMP, T.L. & CHILDRESS, J.F. 1983. *Principles of biomedical ethics*. New York: Oxford University Press.

BEER, P. D. & KOSTER, F. 2009. Sticking together or falling apart: solidarity in an era of individualization and globalization. Amsterdam: Amsterdam University Press.

BELLAMY, R. 2008a. Evaluating Union citizenship: belonging, rights and participation within the EU. *Citizenship Studies*, 12: 597–611.

BELLAMY, R. 2008b. *Citizenship: a very short introduction*. New York: Oxford University Press.

BERTHET, F. *et al.* 2015. Luxembourg: HiT in brief. *Health Systems in Transition*. Available at www.euro.who.int/__data/assets/pdf_file/0006/287943/Mini-HiT_Luxembourg-rev1.pdf [Accessed 24 November 2015].

BEVERIDGE, W.H.B. 1969. *Social insurance and allied services*. New York: Agathon P.

BLACK, H.C. & GARNER, B.A. 2009. *Black's Law Dictionary*. St. Paul, MN: Thomson Reuters.

BLACKBURN, S. 2008. The Oxford dictionary of philosophy. *Oxford reference online*.

BOBBIO, N. 1996. *The age of rights*. Cambridge, UK; Oxford, UK; Cambridge, USA: Polity, Blackwell.

BORGES, D.D.C.L. 2011a. EU health systems and the Internal Market: Reshaping Ideology? *Health Care Analysis*, 19(4): 365–87.

BORGES, D.D.C.L. 2011b. Making sense of human rights in the context of European Union health-care policy: individualist and communitarian views. *International Journal of Law in Context*, 7(3): 335–56.

BOYLE, S. 2011. *Health systems in transition: United Kingdom,* Copenhagen: World Health Organization, on behalf of the European Observatory on Health Systems and Policies.

BRAVEMAN, P. & GRUSKIN, S. 2003. Defining equity in health. *Journal of Epidemiology and Community Health,* 57: 254–8.

BREKKE, K.R., LEVAGGI, R., SICILIANI, L. & STRAUME, O.R. 2011. Patient Mobility, Health Care Quality and Welfare. *Discussion Paper, Norwegian School of Economics.* Available at http://cefup.fep.up.pt/uploads/ECO%20Seminars/2011/OddRune_18_Nov.pdf [Accessed 14 December 2015].

BROWN, L.D. & AMELUNG, V.E. 1999. 'Manacled competition': market reforms in German health care. *Health Affairs,* 18: 76–91.

BROWN, W. 2005. *Edgework: critical essays on knowledge and politics.* Princeton, NJ: Princeton University Press.

BURCHARDT, T. 2007. Welfare: what for? *In:* HILLS, J., LE GRAND, J. & PIACHAUD, D. (eds) *Making social policy work.* Bristol: The Policy Press.

BUSSE, R., GINNEKEN, E.V. & WÖRZ, M. 2011. Access to health care services within and between countries. *In:* WISMAR, M., PALM, W., FIGUERAS, J., ERNST, K. & GINNEKEN, E.V. (eds) *Cross-border health care in the European Union.* Copenhagen: World Health Organization, on Behalf of the European Observatory on Health Systems and Policies.

BUSSE, R., SALTMAN, R.B. & DUBOIS, H.F.W. 2004. Organization and financing of social health insurance systems: current status and recent policy developments. *In:* SALTMAN, R.B., BUSSE, R. & FIGUERAS, J. (eds) *Social health insurance systems in Western Europe.* Maidenhead, UK; New York: Open University Press.

BUSSE, R. & BLÜMEL, M. 2014. Germany: Health System Review. *Health Systems in Transition,* 16(2): 1–296. European Observatory on Health Systems and Policies.

CALLAHAN, D. & WASUNNA, A.A. 2006. *Medicine and the Market: Equity v. Choice.* Baltimore, MD: John Hopkins University Press.

CANNIZZARO, E. 1997. Producing 'Reverse Discrimination' through the Exercise of EC Competences. *Yearbook of European Law,* 17: 29–46.

CAPPELLETTI, M. 1993. *Juízes legisladores?* Porto Alegre: Sérgio Fabris.

CARRIN, G., MATHAUER, I., XUA, K. & EVANSA, D.B. 2008. Universal coverage of health services: tailoring its implementation. *Bulletin of the World Health Organization,* 86: 857–63.

CAVANAGH, S. & CHADWICK, K. 2005. Health needs assessment: A practical guide. Cambridge: National Institute for Health and Clinical Excellence (NICE). Available at www.nice.org.uk/proxy/?sourceUrl=http%3A%2F%2Fwww.nice.org.uk%2Fnicemedia%2Fdocuments%2FHealth_Needs_Assessment_A_Practical_Guide.pdf [Accessed 29 November 2015].

CHERNICHOVSKY, D. 1995. Health System Reforms in Industrialized Democracies: An Emerging Paradigm. *The Milbank Quarterly,* 73: 339–72.

CHEVREUL, K. *et al.* 2010. France: Health system review. *Health Systems in Transition,* 12(6): 1–291.

CLARKE, J., NEWMAN, J., SMITH, N., VIDLER, E. & WESTMARLAND, L. 2007. *Creating citizen-consumers: changing publics and changing public services.* London: Sage.

COHEN, G.A. 1989. On the Currency of Egalitarian Justice. *Ethics,* 99(4): 906–44.

COLLECTIF SSIG-FR. 2006. Les services sociaux et de santé d'intérêt général: droits fondamentaux versus marché intérieur? Une contribution au débat communautaire. Brussels: Bruylant.

CORNELISSEN, R. 1996. The Principle of Territory and the Community Regulations on Social Security (Regulations 1408/71 and 574/72). *Common Market Law Review*, 33: 439–71.

COUSINS, M. 2005. *European welfare states: comparative perspectives*, London; Thousand Oaks, CA: Sage.

CRUZ, J.B. 2011. The Case Law of the European Court of Justice on the Mobility of Patients: An Assessment. *In:* GRONDEN, J.W.V.D., SZYSZCZAK, E., NEERGAARD, U. & KRAJEWSKI, M. (eds) *Health care and EU law*. The Hague: T.M.C. Asser.

CYGAN, A. 2008. Public healthcare in the European Union: still a Service of General Interest? *International and Comparative Law Quarterly*, 57, July 2008: 529–60.

DAMJANOVIC, D. & WITTE, B.D. 2008. Welfare Integration through EU Law: The Overall Picture in the Light of the Lisbon Treaty *EUI Working Papers LAW N. 2008/34*. Available at http://ssrn.com/abstract=1326827 [Accessed 14 December 2015].

DANIELS, N. 2008a. Justice and Access to Health Care. *Stanford Encyclopedia of Philosophy*. Available at http://plato.stanford.edu/entries/justice-healthcareaccess/ [Accessed 14 December 2015].

DANIELS, N. 2008b. *Just health: meeting health needs fairly*. Cambridge; New York: Cambridge University Press.

DAVIES, G. 2006. The Process and Side-Effects of Harmonisation of European Welfare States. *Jean Monnet Working Paper 02/06*. Available at http://jeanmonnetprogram.org/wp-content/uploads/2014/12/060201.pdf [Accessed 14 December 2015].

DE BÚRCA, G. 2005. EU law and the welfare state: in search of solidarity. Oxford: Oxford University Press.

DOCTEUR, E. & OXLEY, H. 2003. Health-Care Systems: Lessons from the Reform Experience. *OECD Health Working Papers*. Organisation for Economic Co-operation and Development.

DONABEDIAN, A. 1972. Models for Organizing the Delivery of Personal Health Services and Criteria for Evaluating Them. *The Milbank Memorial Fund Quarterly*, 50(4): 103–54.

DOORSLAER, E.V., KOOLMAN, X. & JONES, A.M. 2004. Explaining income-related inequalities in doctor utilisation in Europe. *Health Economics*, 13: 629–47.

DOUGAN, M. & SPAVENTA, E. 2005. *Social welfare and EU law*. Oxford: Hart.

DURKHEIM, É. 1932. *De la division du travail social, par Emile Durkheim, professeur à la Sorbonne. 6e édition*, Saint-Germain-lès-Corbeil, impr. Willaume Paris, libr. Félix Alcan, 108, boulevard Saint-Germain.

DWORKIN, R. 1993. Justice in the Distribution of Health Care. *McGill Law Journal*, 38(4): 883–98.

DWYER, P. 2000. *Welfare rights and responsibilities: contesting social citizenship*. Bristol: Policy Press.

DWYER, P. 2004. *Understanding social citizenship: themes and perspectives for policy and practice*. Bristol: Policy Press.

ECONOMOU, C. 2010. Greece: Health system review. *Health Systems in Transition*, 12(7): 1–180.

ESPING-ANDERSEN, G. 1990. *The three worlds of welfare capitalism*. Cambridge: Polity.

ESPING-ANDERSEN, G. 1999. *Social Foundations of Postindustrial Economies*. Oxford: Oxford University Press.

EXPERT PANEL ON EFFECTIVE WAYS OF INVESTING IN HEALTH 175 (EXPH). 2015. Preliminary Report on Access to Health Services in the European Union. Available at http://ec.europa.eu/health/expert_panel/opinions/docs/010_access_healthcare_en.pdf [Accessed 14 December 2015].

EXTER, A.D. & HERMANS, H. 1999. *The right to health care in several European countries.* The Hague; London; Boston: Kluwer Law International.

FAMILIES USA 2009. *Americans at risk: one in three uninsured.* Washington, DC: Families USA. Available at www.ckfindiana.org/files/news/Americans%20At%20Risk%20report%20-%20March%202009.pdf [Accessed 23 November 2015].

FARIA, J.E. (ed.) 2005. *Direitos humanos, direitos sociais e justiça.* São Paulo: Malheiros.

FAULKS, K. 1998. *Citizenship in modern Britain.* Edinburgh: Edinburgh University Press.

FAULKS, K. 2000. *Citizenship.* London: Routledge.

FERRÉ, F. *et al.* 2014. Italy: Health System Review. *Health Systems in Transition,* 16(4): 1–168.

FERRERA, M. 2005. *The boundaries of welfare: European integration and the new spatial politics of social protection.* Oxford: Oxford University Press.

FIDLER, D.P., CORREA, C. & AGINAM, O. 2005. Draft Legal Review of the General Agreement on Trade in Services (GATS) from a Health Policy Perspective. *Globalization, Trade and Health Working Papers Series.* World Health Organization. Available at www.who.int/trade/resource/GATS_Legal_Review_15_12_05.pdf?ua=1 [Accessed 28 November 2015].

FLEAR, M. 2007. Developing Euro-Biocitizens through Migration for Healthcare Services. *Maastricht Journal of European and Comparative Law (MJ),* 14(3): 239–62.

FLEAR, M. 2009. The Open Method of Coordination on health care after the Lisbon Strategy II: Towards a neoliberal framing? *European Integration Online Papers (EIoP),* 13.

FÖLDES, M.É. 2009. *A Legal Analysis of the Influence of Internal Market Implementation on Access to Health Care in Hungary and Slovenia.* Dissertation submitted to the Central European University, Department of Legal Studies and Department of Political Science, in partial fulfilment of the requirements for the degree of Doctor of Philosophy, Central European University.

FOOTMAN, K. *et al.* 2014. *Cross-border healthcare in Europe.* Policy Summary 14, WHO Regional Office for Europe and European Observatory on Health Systems and Policies.

FREEMAN, R. & MORAN, M. 2000. Reforming health care in Europe. *West European Politics,* 23: 35–58.

GARCÍA-ARMESTO, S. *et al.* 2010. Spain: Health system review. *Health Systems in Transition,* 12(4): 1–295.

GERKENS, S. & MERKUR, S. 2010. Belgium: Health system review. *Health Systems in Transition,* 12(5): 1–266.

GIBSON, D.M., GOODIN, R.E. & GRAND, J.L. 1985. Come and get it: distributional biases in social service delivery systems. *Policy and Politics,* 13(2): 109–26.

GINNEKEN, E.V. & BUSSE, R. 2011. Cross-border health care data. *In:* WISMAR, M., PALM, W., FIGUERAS, J., ERNST, K. & GINNEKEN, E.V. (eds) *Cross-border health care in the European Union: mapping and analysing practices and policies.* Copenhagen: World Health Organization, on behalf of the European Observatory on Health Systems and Policies.

GLINOS, I.A. & BAETEN, R. 2006. *A Literature Review of Cross-Border Patient Mobility in the European Union.* Brussels: Observatoire Social Européen. Available at www.ose.be/files/publication/health/WP12_lit_review_final.pdf [Accessed 3 December 2015].

GLINOS, I.A., BAETEN, R., HELBLE, M. & MAARSE, H. 2010. A typology of cross-border patient mobility. *Health Place,* 16(6): 1145–55.

GODDARD, M. & SMITH, P. 2001. Equity of access to health care services: Theory and evidence from the UK. *Social Science & Medicine,* 53: 1149–62.

GOOIJER, W.D. 2007. *Trends in EU health care system.* New York: Springer.

GOSTIN, L.O. 2000. *Public health law: power, duty, restraint*. Berkeley, CA; New York: University of California Press; Milbank Memorial Fund.

GOUDAPPEL, F. 2010. *The effects of EU citizenship*. The Hague: TMC Asser.

GREER, S.L. 2008a. Choosing paths in European Union health services policy: a political analysis of a critical juncture. *Journal of European Social Policy*, 18: 219–31.

GREER, S.L. 2008b. Power: struggle: the politics and policy consequences of patient mobility in Europe. *Observatoire social européen*. Policy Paper n. 2, July 2008.

GREER, S. & JARMAN, H. 2012. Managing risks in EU health services policy: Spot markets, legal certainty and bureaucratic resistance. *Journal of European Social Policy*, 22: 259–72.

GRONDEN, J.V.D. & SAUTER, W. 2011. Taking the temperature: EU Competition Law and Health Care. *Legal Issues of Economic Integration*, 38(3): 213–41.

GROSS, A.M. 2007. The right to health in an era of privatisation and globalisation: national and international perspectives. *In:* BARAK-EREZ, D. & GROSS, A.M. (eds) *Exploring social rights: between theory and practice*. Oxford; Portland, OR: Hart.

GULLIFORD, M. 2003. Equity and access to health care. *In:* GULLIFORD, M. & MORGAN, M. (eds) *Access to health care*. New York: Routledge.

GULLIFORD, M., FIGUEROA-MUÑOZ, J. & MORGAN, M. 2003. Introduction: meaning of 'access' in health care. *In:* GULLIFORD, M. & MORGAN, M. (eds) *Access to health care*. New York: Routledge.

GULLIFORD, M., FIGUEROA-MUNOZ, J., MORGAN, M., HUGHES, D., GIBSON, B., BEECH, R. & HUDSON, M. 2002. What does 'access to health care' mean? *Journal of Health Services Research & Policy*, 7(3): 186–8.

HANCHER, L. & SAUTER, W. 2012. *EU competition and Internal Market Law in the healthcare sector*. Oxford: Oxford University Press.

HARTELOH, P.P.M. 2003. The Meaning of Quality in Health Care: A Conceptual Analysis. *Health Care Analysis*, 11: 259–67.

HATZOPOULOS, V. 2012. *Regulating services in the European Union*. Oxford: Oxford University Press. [Electronic version]

HATZOPOULOS, V. & HERVEY, T. 2013. Coming into line: the EU's Court softens on cross-border health care. *Health Economics, Policy and Law*, 8: 1–5.

HAYNES, R. 2003. Geographical access to health care. *In:* GULLIFORD, M. & MORGAN, M. (eds) *Access to health care*. New York: Routledge.

HEATER, D.B. 1999. *What is citizenship?* Cambridge, UK; Malden, MA: Polity; Blackwell.

HENDRIKS, A. 2012. Health and Human Rights: The European Institutions. *In:* TOEBES, B., HARTLEV, M., HENDRIKS, A. & HERRMANN, J. R. (eds) *Health and human rights in Europe*. Cambridge, Antwerp, Portland, OR: Intersentia.

HERRMANN, J.R. & TOEBES, B. 2012. The European Union and Health and Human Rights. *In:* TOEBES, B., HARTLEV, M., HENDRIKS, A. & HERRMANN, J.R. (eds.) *Health and human rights in Europe*. Cambridge, Antwerp, Portland, OR: Intersentia.

HERVEY, T.K. 2002a. The Legal Basis of European Community Public Health Policy. *In:* MCKEE, M., MOSSIALOS, E. & BAETEN, R. (eds) *The impact of EU Law on health care systems*. Brussels: Presses Interuniversitaires Européenes – Peter Lang.

HERVEY, T.K. 2002b. Mapping the contours of European Union health law and policy. *European Public Law*, 8(1): 69–105.

HERVEY, T.K. 2008. The European Union's Governance of Health Care and the Welfare Modernization Agenda. *Regulation and Governance*, 2: 103–20.

HERVEY, T.K. 2011a. Cooperation between Health Care Authorities in the Proposed Directive on Patients' Rights in Cross-Border Healthcare. *In:* GRONDEN, J.W.V.D.,

SZYSZCZAK, E., NEERGAARD, U. & KRAJEWSKI, M. (eds) *Health care and EU law*. The Hague: T.M.C. Asser.

HERVEY, T.K. 2011b. If Only It Were So Simple: Public Health Services and EU Law. *In:* CREMONA, M. (ed.) *Market integration and public services in the European Union*. Oxford: Oxford University Press.

HERVEY, T.K. & MCHALE, J.V. 2004. *Health law and the European Union*. Cambridge: Cambridge University Press.

HERVEY, T. & TRUBEK, L. 2007. Freedom to Provide Health Care Services within the EU: An Opportunity for a Transformative Directive. *Columbia Journal of European Law*, 13: 623–47.

HIRSCHMAN, A.O. 1970. *Exit, voice, and loyalty: responses to decline in firms, organizations, and States*. Cambridge, MA; London: Harvard University Press.

HOFMARCHER, M. & QUENTIN, W. 2013. Austria: Health system review. *Health Systems in Transition*, 15(7): 1– 291.

HOUDRY, V. 2015. La France et l'action de l'Union en matièere de santé. *In:* BROSSET, E. *Droit européen et protection de la santé: bilan et perspectives*. Brussels: Bruylant, pp. 79–82.

HUNT, P. & BACKMAN, G. 2013. Health Systems and the Right to the Highest Attainable Standard of Health. *In:* GRONDIN, M. *et al.* (eds) *Health and human rights in a changing world*. New York: Routledge.

HURLEY, S. 2007. The 'What' and the 'How' of Distributive Justice and Health. *In:* HOLTUG, N. & LIPPERT-RASMUSSEN, K. (eds) *Egalitarianism: new essays on the nature and value of equality*. Oxford: Oxford University Press.

JELFS, E. & BAETEN, R. 2012. *Simulation on the EU Cross-Border Care Directive (Final Report)*. Brussels: European Social Observatory (OSE), European Health Management Association (EHMA), Association Internationale de la Mutualité (AIM).

JOERGES, C. 2009. A renaissance of the European Constitution? *In:* NEERGAARD, U.B., NIELSEN, R. & ROSEBERRY, L.M. (eds) *Integrating welfare functions into EU law: from Rome to Lisbon*. Copenhagen: DJØF.

JOERGES, C. & RÖDL, F. 2004. 'Social Market Economy' as Europe's Social Model? *In:* MAGNUSSON, L. & STRÅTH, B. (eds) *A European social citizenship?: preconditions for future policies from a historical perspective*. Brussels; New York: P.I.E. – Peter Lang.

JOST, T.S. 2007. *Health Care at Risk: A Critique of the Consumer-Driven Movement*. Durham, NC: Duke University Press.

JOST, T.S., DAWSON, D. & EXTER, A.D. 2006. The role of competition in health care: a western European perspective. *Journal of Health Politics, Policy and Law*, 31(3): 687–703.

KACZOROWSKA, A. 2006. A Review of the Creation by the European Court of Justice of the Right to Effective and Speedy Medical Treatment and its Outcomes. *European Law Journal*, 12: 345–70.

KANAVOS, P. & MACKEE, M. 2000. Cross-border issues in the provision of health services. *Journal of Health Services Research & Policy*, 5(4): 231–6.

KANDIL, F. 2004. European social citizenship and the requirement of European solidarity. *In:* MAGNUSSON, L. & STRÅTH, B. (eds) *A European social citizenship? Preconditions for future policies from a historical perspective*. Brussels; New York: P.I.E. – Peter Lang.

KATTELUS, M. 2014. Implementation of the Directive on the application on patient's rights in cross-border healthcare (2011/24/eu) in Finland. *European Journal of Health Law*, 21(1): 23–32.

KIFMANN, M. & WAGNER, C. 2014. Implications of the EU Patients' Rights Directive in Cross-Border Healthcare on the German Sickness Fund System. *In:* LEVAGGI, R. & MONTEFIORI, M. *Health care provision and patient mobility: health integration in the European Union*. Italy: Springer, pp. 49–66.

KILPATRICK, C. 2011. Internal Market Architecture and the Accommodation of Labour Rights: As Good as it Gets? *EUI Working Papers LAW 2011/04.*

KLEIS, M. & NICOLAIDES, P. 2006. The Concept of Undertaking in Education and Public Health Systems. *European State Aid Law Quarterly*, 505.

KLUTHE, J. 2002. Equity and equality: core values in Canadian health care. *In Touch: Journal of the Provincial Health Ethics Network*, 5(7).

KOIVUSALO, M.T. 2005. The future of European health policies. *Journal of Health Services*, 35(2): 325–42.

KOLB, A.-K. 1999. European social rights towards national welfare states: additional, substitute, illusory? *In:* BUSSEMAKER, J. (ed.) *Citizenship and welfare state reform in Europe.* London; New York: Routledge.

KOSTAKOPOULOU, D. 2005. Ideas, Norms and European Citizenship: Explaining Institutional Change. *The Modern Law Review*, 68: 233–67.

KOSTERA, T. 2008. Europeanizing Healthcare: Cross-Border Patient Mobility and Its Consequences for the German and Danish Health Care Systems. *Bruges Political Research Papers*, 7, Bruges: College of Europe.

KOUTRAKOS, P. 2005. Healthcare as an Economic Service under EU law. *In:* SPAVENTA, E. & DOUGAN, M. (eds) *Social welfare and EU law.* Oxford: Hart.

KRAJEWSKI, M. 2007. Non-economic activities in upstream and downstream markets and the scope of competition law after FENIN. *European Law Review*, 32(1): 111–24.

KROHMAL, B J. & EMANUEL, E.J. 2007. Tiers without tears: the ethics of a two-tier health care system. *In:* STEINBOCK, B. (ed.) *The Oxford handbook of bioethics.* Oxford; New York: Oxford University Press.

KUTZIN, J. 2001. A descriptive framework for country-level analysis of health care financing arrangements. *Health Policy*, 56: 171–204.

LAMPING, W. 2005. European integration and health policy. *In:* STEFFEN, M. (ed.) *Health governance in Europe: issues, challenges, and theories.* London: Routledge.

LAMPING, W. 2010. Mission Impossible? Limits and Perils of Institutionalizing Post-National Social Policy. *In:* ROSS, M. & BORGMANN-PREBIL, Y. (eds) *Promoting solidarity in the European Union.* Oxford; New York: Oxford University Press.

LE GRAND, J. 2003. *Motivation, agency, and public policy: of knights and knaves, pawns and queens.* Oxford: Oxford University Press.

LE GRAND, J. 2007. The other invisible hand: delivering public services through choice and competition. Princeton, NJ: Princeton University Press.

LE GRAND, J. & BARTLETT, W. 1993. *Quasi-markets and social policy.* Basingstoke, UK: Macmillan.

LEE, C.V. & BALABAN, V. 2011. The Pre-Travel Consultation Counseling & Advice for Travelers. *Travelers' Health 2011 Yellow Book.* Centers for Disease Control and Prevention. Available at wwwnc.cdc.gov/travel/yellowbook/2012/chapter-2-the-pre-travel-consultation/medical-tourism.htm [Accessed 14 December 2015].

LEGIDO-QUIGLEY, H., MCKEE, M., NOLTE, E. & GLINOS, I.A. 2008. *Assuring the quality of healthcare in the European Union: A case for action*, Copenhagen: World Health Organization, on behalf of the European Observatory on Health Systems and Policies.

LEGIDO-QUIGLEY, H., MCKEE, M., WALSHE, K., SUÑOL, R., NOLTE, E. & KLAZINGA, N. 2008. How can quality of health care be safeguarded across the European Union? *British Medical Journal*, 336: 920.

LEONARD, E.M. 1900. *The early history of English poor relief (1900).* Cambridge: Cambridge University Press Warehouse. Available at www.archive.org/stream/earlyhistoryofen 00leonrich#page/n5/mode/2up [Accessed 14 December 2015].

LEVAGGI, L. & LEVAGGI, R. 2014. Patients' mobility across borders: a welfare analysis. *In*: LEVAGGI, R. & MONTEFIORI (eds) *Health care provision and patient mobility: health integration in the European Union*. Italy: Springer, pp. 179–200.

LEVAGGI, R. & MENONCIN, F. 2014. Cross-border health care provision: who gains, who loses. *In*: LEVAGGI, R. & MONTEFIORI, M. (eds) *Health care provision and patient mobility: health integration in the European Union*. Italy: Springer, pp. 223–44.

LOPES, J.R.D.L. 2006. *Direitos sociais: teoria e prática*. São Paulo: Editora Método.

LUKES, S. 1999. Solidarity and Citizenship. *In:* BAYERTZ, K. (ed.) *Solidarity*. Dordrecht, Netherlands; London: Kluwer Academic.

MAARSE, H. 2006. The Privatization of Health Care in Europe: An Eight-Country Analysis. *Journal of Health Politics Policy and Law*, 31: 981–1014.

MACINKO, J. & STARFIELD, B. 2002. Annotated Bibliography on Equity in Health, 1980–2001. *International Journal for Equity in Health*, 1: 1.

MAJONE, G. 1996. *Regulating Europe*, London; New York: Routledge.

MARCHILDON, G.P. 2005. The Chaoulli Case: A Two-Tier Magna Carta? *Healthcare Quarterly*, 8(4): 49–52.

MARKS, S. & CLAPHAM, A. 2005. *International human rights lexicon*. Oxford: Oxford University Press.

MARQUAND, D. 2004. *Decline of the public: the hollowing-out of citizenship*. Cambridge: Polity.

MARSHALL, T.H. 1950. *Citizenship and social class and other essays*. Cambridge: Cambridge University Press.

MARSHALL, T.H. 1992. *Citizenship and social class*. London: Pluto.

MAU, S. 2007. Forms and Prospects of European Solidarity. *In:* KARAGIANNIS, N. (ed.) *European solidarity*. Liverpool: Liverpool University Press.

MEYER, H. 2011. Current legislation on cross-border healthcare in the European Union. Petrie-Flom Annual Conference: *The Globalization of Health Care: Legal and Ethical Challenges*. Harvard Law School, Petrie-Flom Center for Health Law Policy, Biotechnology, and Bioethics.

MOONEY, G. & HOUSTON, S. 2008. Equity in health care and institutional trust. *Cadernos de Saúde Pública*, 24(5): 1162–7.

MORTELMANS, K. 2001. Towards convergence in the application of the rules on free movement and on competition? *Common Market Law Review*, 38: 613–49.

MOSSIALOS, E. & DIXON, A. 2002. Funding health care: an introduction. *In:* MOSSIALOS, E., DIXON, A., FIGUERAS, J. & KUTZIN, J. (eds) *Funding health care: options for Europe*. Buckingham, UK; Philadelphia, PA: Open University Press.

MOSSIALOS, E. & LEAR, J. 2012. Balancing economic freedom against social policy principles: EC competition law and national health systems. *Health Policy*, 106: 127–37.

MOSSIALOS, E. & MCKEE, M. 2002. The theoretical basis and historical evolution of health policy in the European Union. *In:* MOSSIALOS, E., PALM, W., KARL, B. & MARHOLD, F. (eds) *EU Law and the social character of health care*. Brussels: P.I.E. – Peter Lang.

MOSSIALOS, E., MCKEE, M., PALM, W.J., KARL, B. & MARHOLD, F. 2002. *EU law and the social character of health care*. Bern; Oxford: P. Lang.

MOSSIALOS, E. & THOMSON, S. 2003. Access to health care in the European Union: the impact of user charges and voluntary health insurance. *In:* GULLIFORD, M. & MORGAN, M. (eds) *Access to health care*. New York: Routledge.MULLARD, M. 1999. Discourses on citizenship: the challenge to contemporary citizenship. *In:* BUSSEMAKER, J. (ed.) *Citizenship and welfare state reform in Europe*. London; New York: Routledge.

MUSGROVE, P. 2000. Health insurance: the influence of the Beveridge Report. *Bulletin of the World Health Organization,* 78: 845–6.

NEERGAARD, U. 2008. Services of General (Economic) Interest and the Services Directive – What is left out, why and where to go? *In:* NEERGAARD, U.B., NIELSEN, R. & ROSEBERRY, L.M. (eds) *The Services Directive: consequences for the welfare state and the European social model.* Copenhagen: DJØF.

NEERGAARD, U. 2009. Services of General Economic Interest: the Nature of the Beast. *In:* KRAJEWSKI, M., NEERGAARD, U.B. & VAN DE GRONDEN, J. (eds) *The changing legal framework for services of general interest in Europe: between competition and solidarity.* The Hague: T.M.C. Asser.

NEERGAARD, U. 2011. EU Health Care Law in a Constitutional Light: Distribution of Competences, Notions of 'Solidarity', and 'Social Europe'. *In:* GRONDEN, J.W.V.D., SZYSZCZAK, E., NEERGAARD, U. & KRAJEWSKI, M. (eds) *Health care and EU law.* The Hague: T.M.C. Asser.

NEERGAARD, U.B., NIELSEN, R. & ROSEBERRY, L.M. 2009. *Integrating welfare functions into EU law: from Rome to Lisbon,* Copenhagen, DJØF.

NEWDICK, C. 2006. Citizenship, free movement and health care: cementing individual rights by corroding social solidarity. *Common Market Law Review,* 43: 1645–68.

NEWDICK, C. 2008. The European Court of Justice, Trans-National Health Care, and Social Citizenship – Accidental Death of a Concept? *Wisconsin International Law Journal,* 26(3): 844.

NEWDICK, C. 2011. Disrupting the Community – Saving Public Health Ethics from the EU Internal Market. *In:* GRONDEN, J.V.D., SZYSZCZAK, E., NEERGAARD, U. & KRAJEWSKI, M. (eds) *Health care and EU law.* The Hague: T.M.C. Asser.

NEWDICK, C. & DERRETT, S. 2006. Access, Equity and the Role of Rights in Health Care. *Health Care Analysis,* 14: 157–68.

NICKEL, J. 2006. Human Rights. *The Stanford Encyclopedia of Philosophy.* Available at http://plato.stanford.edu/entries/rights-human/ [Accessed 14 December 2015].

NICKLESS, J. 2002. The Internal Market and the Social Nature of Health Care. *In:* MOSSIALOS, E., MCKEE, M. & BAETEN, R. (eds) *The impact of EU law on health care systems.* Brussels: P.I.E. – Peter Lang.

NOZICK, R. 1974. Distributive Justice. *In:* AVINERI, S. & DE-SHALIT, A. (eds) *Communitarianism and individualism.* Oxford; New York: Oxford University Press.

NYS, H. 2014. The Transposition of the Directive on Patients' Rights in Cross-Care Healthcare in National Law by the Member States: Still a Lot of Effort to Be Made and Questions to Be Answered. *European Journal of Health Law,* 21: 1–14.

OBERMAIER, A.J. 2009. *The end of territoriality? The impact of ECJ rulings on British, German and French social policy.* Aldershot, UK: Ashgate.

OLEJAZ, M. *et al.* 2012. Denmark: Health system review. *Health Systems in Transition,* 14(2): 1–192.

OLIVER, A. & MOSSIALOS, E. 2004. Equity of access to health care: outlining the foundations for action. *Journal of Epidemiology and Community Health,* 58(8): 655–8.

OLSEN, J.A. 1997. Theories of justice and their implications for priority setting in health care. *Journal of Health Economics,* 16(6): 625–39.

ORGANISATION FOR ECONOMIC CO-OPERATION AND DEVELOPMENT (OECD) 1987. Financing and Delivering Health Care: A Comparative Analysis of OECD Countries. *OECD Social Policy Studies,* 4.

ORGANISATION FOR ECONOMIC CO-OPERATION AND DEVELOPMENT (OECD) 2004. The OECD Health Project. *Private Health Insurance in OECD Countries.*

Available at www.keepeek.com/Digital-Asset-Management/oecd/social-issues-migration-health/private-health-insurance-in-oecd-countries_9789264007451-en#page2 [Accessed 27 November 2015].

OUIGLEY, T., COATE, S. & GUINNANE, T.W. 2001. Incentives, Information, and Welfare: England's New Poor Law and the Workhouse Test. Working Paper. Available at www.russellsage.org/sites/all/files/u4/Besley,%20Coate,%20%26%20Guinnane_Incentives,%20Information,%20and%20Welfare.pdf [Accessed 18 December 2015].

PALM, W. & BAETEN, R. 2011. The quality and safety paradox in the patients' rights directive. *European Journal of Public Health*, 21(3): 272–4.

PENNINGS, F. 2011. The Draft Patient Mobility Directive and the Coordination Regulations of Social Security. *In:* GRONDEN, J.W.V.D., SZYSZCZAK, E., NEERGAARD, U. & KRAJEWSKI, M. (eds) *Health care and EU law*. The Hague: T.M.C. Asser.

PERMANAND, G., MOSSIALOS, E. & MCKEE, M. 2006. Regulating medicines in Europe: the European Medicines Agency, marketing authorisation, transparency and pharmaco vigilance. *Clinical Medicine*, 6(1): 87–90.

POWELL, M. 2002. The Hidden History of Social Citizenship. *Citizenship Studies*, 6(3): 229–44.

PUBLIC HEALTH AGENCY OF CANADA AND WORLD HEALTH ORGANIZATION 2008. Health equity through intersectoral action: An analysis of 18 country case studies. World Health Organization (WHO) and Minister of Health (Canada). Available at www.who.int/social_determinants/resources/health_equity_isa_2008_en.pdf [Accessed 26 November 2015].

QUIGLEY, W.P. 1996. Five Hundred Years of English Poor Laws, 1349–1834: regulating the working and nonworking poor. *Akron Law Review*, 30: 1–63. Available at www.uakron.edu/dotAsset/726694.pdf [Accessed 18 December 2015].

QUINN, P. & HERT, P.D. 2011. The Patients' Rights Directive (2011/24/EU) – Providing (some) rights to EU residents seeking healthcare in other Member States. *Computer Law & Security Review*, 27: 497–502.

RAWLS, J. 1999. *A theory of justice*. Cambridge, MA: Belknap Press of Harvard University Press.

REDDEN, C.J. 2002. Health Care as Citizenship Development: Examining Social Rights and Entitlement. *Canadian Journal of Political Science / Revue canadienne de science politique*, 35(1): 103–25.

REIBLING, N. 2010. Healthcare systems in Europe: towards an incorporation of patient access. *Journal of European Social Policy*, 20: 5–18.

REICH, N. 2001. Union Citizenship—Metaphor or Source of Rights? *European Law Journal*, 7: 4–23.

REISMAN, D. 2010. *Health tourism: social welfare through international trade*. Cheltenham, UK: Edward Elgar.

REQUEJO, M. 2014. Cross-border care in Spain and the implementation of the Directive 2011/24/EU on the application of patients' rights in cross-border healthcare. *European Journal of Health Law*, 21(1): 79–96.

RIAL-SEBBAG, E., CHASSANG, G. & TABOULET, F. 2011. Quelle gouvernance pour les droits des patients en Europe? *Revue des affaires européennes*, 3: 549–61.

RICE, T., ROSENAU, P., UNRUH, L.Y., BARNES, A.J., SALTMAN, R.B. & GINNEKEN, E.V. 2013. United States of America: Health system review. *Health Systems in Transition*, 15(3): 1–431.

RIEDER, C.M. 2010. When Patients Exit, What Happens to Solidarity? *In:* ROSS, M. & BORGMANN-PREBIL, Y. (eds) *Promoting solidarity in the European Union*. Oxford; New York: Oxford University Press.

RINGARD, Å. *et al.* 2013. Norway: Health system review. *Health Systems in Transition*, 15(8): 1–162.

ROSA, S.D.L. 2012. The Directive on Cross-Border Healthcare or the Art of Codifying Complex Case Law. *Common Market Law Review*, 49: 15–46.

ROSCAM ABBING, H.D.C. 2015. EU Cross-Border Healthcare and Health Law. *European Journal Health Law*, 22: 1–12.

RUGER, J.P. 2004. Health and social justice. *The Lancet*, 364: 1075–80.

RUGER, J.P. 2010. *Health and social justice.* Oxford; New York: Oxford University Press.

RYLAND, D. 2007. Freedom, Solidarity and Health Care in the European Union. Paper submitted to the Conference 'The European Constitution and National Constitutions', held at Andrzej Frycz Modrzewski Kraków University, Krakow, Poland (21–24 October 2007). Available at http://eprints.lincoln.ac.uk/3051/1/Freedom_Solidarity_and_Health_Care_in_the_European_Union_Krakow_October_2007.pdf [Accessed 14 December 2015].

SALTMAN, R.B. 1997. Balancing state and market in health system reform. *European Journal of Public Health*, 7(2): 119–20.

SALTMAN, R.B. 2002. The Western European Experience with Health Care Reform. *European Observatory on Health Systems and Policies*. Available at www.teamgrant.ca/M-THAC%20Greatest%20Hits/M-THAC%20Projects/All%20info/mthac%20lectures/Saltman%20Paper.pdf [Accessed 21 December 2015].

SALTMAN, R.B. 2004. Social health insurance in perspective: the challenge of sustaining stability. *In:* SALTMAN, R.B., BUSSE, R. & FIGUERAS, J. (eds) *Social health insurance systems in Western Europe*. Maidenhead, UK; New York: Open University Press.

SALTMAN, R.B. & DUBOIS, H.F.W. 2004. The historical and social base of social health insurance systems. *In:* SALTMAN, R.B., BUSSE, R. & FIGUERAS, J. (eds) *Social health insurance systems in Western Europe*. Maidenhead, UK; New York: Open University Press.

SANTOS, I.S. 2009. *O Mix Público-Privado no Sistema de Saúde Brasileiro: elementos para a regulação da cobertura duplicada.* Thesis submitted for assessment with a view to obtaining the degree of Doctor of Public Health of the Escola Nacional de Saúde Pública Sergio Arouca-ENSP/FIOCRUZ.

SAUTER, W. 2008. Services of General Economic Interest and Universal Service in EU Law. *Services of general economic interest in the single market: what a role for Europe?* Conference held in the European University Institute: Robert Schuman Centre for Advanced Studies.

SAVEDOFF, W. 2004. Tax-based financing for health systems: options and experiences. Geneva: World Health Organization. Available at www.who.int/health_financing/taxed_based_financing_dp_04_4.pdf [Accessed 14 December 2015].

SCHÄFER, W. *et al.* 2010. The Netherlands: Health system review. *Health Systems in Transition*, 12(1): 1–229.

SCHARPF, F.W. 2002. The European Social Model. *Journal of Common Market Studies*, 40: 645–70.

SCHARPF, F.W. 2009. Legitimacy in the Multilevel European Polity. *MPIfG Working Papers*, 09/1.

SCHMITT, J. & ZIPPERER, B. 2007. Is the United States a good model for reducing social exclusion in Europe? *In:* NAVARRO, V. (ed.) *Neoliberalism, globalization, and inequalities: consequences for health and quality of life*. Amityville, NY: Baywood.

SEN, A. 1985. Well-Being, Agency and Freedom: The Dewey Lectures 1984. *The Journal of Philosophy*, 82: 169–221.

SEN, A.K. 2009. *The idea of justice*. London: Allen Lane.

SHISHKIN, S., BURDYAK, A. & POTAPCHIK, E. 2013. Patient choice in the post-semashko health care system. *Working Paper Series: Public Administration*. WP BRP 09/PA/2013, National Research University: Higher School of Economics. Available at www.hse.ru/data/2013/12/24/1341565269/09PA2013.pdf [Accessed 5 Nov 2015].

SHUIBHNE, N.N. 2002. Free Movement of Persons and the Wholly Internal Rule: Time to Move On? *Common Market Law Review*, 39: 731–71.

SHUIBHNE, N.N. 2009. The Outer Limits of EU Citizenship: Displacing Economic Free Movement Rights? *In:* BARNARD, C. & ODUDU, O. (eds) *The outer limits of European law*. Oxford; Portland, OR: Hart.

SIEVEKING, K. 2007. ECJ Rulings on Health Care Services and Their Effects on the Freedom of Cross-Border Patient Mobility in the EU. *European Journal of Migration and Law*, 9: 25–51.

SOMEK, A. 2007. Solidarity Decomposed: Being and time in European citizenship. *University of Iowa Legal Studies Research Paper*, Number 07–13.

SPAVENTA, E. 2007. *Free Movement of Persons in the European Union: Barriers to Movement in their Constitutional Context*. Leiden, Netherlands: Kluwer Law International.

SPAVENTA, E. 2008. Seeing the wood despite the trees? On the scope of Union Citizenship and its Constitutional effects. *Common Market Law Review*, 45: 13–45.

STANTON-IFE, J. 1999. *Health care allocation in ethics and law: a defence of the need principle*. Thesis submitted for assessment with a view to obtaining the degree of Doctor of Laws of the European University Institute.

STJERNØ, S. 2005. *Solidarity in Europe: the history of an idea*. Cambridge: Cambridge University Press.

STUCHLÍK, A. & KELLERMANN, C. 2009. Europe on the Way to a Social Union? The EU Social Agenda in the Context of European Welfarism. *International Policy Analysis*, Available at http://library.fes.de/pdf-files/id/ipa/06013.pdf [Accessed 14 December 2015].

SWEET, A.S. 2000. *Governing with Judges*, Oxford: Oxford University Press.

SZYSZCZAK, E. 2009. Modernising Healthcare: Pilgrimage for the Holy Grail? *In:* KRAJEWSKI, M., NEERGAARD, U.B. & VAN DE GRONDEN, J. (eds) *The changing legal framework for services of general interest in Europe: between competition and solidarity*. The Hague: T.M.C. Asser.

SZYSZCZAK, E. 2011. Patients' Rights: A Lost Cause or Missed Opportunity? *In:* GRONDEN, J.W.V.D., SZYSZCZAK, E., NEERGAARD, U. & KRAJEWSKI, M. (eds) *Health care and EU law*. The Hague: T.M.C. Asser.

TATE, C.N. 1995. When courts go marching in. *In:* TATE, C.N. & VALLINDER, T. (eds) *The global expansion of judicial power*. New York: New York University Press.

TATE, C.N. & VALLINDER, T. (eds) 1995. *The global expansion of judicial power*. New York: New York University Press.

THOMSON, S., FOUBISTER, T. & MOSSIALOS, E. 2009. *Financing health care in the European Union: challenges and policy responses*. Denmark: World Health Organization on behalf of the European Observatory on Health Systems and Policies.

THOMSON, S. *et al.* 2015. *Economic crisis, health systems and health in Europe: impact and implications for policy*. Policy Summary 12, WHO Regional Office for Europe and European Observatory on Health Systems and Policies. Available at www.euro.who.int/__data/assets/pdf_file/0008/257579/Economic-crisis-health-systems-Europe-impact-implications-policy.pdf [Accessed 5 November 2015].

TITMUSS, R.M., OAKLEY, A. & ASHTON, J. 1997. *The gift relationship: from human blood to social policy*. London: London School of Economics & Political Science.

TOTH, F. 2010. Healthcare policies over the last 20 years: Reforms and counter-reforms. *Health Policy*, 95: 82–9.

TRYFONIDOU, A. 2008. Reverse Discrimination in Purely Internal Situations: An Incongruity in a Citizens' Europe. *Legal Issues of Economic Integration*, 35(1): 43–67.

TRYFONIDOU, A. 2009. *Reverse Discrimination in EC Law*. The Netherlands: Kluwer Law International.

UGÁ, M.A.D. & SANTOS, I.S. 2007. An Analysis of Equity in Brazilian Health System Financing. *Health Affairs*, 26: 1017–28.

VAN DER MEI, A.P. 2003. Free movement of persons within the European Community: cross-border access to public benefits. Oxford, UK; Portland, OR: Hart.

WAGSTAFF, A. 2009. Social Health Insurance vs. Tax-Financed Health Systems – Evidence from the OECD. *Policy Research Working Paper 4821*. Washington, DC: The World Bank. Available at www-wds.worldbank.org/external/default/WDSContent Server/IW3P/IB/2009/01/21/000158349_20090121101737/Rendered/PDF/WPS48 21.pdf [Accessed 25 November 2015].

WAGSTAFF, A. & DOORSLAER, E.K.A.V. 1993. Equity in the Finance and Delivery of Health Care: concepts and definitions. *In:* WAGSTAFF, A., RUTTEN, F. & DOORSLAER, E.K.A.V. (eds) *Equity in the finance and delivery of health care: An International Perspective*. Oxford: Oxford University Press.

WENDT, C., JÜRGEN KOHL, M.M. & PFEIFER, M. 2010. How do Europeans perceive their healthcare system? Patterns of satisfaction and preference for state involvement in the field of healthcare. *European Sociological Review*, 26(2): 177–92.

WILLIAMS, A. 1993. Equity in health care: the role of ideology. *In:* WAGSTAFF, A., RUTTEN, F. & DOORSLAER, E.K.A.V. (eds) *Equity in the finance and delivery of health care: an international perspective*. Oxford: Oxford University Press.

WISEMAN, V. 1998. From Selfish Individualism to Citizenship: Avoiding Health Economics' Reputed 'Dead End'. *Health Care Analysis*, 6: 113–22.

WISMAR, M. 2001. ECJ in the driving seat on health policy. But what's the destination? *Eurohealth*, 7(4).

WYATT, D. 2005. Community Competence to regulate Medical Services. *In:* SPAVENTA, E. & DOUGAN, M. (eds) *Social welfare and EU law*. Oxford: Hart.

YAMIN, A.E. 2014. Promoting Equity in Health: What Role for the Courts? *Health and Human Rights Journal*, 16(2): 183–6.

ZANON, E. 2011. Health care across borders: Implications of the EU Directive on cross-border health care for the English NHS. *Eurohealth*, 17: 34–6.

ZIGANTE, V. 2011. Assessing Welfare Effects of the European Choice Agenda: The case of health care in the United Kingdom. *LSE 'Europe in Question' Discussion Paper Series*, LEQS Paper No. 35/2011.

ZUCCA, G. *et al.* 2015. *Evaluative study on the cross-border healthcare Directive (2011/24/EU)*. Luxembourg: Publications Office of the European Union. Available at http://ec.europa.eu/health/cross_border_care/docs/2015_evaluative_study_frep_en.pdf [Accessed 14 December 2015].

Legislation

COUNCIL AND THE MINISTERS FOR HEALTH 1993. Resolution of the Council and the Ministers for Health, meeting within the Council of 27 May 1993 on future action in the field of public health. OJ C 174, 25.06.1993, pp. 0001–3.

COUNCIL OF EUROPE 1950. Convention for the Protection of Human Rights and Fundamental Freedoms as amended by Protocols No. 11 and 14.

COUNCIL OF EUROPE 1961. European Social Charter.

COUNCIL OF EUROPE 1997. Convention for the protection of human rights and dignity of the human being with regard to the application of biology and medicine: Convention on human rights and biomedicine.

COUNCIL OF THE EUROPEAN COMMUNITIES 1958. Regulation (EEC) No 3 on social security for migrant workers. OJ N. 30, 16.12.1958, pp. 561–8.

COUNCIL OF THE EUROPEAN COMMUNITIES 1971. Regulation (EEC) No 1408/71 on the application of social security schemes to employed persons and their families moving within the Community OJ L 149, 05.07.1971, pp. 2–50.

EUROPEAN PARLIAMENT AND THE COUNCIL OF THE EUROPEAN UNION 1996. Decision No 645/96/EC of the European Parliament and of the Council of 29 March 1996 adopting a programme of Community action on health promotion, information, education and training within the framework for action in the field of public health (1996 to 2000).

EUROPEAN PARLIAMENT AND THE COUNCIL OF THE EUROPEAN UNION 1996. Decision No 646/96/EC of the European Parliament and of the Council of 29 March 1996 adopting an action plan to combat cancer within the framework for action in the field of public health (1996 to 2000).

EUROPEAN PARLIAMENT AND THE COUNCIL OF THE EUROPEAN UNION 1996. Decision No 647/96/EC of the European Parliament and of the Council of 29 March 1996 adopting a programme of Community action on the prevention of AIDS and certain other communicable diseases within the framework for action in the field of public health (1996 to 2000).

EUROPEAN PARLIAMENT AND THE COUNCIL OF THE EUROPEAN UNION 2000. Charter of Fundamental Rights of the European Union (2000/C 364/01).

EUROPEAN PARLIAMENT AND THE COUNCIL OF THE EUROPEAN UNION 2002. Decision No 1786/2002/EC of the European Parliament and of the Council of 23 September 2002 adopting a programme of Community action in the field of public health (2003–2008).

EUROPEAN PARLIAMENT AND THE COUNCIL OF THE EUROPEAN UNION 2004. Regulation (EC) No 883/2004 of the European Parliament and of the Council of 29 April 2004 on the coordination of social security systems. *L 166*.

EUROPEAN PARLIAMENT AND THE COUNCIL OF THE EUROPEAN UNION 2005. Directive 2005/36/EC on the recognition of professional qualifications.

EUROPEAN PARLIAMENT AND COUNCIL OF THE EUROPEAN UNION 2006. Directive 2006/123/EC on services in the internal market.

EUROPEAN PARLIAMENT AND THE COUNCIL OF THE EUROPEAN UNION 2007. Decision No 1350/2007/EC of the European Parliament and of the Council of 23 October 2007 establishing a second programme of Community action in the field of health (2008–13).

EUROPEAN PARLIAMENT AND THE COUNCIL OF THE EUROPEAN UNION 2011. Directive 2011/24/EU on the application of patients' rights in cross-border healthcare.

EUROPEAN PARLIAMENT AND THE COUNCIL OF THE EUROPEAN UNION 2014. Regulation (EU) 282/2014 of the European Parliament and of the Council of 11 March 2014 on the establishment of a third Programme for the Union's action in the field of health (2014–2020) and repealing Decision No 1350/2007/EC (Text with EEA relevance).

UNITED KINGDOM 2009. Health Act 2009. Available at www.opsi.gov.uk/acts/acts 2009/ukpga_20090021_en_1#Legislation-Preamble [Accessed 26 November 2015].

Institutional documents

Council of Europe

COUNCIL OF EUROPE 1996. Explanatory Report to the Convention on human rights and biomedicine. Available at https://rm.coe.int/CoERMPublicCommonSearch Services/DisplayDCTMContent?documentId=09000016800ccde5 [Accessed 3 December 2015].

COUNCIL OF EUROPE 2008. Digest of the Case Law of the European Committee of Social Rights. Available at www.coe.int/t/dghl/monitoring/socialcharter/Digest/Digest Sept2008_en.pdf [Accessed 3 December 2015].

Council of the European Union

COUNCIL OF THE EUROPEAN UNION 2006. Council Conclusions on Common values and principles in European Union Health Systems. 2006/C 146/01.

COUNCIL OF THE EUROPEAN UNION 2010. Council conclusions on Equity and Health in All Policies: Solidarity in Health. Adopted by the Council of the European Union on 8 June 2010 at the 3019th Employment, Social Policy, Health and Consumer Affairs Council meeting. Available at www.consilium.europa.eu/uedocs/cms_data/docs/pressdata/en/lsa/114994.pdf [Accessed 7 January 2016].

European Commission

EUROPEAN COMMISSION 2001. Report of the High Level Committee on Health 'The Internal Market and Health Services'. Available at http://ec.europa.eu/health/ph_overview/Documents/key06_en.pdf [Accessed 3 December 2015].

EUROPEAN COMMISSION 2003. High level process of reflection on patient mobility and healthcare developments in the European Union. Available at http://ec.europa.eu/health/ph_overview/Documents/key01_mobility_en.pdf [Accessed 3 December 2015].

COMMISSION OF THE EUROPEAN COMMUNITIES 2003. Green paper on services of general interest. COM (2003) 270.

COMMISSION OF THE EUROPEAN COMMUNITIES 2004a. Communication from the Commission – Follow-up to the high level reflection process on patient mobility and healthcare developments in the European Union. COM/2004/0301 final. Available at http://eur-lex.europa.eu/LexUriServ/LexUriServ.do?uri=COM:2004:0301: FIN:EN:PDF [Accessed 6 January 2016].

COMMISSION OF THE EUROPEAN COMMUNITIES 2004b. White Paper on services of general interest. COM (2004) 374.

COMMISSION OF THE EUROPEAN COMMUNITIES 2006a. Communication from the Commission. Consultation regarding community action on health services. SEC (2006) 1195/4.

COMMISSION OF THE EUROPEAN COMMUNITIES 2006b. Implementing the Community Lisbon programme. Social services of general interest in the European Union. COM (2006) 177.

COMMISSION OF THE EUROPEAN COMMUNITIES 2007. White Paper – Together for Health: A Strategic Approach for the EU 2008–2013. COM (2007) 630 final.

COMMISSION OF THE EUROPEAN COMMUNITIES 2008a. Proposal for a directive of the European parliament and of the Council on the application of patients' rights in cross-border healthcare. 2008/0142 (COD).

COMMISSION OF THE EUROPEAN COMMUNITIES 2008b. Renewed social agenda: Opportunities, access and solidarity in 21st century Europe. COM (2008) 412 final.

COMMISSION OF THE EUROPEAN COMMUNITIES 2011. Communication from the Commission to the European Parliament, the Council, the European Economic and Social Committee and the Committee of the Regions – A Quality Framework for Services of General Interest in Europe. COM (2011).

EUROPEAN COMMISSION 2012. Standard Eurobarometer 77: The values of Europeans.

EUROPEAN COMMISSION 2014. Report from the Commission to the Council and the European Parliament compliant with the obligations foreseen under Article 20(3) of Directive 2011/24/EU of the European Parliament and of the Council of 9 March 2011 on the application of patients' rights in cross-border healthcare. COM (2014) 044 final.

EUROPEAN COMMISSION 2014. Impact of information on patients' choice within the context of the Directive 2011/24/EU of the European Parliament and of the Council on the application of patients' rights in cross-border healthcare (Final Report). Available at http://ec.europa.eu/health/cross_border_care/docs/cbhc_information_patients choice_en.pdf [Accessed 14 December 2015].

EUROPEAN COMMISSION 2014. Special Eurobarometer 425. Available at http://ec.europa.eu/public_opinion/archives/ebs/ebs_425_en.pdf [Accessed 10 December 2015].

EUROPEAN COMMISSION 2015. Report from the Commission to the European Parliament and the Council. Commission report on the operation of Directive 2011/24/EU on the application of patients' rights in cross-border healthcare. COM (2015) 421 final.

EUROPEAN COMMISSION 2015. Expert Panel on effective ways of investing in Health 175 (EXPH). Preliminary Report on Access to Health Services in the European Union. Available at http://ec.europa.eu/health/expert_panel/opinions/docs/010_access_healthcare_en.pdf [Accessed 14 December 2015].

European Parliament

EUROPEAN PARLIAMENT 2007a. European Parliament resolution of 15 March 2007 on Community action on the provision of cross-border healthcare. B6–0098/2007.

EUROPEAN PARLIAMENT 2007b. The Impact of the European Court of Justice Case Law on National Systems For Cross-Border Health Service Provision. DG Internal Policies of the Union – Policy Department Economic and Scientific Policy.

EUROPEAN PARLIAMENT 2007c. Report on the impact and consequences of the exclusion of health services from the Directive on services in the internal market, 10 May 2007. A6–0173/2007.

EUROPEAN PARLIAMENT 2009. Committee on the Environment, Public Health and Food Safety. Report on the proposal for a directive on the application of patients' rights in cross-border healthcare (Explanatory Statement). A6–0233/2009. Available at www.europarl.europa.eu/sides/getDoc.do?type=REPORT&reference=A6–2009–0233 &language=EN#title2 [Accessed 3 December 2015].

UK Department of Health

UNITED KINGDOM DEPARTMENT OF HEALTH. *The NHS Constitution*. Available at www.nhs.uk/choiceintheNHS/Rightsandpledges/NHSConstitution/Documents/2013/the-nhs-constitution-for-england-2013.pdf [Accessed 24 November 2015].

United Nations (UN)

UNITED NATIONS (UN). International Covenant on Economic, Social and Cultural Rights 1966. Available at www.ohchr.org/EN/ProfessionalInterest/Pages/CESCR.aspx [Accessed 6 January 2016].

UNITED NATIONS (UN). Convention on the Elimination of All Forms of Discrimination against Women (CEDAW) 1979. Available at www.un.org/womenwatch/daw/cedaw/ [Accessed 6 January 2016].

UNITED NATIONS (UN). Convention on the Rights of the Child (CRC) 1989. Available at www.ohchr.org/en/professionalinterest/pages/crc.aspx [Accessed 6 January 2016].

UNITED NATIONS (UN) COMMITTEE ON ECONOMIC SOCIAL AND CULTURAL RIGHTS – CESCR 2000. Substantive issues arising in the implementation of the International Covenant on Economic, Social and Cultural Rights – General Comment No. 14 (E/C. 12/2000/4). Available at www.unhchr.ch/tbs/doc.nsf/(Symbol)/40d0099013586b0e2c1256915005090be?Opendocument [Accessed 8 December 2015].

World Health Organization (WHO)

WORLD HEALTH ORGANIZATION 1946. Constitution of the World Health Organization. Available at www.who.int/about/mission/en/ [Accessed 6 January 2016].

WORLD HEALTH ORGANIZATION 2000. The world health report 2000 – Health systems: improving performance. Geneva.

WORLD HEALTH ORGANIZATION 2002. Understanding the BSE threat. Geneva. Available at www.who.int/csr/resources/publications/bse/BSEthreat.pdf [Accessed 6 January 2016].

Index